SECTIONS 409A AND 457

ANSWERS TO
300 FREQUENTLY
ASKED QUESTIONS

FOURTH
EDITION

BRIAN W. BERGLUND
& LOUIS R. RICHEY

SECTIONS 409A AND 457

ANSWERS TO
300 FREQUENTLY
ASKED QUESTIONS

**FOURTH
EDITION**

ABA
AMERICAN**BAR**ASSOCIATION
ABA Publishing

Cover design by ABA Design

The materials contained herein represent the opinions of the authors and/or the editors and should not be construed to be the views or opinions of the law firms or companies with whom such persons are in partnership with, associated with, or employed by, nor of the American Bar Association, unless adopted pursuant to the bylaws of the Association.

Nothing contained in this book is to be considered as the rendering of legal advice for specific cases, and readers are responsible for obtaining such advice from their own legal counsel. This book is intended for educational and informational purposes only.

© 2021 American Bar Association. All rights reserved.

No part of this publication may be reproduced, stored in a retrieval system, or transmitted in any form or by any means, electronic, mechanical, photocopying, recording, or otherwise, without the prior written permission of the publisher. For permission, complete the request form at www.americanbar.org/reprint or email ABA Publishing at copyright@americanbar.org.

Printed in the United States of America.

25 24 23 22 21   5 4 3 2 1

ISBN: 978-1-64105-974-9
e-ISBN: 978-1-64105-975-6

Discounts are available for books ordered in bulk. Special consideration is given to state bars, CLE programs, and other bar-related organizations. Inquire at Book Publishing, ABA Publishing, American Bar Association, 321 N. Clark Street, Chicago, Illinois 60654-7598.

www.shopABA.org

CONTENTS

ABOUT THE AUTHORS   XXXVII

NOTES ON CITATIONS   XLI

INTRODUCTION   XLIII

PLANS SUBJECT TO SECTIONS 409A AND 457   1

  Q.1 What types of compensation and benefit plans are subject to Section 409A?   1

  Q.2 What plans are not subject to Section 409A?   3

  Q.3 What constitutes a deferral of compensation for purposes of Section 409A?   4

  Q.4 When is it determined whether a plan is subject to Section 409A?   6

  Q.5 When is a plan legally binding for purposes of Section 409A?   6

  Q.6 Who is the service recipient for purposes of Section 409A?   7

  Q.7 Who is a service provider for purposes of Section 409A?   8

  Q.8 If a business engages an individual to write a book, song, software program, or similar item, and the parties agree that the business will acquire ownership of or distribution rights to the property produced in exchange for a monetary payment, does Section 409A apply to the arrangement?   9

Q.9 Are compensation and benefit plans of tax-exempt organizations subject to Section 409A?   9

Q.10 Are arrangements involving partnerships subject to Section 409A?   10

Q.11 What constitutes disability pay exempt from Section 409A?   11

Q.12 What constitutes a bona fide death benefit plan exempt from Section 409A?   12

Q.13 What constitutes a bona fide vacation or leave plan?   13

Q.14 What are the general requirements for nonqualified deferred compensation plans subject to Section 409A?   13

DOCUMENTATION REQUIREMENTS   15

Q.15 Are plans subject to Section 409A required to be in writing?   15

Q.16 When must a plan subject to Section 409A be documented?   15

Q.17 Are there specific features prohibited in plans subject to Section 409A that were frequently included in nonqualified plans before enactment of Section 409A?   16

Q.18 Is it appropriate to document the provisions of a plan designed to fall outside the scope of Section 409A?   17

Q.19 What are the minimum documentation requirements for a plan subject to Section 409A?   18

SHORT-TERM DEFERRALS EXEMPT FROM SECTION 409A   23

Q.20 Do amounts that are paid shortly after they are earned constitute deferred compensation subject to Section 409A?   23

Q.21 What is the short-term deferral rule?   24

Q.22 When is payment considered to have been made for purposes of the short-term deferral rule? **27**

Q.23 What situations justify delay in payment of compensation designed to qualify as a short-term deferral beyond 2½ months after the end of the taxable year in which the compensation is earned? **27**

Q.24 What is a substantial risk of forfeiture, and how does it relate to satisfaction of the short-term deferral rule for purposes of Section 409A? **28**

Q.25 If a compensation arrangement qualifies as a short-term deferral exempt from Section 409A, can the parties change the form and time of payment under the arrangement after the services relating to the compensation have been performed without becoming subject to Section 409A? **31**

Q.26 What is the relationship between the definitions of substantial risk of forfeiture under Section 409A, Section 83, and Section 457(f)? **32**

Q.27 What is a vest and pay lump sum SERP? **33**

DISTRIBUTION EVENTS UNDER SECTION 409A **35**

Q.28 What are the primary permissible distribution events for purposes of Section 409A? **35**

Q.29 What type of separation from service qualifies as a permissible distribution event for an employee under Section 409A? **36**

Q.30 Will a service provider experience a separation from service if he or she goes on a leave of absence? **38**

Q.31 Will a service provider experience a separation from service in connection with an asset sale? **39**

Q.32 Will a spin-off or stock sale of a subsidiary cause the affected employees to experience a separation from service? **39**

VIII SECTIONS 409A AND 457

Q.33 May a transaction that is treated as a deemed asset sale under Section 338 be treated as an asset sale for purposes of the special separation from service rules described in Q.31?   **40**

Q.34 What constitutes a separation from service of an independent contractor for purposes of Section 409A?   **40**

Q.35 How is a separation of service defined when a service provider performs services for a service recipient both as an employee and independent contractor?   **41**

Q.36 Must a plan governed by Section 409A that is maintained by a publicly traded company require delayed payments to some plan participants, called "specified employees," even though there is a valid separation from service?   **43**

Q.37 Who are "specified employees" of a publicly traded company, its subsidiaries, and its affiliates, for purposes of the six-month delay rule?   **44**

Q.38 Can a nonemployee director constitute a specified employee of a service recipient as a result of the director's ownership interest in the service recipient?   **47**

Q.39 How are specified employees identified following a corporate transaction involving two public companies?   **47**

Q.40 How are specified employees identified following a transaction involving a public company and a nonpublic company?   **49**

Q.41 How are specified employees identified following a spin-off?   **50**

Q.42 How are specified employees identified following an initial public offering?   **50**

Q.43 Are there alternative rules for identifying specified employees following a corporate transaction?   **50**

Q.44 Is it possible to comply with the requirement that payments to specified employees on account of separation from service must be delayed for six months after separation by requiring that payments to all service providers on account of separation from service be delayed for six months after separation?   **51**

Q.45 Could a specified employee have a claim for post-employment discrimination or retaliation against a service recipient for complying with the six-month delay requirement under Section 409A?   **51**

Q.46 What is the definition of disability for purposes of Section 409A?   **52**

Q.47 Can a plan's form and time of payment on account of disability be different from the plan's form and time of payment on account of separation from service?   **53**

Q.48 Once a distribution event that entitles a plan participant to receive payment occurs, when must the payment be made?   **53**

PAYMENTS   **55**

Q.49 When is a payment considered to have been made?   **55**

Q.50 Is the transfer of property that is subject to a substantial risk of forfeiture considered a payment under Section 409A?   **56**

Q.51 If a payment is to be made upon death, when must the payment be made?   **56**

Q.52 If a payment is to be made upon death, may the beneficiary select the year of payment?   **56**

Q.53 If the plan document specifies a more restrictive period for payment of death benefits than is permitted under the rules described in Q.51, may the plan be amended to expand the period for payment of death benefits?   **57**

Q.54 Must the plan document specify the period during which death benefits may be paid?   **57**

Q.55 Do the rules applicable to payments upon the death of a participant apply upon the death of a beneficiary?   **58**

Q.56 Can the time of payment depend on the time the service provider executes a release?   **58**

Q.57 Can a plan provide that distribution occurs on the earliest of two or more permissible events?   **59**

Q.58 What is the anti-toggling rule and how is it applied?   **59**

Q.59 Can a plan provide for different forms of payment depending on whether the service provider is married or not when payment begins?   **61**

Q.60 Can a plan provide that distribution occurs on the earlier of a narrowly defined involuntary separation from service and another permissible distribution event?   **62**

Q.61 Are there any situations in which a late payment will be excused because of administrative impracticability?   **62**

Q.62 Are there any situations in which a late payment will be excused because of financial difficulties of the service recipient?   **63**

Q.63 What constitutes a downturn in the financial health of a service recipient?   **63**

Q.64 May a service recipient delay making a payment to avoid violating a law?   **63**

Q.65 May payment be delayed to avoid the loss of a deduction under I.R.C. § 162(m)?   **64**

Q.66 Can a plan provide that the form of distribution is based on the value of the service provider's benefit at the time distribution commences?   **64**

Q.67 If distribution of deferred compensation is scheduled to be made in cash, can the service recipient and service provider agree after the services related to the deferred compensation have been performed that distribution will instead be made in the form of restricted stock?   **65**

Q.68 May a distribution of deferred compensation be made in the form of a stock option?   **66**

Q.69 May a service provider and service recipient agree to cancel a deferred compensation arrangement and replace it with a split-dollar arrangement?   **66**

Q.70 Can distributions scheduled on account of separation from service under a deferred compensation plan subject to Section 409A be suspended if the employee is rehired and resumes eligibility under the plan?   **66**

Q.71 Does a 409A violation always occur if the service recipient refuses or inadvertently fails to make a payment of deferred compensation when due?   **67**

ACCELERATION OF BENEFITS   **69**

Q.72 May deferred compensation distributions be accelerated?   **69**

Q.73 What is an unforeseeable emergency for purposes of Section 409A?   **70**

Q.74 When can a plan be amended to provide for acceleration of distribution incident to unforeseeable emergency, death, or disability? **71**

Q.75 If a designated beneficiary has become entitled to payments upon the death of the participant, are there any situations in which the payments due to the beneficiary may be accelerated? **72**

Q.76 May a service provider who has elected to receive benefits in the form of a periodic benefit measured by joint life expectancies change beneficiaries without causing an acceleration of benefits? **72**

Q.77 May benefits be accelerated to comply with conflict of interest or foreign ethics laws? **73**

Q.78 What constitutes a cash-out that can be accelerated and paid in a lump sum without violating Section 409A? **73**

Q.79 May a cash-out of small benefits be conditioned on the election or consent of the service provider? **74**

Q.80 May a plan provide that installment or annuity payments will be cashed out in a single sum if the present value of the service provider's remaining benefit falls below a specified level set forth in the plan? **74**

Q.81 May a plan provide for a distribution of benefits upon a change of control? **75**

Q.82 How is a change in ownership or effective control defined for purposes of Section 409A? **75**

Q.83 What are the requirements for enforceability of a domestic relations order directing acceleration of distribution of amounts deferred by a participant under a plan governed by Section 409A? **76**

Q.84 Is a deferred compensation plan subject to Section 409A required to accelerate distribution of amounts deferred by a participant or to divide the participant's account in favor of the adverse party named in a domestic relations order that satisfies the requirements for enforceability under Section 409A? **78**

Q.85 In what circumstances may an employer terminate or liquidate a plan that is subject to Section 409A? **79**

Q.86 Can an existing plan without a provision for termination be amended to provide for plan termination? **81**

Q.87 Can a service recipient voluntarily terminate a plan with respect to one or more, but not all, service recipients participating in the plan? **81**

Q.88 Must a specified employee of a public company wait at least six months to receive distribution due upon a plan termination? **82**

Q.89 Does acceleration of vesting of deferred compensation alone cause a problem under Section 409A? **83**

Q.90 What is the substitution rule? **83**

Q.91 May a service provider borrow money from his or her nonqualified plan or pledge nonqualified plan benefits as security for a loan or other amount due creditors? **84**

Q.92 Does Section 409A prohibit forfeiture, reduction, or voluntary relinquishment of deferred compensation? **84**

Q.93 Does Section 409A permit offset of the amount due the service provider on distribution by the amount the service provider owes the service recipient? **85**

Q.94 Does Section 409A permit offsets of deferred compensation to comply with federal debt collection laws?   86

Q.95 May deferred compensation be reduced to reflect required tax withholding amounts relating to such deferred compensation?   86

Q.96 May payment of deferred compensation be accelerated if the plan violates the requirements of Section 409A?   86

Q.97 May payment of deferred compensation be accelerated to prevent a nonallocation year under I.R.C. Section 409(p)?   87

Q.98 May payment of deferred compensation be accelerated pursuant to the settlement of a dispute regarding the service provider's entitlement to receive such deferred compensation?   87

Q.99 Is an election change under a cafeteria plan that results in an acceleration of deferred compensation problematic?   88

Q.100 If a service recipient determines that a service provider who is a member of a top hat plan is no longer a member of a select group of management or highly compensated employees, may the service recipient cancel the service provider's deferral elections and immediately distribute his or her plan benefits?   89

TAX CONSEQUENCES   91

Q.101 What constitutes a violation of Section 409A that causes a service provider to incur tax liability under Section 409A?   91

Q.102 What is the general federal income tax scheme for plans subject to Section 409A?   91

Q.103 What are the federal income tax consequences of a breach of Section 409A?   93

Q.104 Are there situations in which a substantial risk of forfeiture will be disregarded for purposes of determining whether an amount is includible in income under Q.103? **94**

Q.105 Who is responsible for payment of the taxes imposed on account of a breach of Section 409A? **94**

Q.106 Is an employer required to indemnify plan participants against the taxes imposed by Section 409A if the related violation of Section 409A is due to the employer's own action or inaction? **95**

Q.107 What is the aggregation rule, and how does it apply to determine federal income tax liability on account of a violation of Section 409A? **95**

Q.108 Do the plan aggregation rules apply for other purposes under Section 409A? **97**

Q.109 What is a documentary violation of Section 409A? **97**

Q.110 What is the effect of a documentary violation of Section 409A? **97**

Q.111 What is an operational violation of Section 409A? **98**

Q.112 What is the effect of an operational violation of Section 409A? **98**

Q.113 If a plan fails to comply with Section 409A in one year but deferrals continue under the plan in subsequent years during which the plan otherwise fully complies with Section 409A both in form and operation, does the 409A failure adversely impact the subsequent deferrals? **99**

Q.114 Does Section 409A replace all prior law governing federal income taxation of unfunded deferred compensation arrangements? **99**

Q.115 Have any states imposed a personal income tax that parallels Section 409A? **100**

Q.116 Can the negative income tax consequences of a breach of Section 409A be mediated? **100**

DEFERRED COMPENSATION PLANS SUBJECT TO 409A **101**

Q.117 How are participant account balance plans treated for purposes of Section 409A? **101**

Q.118 How are employer account balance plans treated for purposes of Section 409A? **101**

Q.119 How are employer non-account balance plans treated for purposes of Section 409A? **102**

SERVICE PROVIDER ELECTIONS **103**

Q.120 What types of service provider elections are typically provided for under deferred compensation plans subject to Section 409A? **103**

Q.121 When must initial elections to defer and to designate the time and form of payment be made under Section 409A? **104**

Q.122 Must the method for calculating installment payments under a nonqualified plan be specified in writing at the time of an initial deferral election? **108**

Q.123 Which year's deferral election applies to base pay earned during the final payroll period of one year and paid on the first pay date of the next year in accordance with the service recipient's standard payroll practice? **109**

Q.124 How is performance-based compensation defined for purposes of Section 409A? **109**

Q.125 Is a bonus deferral election that is subject to Section 409A canceled if the service provider separates from service after the election is made or becomes final, but before the date the bonus amount is credited to the service provider's account? 110

Q.126 Does a service provider's ability to elect that compensation earned in a nine- or ten-month period, typically an academic year, be paid over a twelve-month period spanning two taxable years create nonqualified deferred compensation subject to Section 409A? 111

Q.127 Can a participant make a subsequent election to change the time or form of payment specified in an earlier election? 114

Q.128 May a participant revoke a subsequent election to change the time or form of payment specified in an earlier election? 116

Q.129 If a plan does not include a provision permitting a participant to make a subsequent election to change the time or form of payment specified in an earlier election, may the plan be amended to add such a provision? 116

Q.130 Is a change of form of payment from one type of annuity to another actuarially equivalent annuity commencing at the same time subject to the requirements that apply to subsequent elections? 117

Q.131 May a service recipient amend a plan to change actuarial assumptions applicable to annuity payment forms available under the plan without triggering the subsequent election rules or otherwise violating Section 409A? 117

Q.132 Can a participant make a subsequent election to defer only a portion of an amount previously deferred? — 118

Q.133 Can a participant make a subsequent election to defer periodic installments after distribution has begun? — 118

Q.134 Can a participant make a subsequent election to change the form of payment from periodic installments to a single sum? — 119

Q.135 Can a participant cancel an election to defer compensation during the plan year in which the compensation would otherwise have been paid in the absence of the election? — 120

Q.136 Can a plan permit a service provider to elect multiple forms of payment with respect to various portions of a deferred amount? — 121

Q.137 If a service provider is allowed to elect different deferral percentages for different types of compensation during a year, such as base pay, annual bonus and long-term bonus, will a Section 409A violation occur if the mix of the service provider's compensation changes mid-year? — 121

Q.138 Can the subsequent election rule be used to increase participant flexibility in a plan with multiple annual election options? — 122

Q.139 Can the subsequent election rule and the single or multiple payment election be used in combination to increase the security of benefits accrued under a participant individual account plan benefit? — 123

Q.140 What is a rolling risk of forfeiture and how do the 409A rules apply to a rolling risk of forfeiture? — 124

Q.141 How is the term "materially greater" defined for purposes of Section 409A in the context of rolling risks of forfeiture? **125**

SEVERANCE PLANS **127**

Q.142 What severance payments are exempt from Section 409A? **127**

Q.143 May the severance plan exemption apply to service providers whose employment begins and ends in the same year? **128**

Q.144 Must the design of a severance pay program use only the short-term deferral rule or only the severance plan rules, or can the two rules be used in combination? **128**

Q.145 Is there any other exemption that could apply to severance payments under Section 409A? **129**

Q.146 Can severance amounts payable on account of voluntary termination or termination for good reason qualify as severance pay or short-term deferrals for purposes of Section 409A? **130**

Q.147 When is termination for good reason considered equivalent to involuntary severance? **130**

Q.148 If a severance arrangement is exempt from Section 409A, can the parties modify the form and time of payment under the arrangement without making the arrangement subject to Section 409A? **132**

Q.149 Is a mitigation provision permitted in a severance agreement that is subject to Section 409A? **132**

Q.150 If all payments due under a severance arrangement do not meet the short-term deferral exception, the separation pay exception, or the small distribution exception, does the arrangement violate Section 409A? **132**

Q.151 Can severance payments substitute for nonqualified deferred compensation payments that are being forfeited? **133**

Q.152 What is a window program for purposes of the severance pay exception to Section 409A? **134**

Q.153 Do collectively bargained severance plans and foreign severance plans required by local law get special treatment? **134**

STOCK-BASED COMPENSATION **135**

Q.154 Does Section 409A apply to incentive stock options or to options issued under a statutory employee stock purchase plan? **135**

Q.155 Does Section 409A apply to nonstatutory stock options and stock appreciation rights (SARs)? **135**

Q.156 How are a service provider's rights to receive nonvested stock on the exercise of a stock right and to pay the exercise price with previously acquired shares treated under Section 409A? **137**

Q.157 What constitutes service recipient stock for purposes of the stock-based compensation exception to Section 409A? **137**

Q.158 May a service recipient grant stock rights to an individual before the individual becomes a service provider and still have the underlying stock qualify as service recipient stock? **138**

Q.159 Can stock that is subject to a mandatory repurchase obligation upon a service recipient's termination for cause or violation of a restrictive covenant qualify as service recipient stock? **139**

Q.160 How is fair market value of service recipient stock calculated for purposes of determining the exercise price of an option or SAR? **139**

Q.161 What is the relationship between Section 409A and ASC 718? **141**

Q.162 Can the exercise period be extended or the option or SAR modified without causing loss of the exception from Section 409A coverage? **142**

Q.163 How can a nonqualified stock option or SAR become subject to Section 409A? **143**

Q.164 If a nonqualified stock option or SAR is intended to be exempt from Section 409A, may the option or SAR include dividend equivalent rights which are contingent upon exercise? **144**

Q.165 If a nonqualified stock option or SAR is intended to be exempt from Section 409A, may the option or SAR include dividend equivalent rights that expire upon exercise? **144**

Q.166 If a nonqualified stock option or SAR is intended to be exempt from Section 409A, may the option or SAR be adjusted to reflect a stock split or stock dividend? **145**

Q.167 How can a nonqualified stock option or SAR be structured to comply with Section 409A? **145**

Q.168 Does Section 409A apply to restricted stock, restricted stock units, or phantom stock units? **146**

Q.169 Is a deferred compensation plan subject to Section 409A required to specify a valuation date for restricted stock units granted under the plan? **147**

Q.170 Can dividend-equivalent distributions on phantom or restricted stock units qualify as current compensation or short-term deferrals? **147**

Q.171 What are transaction-based compensation payments? **148**

Q.172 What special payment rules apply to transaction-based compensation? **148**

Q.173 How do the transaction-based compensation rules apply to stock options or stock appreciation rights that were exempt from Section 409A when issued? **149**

EMPLOYMENT AGREEMENTS 151

Q.174 Which common provisions of an employment agreement might create issues under Section 409A? **151**

Q.175 What issues do fringe benefit arrangements pose under Section 409A? **151**

Q.176 If a former highly paid service provider is allowed to continue self-insured medical coverage for life by paying the full cost of coverage, is the arrangement subject to Section 409A? **153**

Q.177 Is a provision in an employment agreement for a tax gross-up payment, such as to compensate an executive for golden parachute taxes, permitted under Section 409A? **153**

Q.178 Are payments made pursuant to a settlement with an employer, payments made under indemnification agreements, or payments made to acquire directors' and officers' insurance treated as nonqualified deferred compensation subject to Section 409A? **154**

Q.179 Are payments of employment-related legal fees and expenses deferred compensation subject to Section 409A? **155**

SPLIT-DOLLAR AND OTHER LIFE INSURANCE ARRANGEMENTS 157

Q.180 Which split-dollar life insurance arrangements are subject to or exempt from Section 409A coverage? **157**

Q.181 Are split-dollar life insurance programs subject to grandfathering under Section 409A? **158**

Q.182 What is a bonus life insurance or annuity plan, and how can it be used as a substitute for a nonqualified deferred compensation plan subject to Section 409A? 158

Q.183 Is a key person life insurance policy owned by the service recipient subject to Section 409A? 161

Q.184 Are other life insurance plans subject to Section 409A? 161

Q.185 Could Section 409A apply in connection with termination of a split-dollar life insurance arrangement that is generally exempt from Section 409A? 162

FOREIGN PLANS 163

Q.186 Does Section 409A apply to deferred compensation attributable to services rendered outside the United States? 163

Q.187 What are the requirements for the treaty exemption from Section 409A? 165

Q.188 What are the requirements for exemption from Section 409A for amounts subject to tax equalization agreements? 165

Q.189 What are the requirements for exemption from Section 409A for foreign social security arrangements? 166

Q.190 What are the requirements for exemption from Section 409A for broad-based foreign retirement plans? 166

Q.191 Can foreign earned income be subject to exemption from Section 409A under the generally applicable rules? 167

Q.192 How does Section 457A compare to Section 409A? 167

Q.193 If a plan is subject to Section 457A, may it also be subject to Section 409A? 169

LIMITATIONS ON LINKING PLANS 171

Q.194 Can participant elections under a nonqualified deferred compensation plan that is an excess plan be linked to and controlled by a qualified retirement plan? 171

Q.195 Can the benefits from one nonqualified plan be offset against the benefits of another nonqualified plan? 172

FUNDING 175

Q.196 Is a plan subject to Section 409A required to be funded? 175

Q.197 Does Section 409A permit assets in a rabbi trust or other trust to be applied exclusively to fund a nonqualified deferred compensation plan incident to a change in the employer's financial condition? 176

Q.198 May an employer use an offshore trust to hold assets acquired in connection with a nonqualified deferred compensation plan covered by Section 409A? 177

Q.199 May a nonqualified deferred compensation plan be informally funded through a rabbi trust while the plan sponsor maintains an underfunded tax-qualified defined benefit retirement plan? 177

Q.200 Do the Section 409A funding restrictions apply to grandfathered plans? 179

PANDEMICS AND OTHER CRISES THAT DISRUPT THE ECONOMY 181

Q.201 What issues and concerns arose during the Covid-19 pandemic as a result of restrictions imposed by Section 409A? 181

Q.202 What legislative or regulatory relief was issued to address the Section 409A challenges that arose during the Covid-19 pandemic? 182

Q.203 May a service provider access his or her nonqualified plan benefits due to a pandemic? **182**

Q.204 Under what circumstances may a service provider access nonqualified plan benefits during a pandemic due to unforeseeable emergency, and how do these circumstances differ from those applicable to hardship withdrawals from 401(k) plans? **183**

Q.205 Under what circumstances may a service provider access nonqualified plan benefits during a pandemic due to disability? **184**

Q.206 Under what circumstances may a service provider be provided access to nonqualified plan benefits during a pandemic due to plan termination? **184**

Q.207 May a service provider modify or cancel his or her nonqualified plan deferral election as a result of a pandemic? **185**

Q.208 If a service recipient reduces a service provider's regular compensation during a pandemic, does the service provider have the option of cancelling his or her nonqualified deferral election? **186**

Q.209 If a service recipient reduces a service provider's compensation during a pandemic, may the service recipient promise to pay the compensation reduction to the service provider in the future? **187**

Q.210 If a service recipient reduces a service provider's bonus opportunity during a pandemic, does the service provider have the option of modifying or cancelling his or her bonus deferral election if the bonus is not performance based? **188**

Q.211 If a service recipient reduces or otherwise modifies a service provider's opportunity to earn a performance-based bonus during a pandemic, does the service provider still have the option of making a delayed election in accordance with the performance-based bonus rules? **188**

Q.212 If a service recipient reduces or otherwise modifies a service provider's opportunity to earn a performance-based bonus more than six months into the performance period due to a pandemic, what impact does this have on a service provider's delayed election pursuant to the performance-based bonus rules? **189**

Q.213 What impact does a temporary shutdown of all business operations during a pandemic have on service provider deferrals under a nonqualified plan? **190**

Q.214 May a service recipient reduce or cancel matching or other employer credits to a nonqualified plan during a pandemic without violating Section 409A? **190**

Q.215 To help preserve cash flow during a pandemic, may a service recipient reduce or cancel asset contributions to a rabbi trust used to informally track the liabilities of a plan without violating Section 409A? **191**

Q.216 If a service recipient furloughs service providers during a pandemic, does a separation from service occur for purposes of Section 409A? **191**

Q.217 If a service provider takes a leave of absence during a pandemic, does a separation from service occur for purposes of Section 409A? **192**

ENFORCEMENT **193**

Q.218 Can an employer obtain an IRS letter ruling that a deferred compensation plan satisfies the requirements of Section 409A? **193**

Q.219 Are there any issues involving deferred compensation plans subject to Section 409A on which the IRS will issue rulings? **194**

Q.220 When will the IRS actively audit and enforce the requirements of Section 409A with respect to covered plans? **194**

Q.221 Does the service recipient have income tax reporting obligations with respect to amounts accrued by service providers under its deferred compensation plans that are subject to Section 409A? **195**

Q.222 What penalties may be imposed on a service recipient when a Section 409A violation occurs? **196**

Q.223 In determining compliance with the various timing requirements in the Section 409A rules, how does the IRS count days, months, and years? **196**

MITIGATION—DOCUMENTARY ERRORS **197**

Q.224 Are there ways to limit the negative tax consequences of documentary errors under Section 409A? **197**

Q.225 What types of documentary errors are subject to correction under Notice 2010-6? **197**

Q.226 What types of plans are not eligible for correction of documentary errors under Notice 2010-6? **198**

Q.227 What documentary ambiguities in a plan can be addressed by interpreting the ambiguous provision consistent with Section 409A without having to amend the plan? **198**

Q.228 What types of errors in plan documentation can be corrected by plan amendment without recognition of income by a service provider? **200**

Q.229 What types of documentary errors can be corrected by plan amendment with limited recognition of income for service providers who were subject to the documentary error before the corrective amendment? **201**

Q.230 What type of documentary errors can be corrected by plan amendment with recognition of Section 409A income by affected service providers without exception? — 205

Q.231 What special rules apply to stock plans? — 206

Q.232 In what circumstances can a documentary error relating to a stock right intended to be exempt from Section 409A be corrected? — 206

Q.233 What special rules apply to linked plans? — 207

Q.234 When is correction deemed to occur for purposes of Notice 2010-6? — 207

Q.235 What are the rules for recognition of service provider income incident to a documentary correction pursuant to Notice 2010-6? — 207

Q.236 What additional reporting and disclosure requirements are imposed in connection with correction of a documentary error that requires a plan amendment? — 208

Q.237 Can a documentary error in a new plan be corrected by plan amendment without being subject to the tax and reporting requirements generally required? — 209

Q.238 What correction is available in the event of a scrivener's error? — 210

Q.239 Are there any circumstances in which a documentary error in a plan subject to Section 409A can be corrected without complying with Notice 2010-6? — 210

MITIGATION OF CONSEQUENCES— OPERATIONAL ERRORS — 213

Q.240 Has the IRS published guidance on correction of inadvertent errors in the administration of deferred compensation plans subject to Section 409A? — 213

Q.241 Is there a minimal level of administrative error under Section 409A for which the IRS does not require formal correction and reporting? **214**

Q.242 Are there any plans for which the correction of operational defects pursuant to Notice 2008-113 does not apply? **215**

Q.243 What analysis should be done to determine whether correction of an operational error pursuant to Notice 2008-113 is necessary? **215**

Q.244 What correction is available for failure to defer compensation pursuant to the plan, the service provider's deferral election, and Section 409A? **217**

Q.245 What correction is available for late distribution of previously deferred compensation? **223**

Q.246 What correction is available in the case of otherwise proper payment of amounts due a specified employee upon separation from service during the six months following the separation? **228**

Q.247 What correction is available if the amount deferred on behalf of a service provider under the plan is greater than provided for in the plan or the service provider's deferral election? **234**

Q.248 What correction is available for payment of deferred compensation before the calendar year it is scheduled to be paid? **239**

Q.249 What correction is available if distribution occurs in the correct calendar year but earlier than the scheduled distribution date? **246**

Q.250 What correction is available for erroneously establishing the exercise price of a stock right below fair market value of the underlying stock on the date of grant? **253**

Q.251 What is the limitation on elective deferrals under Section 402(g)(1)(B) of the Code? **255**

Q.252 Who is an insider under Notice 2008–113? **255**

Q.253 If the term "officer" is determined by reference to the Section 16 rules identifying who is an "insider" for 409A correction purposes, which individuals would be considered officers? **256**

Q.254 If earnings or losses are to be credited in connection with an applicable correction, but it is administratively impracticable to make the adjustment for earnings or losses by the deadline for corrections set forth in Notice 2008–113, is any relief available? **256**

Q.255 What are the additional reporting and disclosure requirements regarding corrections pursuant to Notice 2008–113? **257**

MITIGATION—DISQUALIFICATION BY IRS EXAMINATION **259**

Q.256 When is a service recipient considered to be under IRS examination for purposes of the documentary and operational correction programs? **259**

Q.257 When is a service provider considered to be under IRS examination for purposes of the documentary and operational corrections programs? **260**

Q.258 How should a service recipient that uses a correction procedure address the audit status of its affected service providers? **260**

Q.259 When will a correction be considered complete for purposes of determining whether the service provider or service recipient is under IRS examination at the time of correction? **261**

Q.260 What should a taxpayer do if the IRS audits the taxpayer's return for a year in which a correction after the year of error occurred? **262**

Q.261 Will participation in a correction program increase a taxpayer's audit risk? **262**

Q.262 If an operational failure is corrected under the principles described in Notice 2008-113 and a substantially similar operational failure subsequently occurs, can the subsequent failure be corrected by applying these principles again? **263**

Q.263 Why doesn't the IRS offer a Section 409A correction program like the Employee Plans Compliance Resolution System (EPCRS) for tax-qualified retirement plans? **263**

Q.264 What options are available if a 409A failure is discovered when correction is no longer available under the IRS correction guidance? **264**

Q.265 What is the statute of limitations for breach of Section 409A? **264**

Q.266 How do statute of limitations principles apply in the context of 409A violations? **265**

Q.267 May a service recipient take the position that the assessment of 409A tax liabilities is time-barred when such liabilities arise from a failure to timely distribute nonqualified deferred compensation in a closed tax year? **265**

Q.268 If a service provider fails to properly include amounts in income arising from a Section 409A failure, and assessment of taxes becomes barred by the statute of limitations, can the taxpayer claim that such amounts can never be taxed? **266**

EFFECTIVE DATES **269**

Q.269 What was the statutory effective date of Section 409A? **269**

Q.270 When is a grandfathered plan considered to have been materially modified? **269**

Q.271 Can a grandfathered plan be amended to permit addition of a life insurance contract for notional investment crediting purposes without causing the plan to lose grandfathered status? **272**

Q.272 If a grandfathered plan is amended to change the form and time of payments under the plan, will such a material modification result in a violation of Section 409A? **272**

Q.273 How are amounts eligible for grandfathering determined? **273**

Q.274 Are grandfathered amounts subject to any restrictions on distribution? **274**

Q.275 What was the effective date for actual compliance with Section 409A? **275**

Q.276 What were the standards for compliance with Section 409A for the transition period between the statutory effective date, January 1, 2005, and December 31, 2008? **275**

Q.277 Has Congress ever introduced legislation to repeal Section 409A? **276**

PLANS OF TAX-EXEMPT ENTITIES **277**

Q.278 What regulatory guidance has been issued with respect to deferred compensation plans of tax-exempt and governmental entities, and when is the regulatory guidance effective? **277**

Q.279 What are the general tax rules governing nonqualified deferred compensation arrangements of tax-exempt entities? **278**

Q.280 Why are the rules associated with the taxation of deferred compensation for tax-exempt entities different from the rules applicable to taxable employers? **278**

Q.281 What is the definition of deferred compensation in the tax-exempt employer context? **279**

Q.282 If a plan is subject to Section 457, may it also be subject to Section 409A? **279**

Q.283 What plans are treated as not providing for a deferral of compensation for purposes of Section 457? **279**

Q.284 When is a plan legally binding for purposes of Section 457? **280**

Q.285 What is a bona fide severance pay plan for purposes of Section 457? **280**

Q.286 How does the definition of "bona fide severance pay plan" differ for purposes of Sections 409A and 457? **281**

Q.287 What constitutes a bona fide death benefit plan exempt from Section 457? **282**

Q.288 What is a bona fide disability pay plan for purposes of Section 457? **282**

Q.289 What is a bona fide sick and vacation leave plan? **283**

Q.290 What is the short-term deferral rule in the context of Section 457? **284**

Q.291 How does the definition of "substantial risk of forfeiture" differ for purposes of Sections 409A and 457? **284**

Q.292 What is recurring part-year compensation? **286**

Q.293 May an employee of a tax-exempt organization elect to defer salary or other vested compensation subject to a substantial risk of forfeiture and thereby achieve deferral of income taxation under Section 457? **287**

Q.294 May an employee of a tax-exempt employer achieve a deferral of income taxation of an amount subject to a substantial risk of forfeiture by extending the substantial risk of forfeiture to a future date? **288**

Q.295 How do the rules under Section 457 relating to rolling risks of forfeiture differ from the Section 409A rules? **289**

Q.296 If an amount is includable in income under Section 457(f) before payment of the deferred amount is made, how is the taxable amount of compensation determined? **290**

Q.297 How is the present value of compensation deferred under an account balance plan determined for purposes of Section 457? **291**

Q.298 How is the present value of deferred compensation under a plan that is not an account balance plan determined? **291**

Q.299 If an amount is includable in income under Section 457 before payment is made, how are earnings accruing after the date of income inclusion treated? **291**

Q.300 If an amount is includable in income under Section 457(f) before payment is made, may benefits under the plan be reduced to pay required tax withholdings? **292**

APPENDIX A CHECKLIST FOR STRUCTURING NONQUALIFIED DEFERRED COMPENSATION AND BENEFITS **293**

APPENDIX B CHECKLIST FOR DRAFTING PLANS SUBJECT TO SECTION 409A **295**

APPENDIX C UNFORESEEABLE
	EMERGENCY DISTRIBUTION
	REQUEST FORM	**301**

APPENDIX D DOMESTIC RELATIONS ORDER	**307**

APPENDIX E CHECKLIST FOR
	PERMISSIBLE DISTRIBUTIONS
	AND ACCELERATIONS	**311**

APPENDIX F CORRECTION OF
	DOCUMENTARY FAILURES
	SAMPLE STATEMENTS	**315**

APPENDIX G CORRECTION OF
	OPERATIONAL FAILURES
	SAMPLE STATEMENTS	**317**

APPENDIX H SUPER SUMMARY
	FOR CORRECTION OF
	OPERATIONAL VIOLATION
	OF SECTION 409A	**319**

TABLE OF AUTHORITIES	**323**

INDEX	**337**

ABOUT THE AUTHORS

BRIAN W. BERGLUND, BRYAN CAVE LEIGHTON PAISNER LLP

Mr. Berglund is Of Counsel in the Denver, Colorado, office of Bryan Cave Leighton Paisner LLP, an international law firm. Mr. Berglund has spent his entire legal career with Bryan Cave, encompassing more than 40 years. He is a member of the firm's Employee Benefits and Executive Compensation Group and its Tax Advice and Controversy Group. He has primarily represented large employers with sophisticated plans and counseled clients on tax law (especially regarding Code Section 409A), ERISA, securities law, and other issues relating to the design and structure of most types of executive and employee benefit plans. These include appropriate structures for employment agreements, severance plans, stock option plans, nonqualified deferred compensation plans, qualified plans, cafeteria and fringe benefit, and other welfare benefit plans. Mr. Berglund is a fellow in the American College of Employee Benefits Counsel.

Mr. Berglund graduated magna cum laude and Phi Beta Kappa with a degree in mathematics from Carleton College in Minnesota and graduated Order of the Coif from the Washington University School of Law in St. Louis. He was an adjunct professor of law at the Washington University School of Law for five years, where he taught a course in the graduate tax program titled "Advanced Topics in Employee Benefits." He has served as president of the Employee Benefits Association of St. Louis, Missouri.

Mr. Berglund frequently lectures on executive and employee benefits and tax-related topics to various law and bar groups. He has spoken regularly at American Law Institute-American Bar Association (ALI-ABA) programs, other programs covering executive and employee benefits, and St. Louis and Missouri Bar Association sponsored events.

Mr. Berglund has written several articles, which have appeared in a number of ALI-ABA program materials, including the *Employment Law Journal, Corporate Law Counselor,* and *St. Louis Bar Association Journal*. His article titled, "Correcting 409A Violations to Minimize Deferred Compensation Taxes," appeared in the *St. Louis Bar Association Journal*, Winter 2009 edition.

Mr. Berglund can be reached at bwberglund@bclplaw.com.

LOUIS R. RICHEY, JD, EXECUTIVE AND EMPLOYEE COMPENSATION & BENEFITS CONSULTANT

Mr. Richey is currently an Independent executive and employee compensation and benefits consultant, including technology applications for marketing and documenting such programs located north of Atlanta, GA in Blairsville, GA. He retired in 2020 as a legacy senior vice president and in-house attorney with Infosys McCamish Systems LLC, located in Atlanta, Georgia. McCamish Systems is one of the nation's leading providers of outsourced administrative and other back-office support services for life insurance carriers and other major financial services organizations, such as banks and brokerage companies. Infosys is a leading global information technology and administration business process outsourcing company. Mr. Richey helped lead the McCamish Retirement Services Group. Mr. Richey was the legal and content expert for all of McCamish's executive, employee and qualified and nonqualified pension benefit web-based marketing, design and plan administration platforms for some 20 years.

Mr. Richey is widely known as an author and a financial and executive compensation and benefits products and services marketing innovator. He is also recognized as an experienced executive and employee benefits attorney and consultant, with special expertise on insurance-related techniques and Section 409A nonqualified deferred compensation plans and other retirement plans. He has over 35 years' experience in executive and employee benefits compensation consulting, planning and insurance for Fortune 1000 public, closely held and tax-exempt organizations, and their employees. Prior to his employment with

Infosys McCamish, Mr. Richey served as a senior marketing officer or senior technical executive & employee compensation consultant with the American Express Company, the General American Life Insurance Company, William M. Mercer, Magner Network, and several offices of the Management Compensation Group (MCG) and M Group.

Mr. Richey is a graduate of Wabash College in Crawfordsville, Indiana, a cum laude graduate of the McKinney Indiana University Law School in Indianapolis, He is a member of the Georgia and Federal Bar, and a retired member of the Indiana Bar. He is also a Georgia registered neutral for civil arbitration and mediation. He is currently a member of the BNA and the National Underwriter Editorial Advisory Boards. He is also a retired chairman of the Board of Visitors of the McKinney Indiana University Law School, Indianapolis. He has been named a Kentucky Colonel and an Arkansas Traveler in recognition of his educational contributions to the legal profession.

Mr. Richey continues to lecture widely on the impact and implications of Section 409A, executive and employee benefit topics, retirement planning, financial services marketing, insurance, and financial planning. Over his long career, he has lectured at major conferences and institutes, including the New York University Federal Tax Institute (2X), the Southwest Federal Tax Conference, the Notre Dame Estate Planning Institute (2X), the American Society of Actuaries Annual Conference, the LIMRA Advance Marketing Conference (5X), the IMRA/LOMA Conference, the NACD, and a host of other conferences and local meetings.

Mr. Richey's comments have appeared in *Business Week*, *The Wall Street Journal*, *Forbes Magazine*, and *Investor's Daily*. He has appeared on the *Financial News Network* for National Public Radio. He has authored or co-authored a number of books and BNA portfolios, and more than five hundred articles, audios, and videos on compensation and tax topics in publications like BNA's *Compensation Planning Journal and its Estate Planning Journal.*

Mr. Richey is widely known for authoring or co-authoring popular practice-oriented publications, including BNA Tax Management Portfolios #393, entitled *Executive Compensation, a Practical Guide; as well as* #386 5th, and #282 3rd, entitled, *Insurance-Related Compensation.* This last publication was cited in a U.S. Tax Court opinion. For ALM

NUCO, he published *The Advisor's Guide to Nonqualified Deferred Compensation*, 2014-5th Edition, *The Advisor's Guide to 401(k) Plans*, 2014-1st Edition, and *Retirement Plan Facts*, 2016 Edition, all originally available from the ALM National Underwriter Company. Mr. Richey is also a 15-year advisor and editor on the deferred compensation, retirement plan and executive compensations sections of the ALM NUCO *Tax Fact*. In the 1980s, the Internal Revenue Service (IRS) included one of his published articles in training materials for its own estate and gift tax agents and attorneys. Mr. Richey can be reached at **LouRichey@AOL.com**.

The authors gratefully acknowledge the contributions of Carolyn Wolff and Caitlin Lucey in drafting this work.

NOTES ON CITATIONS

Citations to provisions of the Internal Revenue Code, final Treasury Regulations and other Internal Revenue Service publications are abbreviated.

Examples: I.R.C. § 409A; Treas. Reg. § 1.409A-1; Rev. Rul. 2010–27; Notice 2010–6; IR-2012–77; PLR 9030028.

Citations to proposed regulations and preambles to final and proposed regulations refer to the year issued and the relevant section number.

Examples: Preamble to Final 409A Regulations, § II.B (2007); Preamble to 2016 Proposed 409A Regulations § IV.E; Prop. Treas. Reg. § 1.457-11 (2016).

Citations to special materials.

Annotated final regulations. Comments on the application of Section 409A to topics other than calculation and payment of income tax made by Internal Revenue Service (IRS) representatives speaking at professional meetings have been compiled in the form of annotations to the final regulations. The annotations are updated periodically. Citations are to the annotated regulations published in the BNA Pension & Benefits Daily on July 12, 2012.

Example: Annotated Final Regulations, comments by [speaker's name], following Treas. Reg. § [1.409A-xxx], followed by a direct quotation in some cases. The form varies slightly if several speakers have commented on the same provision of the regulations.

Annotated Notice 2010–6. Comments on the correction of documentary errors in plans subject to Section 409A made by IRS representatives speaking at professional meetings have been compiled in the form of annotations to Notice 2010–6. These annotations are updated periodically as additional comments are made. Citations are to the annotated notice published in the BNA Pension & Benefits Daily on January 27, 2012.

Example: Annotated Notice 2010-6, comments by [speaker name], following § [yy].

American Bar Association Annual Meeting, Section of Taxation, Committee on Employee Benefits, Joint Committee on Employee Benefits, Internal Revenue Service, Questions and Answers. At this annual meeting held each May in Washington, D.C, members of the employee benefits bar present questions to the IRS regarding open issues. Citations to these questions and the answers provided by the IRS representatives include the year, the reference ABA JCEB Questions, and the question number.

Example: 2008 ABA JCEB Questions, Q&A 41.

The materials can be found by entering the terms "Joint Committee on Employee Benefits," "Internal Revenue Service," and the meeting year in a search engine.

Other citations are in standard form.

INTRODUCTION

When we published the first edition of this book back in early 2011 covering the basics of Section 409A, we expressed our understanding that our publication could only be a start to dealing with the many questions that would be encountered in creating, operating and amending plans subject to or designed to avoid the far-reaching scope of Section 409A. At that time, we asked you to contact us with questions that you routinely encountered. You responded so well, in fact, that we found ourselves with many more questions and answers. This fourth edition now covers 300 of your most frequently asked questions about Sections 409A and 457.

As we anticipated, new and important developments have continued to emerge in the form of IRS guidance and case law since the first edition was published. As a consequence, a prior edition included significantly more guidance on questions regarding procedures for correcting errors in documentation that resulted from the release of IRS Notices 2010–6 and 2010–80 as well as questions regarding administrative error corrections arising from the operation of nonqualified deferred compensation plans under the complex and often confusing guidance under Section 409A. Then, in June 2016, the IRS released additional proposed Section 409A Regulations, including the long-overdue proposed regulations for Section 457 relating to nonqualified plans of tax-exempt organizations.

In addition to providing correction procedures, the 2010 IRS Notices provide guidance on drafting documents subject to Section 409A by highlighting language that gives rise to documentary errors under Section 409A. Of course, with that guidance came a host of additional questions.

Even though more than 15 years have passed since the enactment of Section 409A, little or no official guidance has yet been issued with respect to some parts of the law. For example, the IRS and the

Department of the Treasury (Treasury) have not issued proposed regulations with respect to the funding rules under Section 409A(b). Important Section 409A regulations governing the calculation of the tax in case of a violation have not been finalized, even though the proposed regulations were released in 2008 (note that amendments to the proposed regulations regarding Section 409A income inclusion principles were issued in 2016). In addition, new law has been passed since the prior edition, such as the changes to Section 162(m) compensation deductions, and the addition of Section 4960 imposing a 21 percent excise tax on executive compensation of certain tax-exempt organizations, which has resulted in the need to "adjust," or even amend 409A-covered plans.

Finally, in 2020, the Covid-19 pandemic caused tremendous focus on the ability under 409A of both plan sponsors and participants to deal with their plans, stop contributions and access benefits to address the financial problems of both groups generated by the negative financial impact and chaos created by the pandemic. However, Congress provided no special relief for either group as to their 409A-covered plans, especially employee account balance plans. And, in IRS Notice 2020-50, Section 6, the IRS provided only minimal relief regarding a participant's ability to suspend deferrals (not access account balances) when the participant has first accessed their qualified 401(k) accounts under special pandemic financial hardship provisions. Therefore, parties were left to carefully nuance the existing law and regulations for 409A-permissible solutions for deferral cancellations and acceleration of account balance distributions.

So, much guidance is still yet to come on Section 409A from the government, new laws may require changes, and case law, like *Wilson v Safelite,* will undoubtedly proliferate as disputes relating to Section 409A arise. Each release of new law, new guidance and each new case opinion will inevitably lead to additional questions. We also note that the answers to the additional 50 question in this edition evidence a growing subtlety and sophistication that try solid analysis. All practitioners may not agree with an interpretation in an answer in some cases as we note in the copy where appropriate.

In this process, we recognize that this fourth edition will only be another step—hopefully a very helpful step—toward addressing the important questions routinely raised by this complicated and broadly applicable law. We trust that you will find this book useful to your practice when dealing with plans subject to and exempt from Sections 409A and 457. But if you find that this guide does not answer a Section 409A- or 457-related question, please contact us at bwberglund@bclplaw.com (Brian Berglund) and Lou_Richey@AOL.com (Lou Richey).

Finally, thanks for buying all our prior editions, and now this fourth edition. We are truly honored by your trust in our work product and seek to make each edition more helpful to you.

PLANS SUBJECT TO SECTIONS 409A AND 457

Q.1 WHAT TYPES OF COMPENSATION AND BENEFIT PLANS ARE SUBJECT TO SECTION 409A?

Anyone hoping to find a clear definition of exactly what types of compensation are subject to Section 409A of the Internal Revenue Code of 1986 ("Code") will be disappointed. As more fully explained in **Q.3**, the Section 409A regulations start with the proposition that almost every type of compensation arrangement constitutes a "deferral of compensation" potentially subject to Section 409A. It then sets forth a series of exceptions and exclusions under Section 409A for specific categories of compensation. This construct requires that a practitioner begin with the assumption that the compensation in question is subject to Section 409A. The practitioner must then determine whether an exception or exclusion applies.

A deferred compensation plan subject to Section 409A can include any compensation arrangement, written or oral, including an arrangement for one individual, or an arrangement which has not vested. As long as there is a promise — even a contingent promise — to pay compensation in a future taxable year, the applicability of Section 409A must be analyzed.

The service recipient can be an individual, partnership, corporation or any variation of those forms. It can be for-profit or not-for-profit, taxable or tax-exempt. The size, legal form and purpose of the service recipient are not material (see **Q.6**).

The service provider can be an employee of an employer, a director of a corporation, a partner of a partnership, an unrelated independent contractor, a cash-basis corporation, or a personal service organization or an entity (see **Q.7**).

Because nonqualified deferred compensation is defined so broadly under Section 409A and subject to so many exceptions, it is difficult to list all of the types of plans or arrangements subject to Section 409A. Having said this, the following types of plans historically classified as nonqualified deferred compensation plans are almost always subject to Section 409A:

- Unfunded participant account balance plans (nonqualified defined contribution plans based on participant elective deferrals)
- Unfunded employer account balance plans (nonqualified defined contribution matching plans, employer awards of additional deferred compensation under nonqualified defined contribution plans)
- Unfunded employer non-account balance plans (nonqualified defined benefit plans)

The following plans or arrangements have not historically been classified as nonqualified deferred compensation plans, but could be subject to Section 409A unless structured to fit within an exception or exclusion:

- Equity plans (stock option plans, stock appreciation rights)
- Split-dollar life insurance plans
- Severance and separation pay plans
- Post-employment expense reimbursement and fringe benefit plans
- Change of control plans
- Bonus plans
- Foreign plans

Deferred compensation arrangements potentially subject to Section 409A are frequently embedded in employment agreements, employment offer letters, commission arrangements, bonus arrangements, Section 457(f) top-hat plans sponsored by Section 501(c)(3) organizations, post-employment medical reimbursement arrangements, and partnership plans.

Citation: I.R.C. § 409A(d); Treas. Reg. §§ 1.409A-1(a)-(b); Preamble to 2016 Proposed 409A Regulations § VIII.

Q.2 WHAT PLANS ARE NOT SUBJECT TO SECTION 409A?

Exceptions to Section 409A are identified in the statute and regulations.

Statutory Exceptions:

- Tax-qualified employer retirement plans that satisfy the requirements of Code Section 401(a) (e.g., 401(k) plans, defined benefit pension plans and employee stock ownership plans (ESOPs)).
- Simple retirement plans described in Code Section 408(p) and simplified employee pension plans (SEPs) described in Code Section 408(k).
- Tax-deferred annuities that satisfy the requirements of Code Section 403(b).
- Eligible plans maintained by governmental and tax-exempt Section 501(c)(3) entities that satisfy the requirements of Code Section 457(b), sometimes called eligible 457 plans.
- Bona fide vacation and leave plans (see **Q.13**), disability pay plans (see **Q.11**), compensatory time plans, and death benefit plans (many split-dollar life insurance plans do not fit within this exception (see **Q.12** and **Q.180**)).
- Code Section 223 health savings accounts, Code Section 220 Archer medical savings accounts, flexible spending accounts, and certain medical reimbursement arrangements.

Regulatory Exceptions:

- Short-term deferrals (see **Q.21**).
- Equity plans that meet the requirements of Code Sections 422 (incentive stock options) and 423 (employee stock purchase plans) (see **Q.154**).
- Nonqualified stock options and stock appreciation rights with a strike price no less than fair market value on the date of grant that meet certain requirements (see **Q.155**).
- Non-collectively bargained severance plans that provide benefits for involuntary separation, separation for good reason, or separation

during limited window periods, with limits on the amount payable and the period of payment (see **Q.142**).
- Collectively bargained severance plans (see **Q.153**).
- Non-taxable benefits under Code Sections 104–106 (medical, dental, vision), 117 (tuition benefits), 119 (meals and lodging), 127 (educational assistance programs), 129 (dependent care assistance benefits), and 132 (certain fringe benefits) (see **Q.175**).
- Taxable education benefits (e.g., books, tuitions, and fees) for courses other than those involving sports, games, or hobbies.
- Endorsement and bona fide loan split-dollar arrangements (see **Q.180**).
- Teacher employment contracts that permit payment of compensation over twelve months rather than the nine- or ten-month school year during which it is earned (see **Q.126**).
- Certain indemnification and liability insurance agreements (see **Q.178**).
- Certain settlement agreements between the service recipient and the service provider (see **Q.178**).
- Normal end-of-period payroll payments overlapping two tax years (see **Q.20**).
- Section 83 restricted property transfers (see **Q.168**).
- Foreign plans that satisfy an otherwise applicable exception or that cover only non-resident aliens with no U.S. source income (see **Q.186**).
- Arrangements between accrual method taxpayers (see **Q.7**).
- Deferred compensation to independent contractors serving multiple non-affiliated service recipients (see **Q.7**).

Citation: I.R.C. § 409A(d); Treas. Reg. §§ 1.409A-1(a)-(b).

Q.3 WHAT CONSTITUTES A DEFERRAL OF COMPENSATION FOR PURPOSES OF SECTION 409A?

For purposes of Section 409A, a deferral of compensation occurs when, under the terms of the agreement and the relevant facts and circumstances, the plan participant acquires a legally binding right in one year to receive compensation that is or may be due and payable in a later year.

A substantial risk of forfeiture or other contingency does not diminish a payee's legally binding right to deferred compensation for this purpose.

However, no deferral of compensation occurs if the service recipient has unilateral unqualified discretion to reduce or eliminate the compensation after the services have been performed, unless it is unlikely that the service recipient will ever exercise this right or the service recipient's exercise of the right is tied to objective criteria (see **Q.5**).

The only types of compensation that will not fit within this extremely broad definition are compensation that must be paid in the calendar year in which the legally binding right to compensation arises and compensation that is subject to the sole discretion of the employer or other service recipient (see **Q.5**). For example, if an employer advises an employee that the employer may pay the employee a bonus sometime in the future at the sole discretion of the employer using subjective criteria such that the employee will have no legal recourse if the employer chooses not to pay a bonus, then the discretionary bonus would generally not fall within the definition of deferred compensation.

Note the breadth of the general definition. It may include virtually any type of compensation that an employer or other service recipient has a contractual obligation to pay in a future taxable year, including an obligation subject to contingencies.

Even base pay could constitute a deferral of compensation under this very broad definition. For example, assume an employee renders services to an employer in late December 2010 and will not receive payment for those services until the end of the first pay period in January 2011. Under the general broad definition, a deferral of compensation has occurred because the employee has a legally binding right to compensation payable in a later taxable year. However, this pay pattern is an exception to the general definition of deferred compensation for amounts paid shortly after they are earned pursuant to customary payroll practices (see **Q.20**).

Citation: I.R.C. § 409A(d)(1); Treas. Reg. §§ 1.409A-1(a)(1) and (b)(1); Annotated Final Regulations, comments by Daniel L. Hogans, following Treas. Reg. § 1.409A-1(a)(1), "A legally binding right can include, and often does include, a contingent right. Just because there is a contingency does not mean that there is no legally binding right. It does not mean a vested or perfected right—it just means a legally binding contingent right in a lot of cases. So, as a starting point, as long as you've got the promise—even if it is a contingent promise—to pay compensation in a future taxable year, you have a 409A issue. Further analysis is required."

Q.4 WHEN IS IT DETERMINED WHETHER A PLAN IS SUBJECT TO SECTION 409A?

This determination is made when the participant obtains a legally binding right to the deferred compensation. A plan generally becomes binding when it is no longer subject to reduction in benefits or termination by the unilateral act of the service recipient (see **Q.5**).

Citation: Treas. Reg. § 1.409A-1(c)(3).

Q.5 WHEN IS A PLAN LEGALLY BINDING FOR PURPOSES OF SECTION 409A?

A service provider has a legally binding right to compensation under a plan of a service recipient unless the service recipient can unilaterally reduce or eliminate the duty to pay the compensation. Even in that case, if the facts and circumstances suggest that the right to reduce or eliminate compensation lacks substantial significance or can be exercised only upon a condition, the right to deferred compensation is treated as legally binding for purposes of Section 409A.

In general, there is no substantial significance to a power to reduce or eliminate a service provider's right to deferred compensation if the service provider (i) has effective control over the person retaining the discretion; (ii) has effective control over any part of the compensation of the person retaining the discretion; or (iii) is a member of the family of the person retaining discretion (determined under Code Section 267(c)(4), applied as if the family also includes the spouse of any family member). There is no unilateral power to reduce or eliminate compensation if the criteria for reduction or elimination are by operation of the plan's terms, although this could qualify as a substantial risk of forfeiture for purposes of Section 409A (see **Q.24**). Also, the service recipient has a legally binding obligation under a plan (typically an excess plan), even if the plan's benefit formula provides for offset by tax-qualified plan benefits or benefits are reduced by actual or notional losses or by subsequent decreases in compensation used to calculate final average compensation.

Example. An employer maintains a nonqualified deferred compensation plan that provides that an employee who retires from the employer at age 65 or later will receive a lump sum benefit on retirement equal to one times the employee's annual base compensation at the time of retirement. The plan also provides that the employer may, in its sole discretion, reduce or eliminate benefits under the plan. All employees of the employer, including non-highly paid employees, are eligible for benefits under the plan. Based on all of the surrounding facts and circumstances, the employer's purported right to eliminate compensation lacks substantial significance. Because the arrangement covers all employees of the employer, including non-highly paid employees, it constitutes a pension plan subject to ERISA, including ERISA Section 204(g), which prohibits cutbacks in benefits. Based on the facts and circumstances, the employer cannot reduce or eliminate benefits, and therefore the plan is subject to Section 409A. (It also violates ERISA in several respects.)

Citation: Treas. Reg. § 1.409A-1(b)(1).

Q.6 WHO IS THE SERVICE RECIPIENT FOR PURPOSES OF SECTION 409A?

The service recipient is an individual or any type of legal entity that is the recipient of services rendered in exchange for a legally binding commitment to pay deferred compensation.

The size, legal form, and purpose of the recipient of the services are not material. The recipient can be an individual, partnership, corporation or any variation of those forms. It can be for-profit or not-for-profit, taxable or tax-exempt. The service recipient includes all entities aggregated with the direct service recipient as a single employer for purposes of Code Section 414(b) or (c). For example, if an employee provides services to ABC Corporation, then the service recipient includes both ABC Corporation and all entities aggregated with ABC Corporation as a single employer for purposes of Sections 414(b) and (c). If the parent of ABC Corporation provides a nonqualified deferred compensation plan for the benefit of a direct employee of ABC Corporation, then Section 409A applies to that plan even though the compensation is owed by the parent, not ABC Corporation.

For nonqualified stock options and stock appreciation rights, the Sections 414(b) and (c) aggregation rules are applied to determine whether stock constitutes service recipient stock, except that as little as a 20 percent interest can be considered a controlling interest for purposes of these aggregation rules (see **Q.107**).

Citation: Treas. Reg. § 1.409A-1(g).

Q.7 WHO IS A SERVICE PROVIDER FOR PURPOSES OF SECTION 409A?

A service provider can be an employee of an employer, a director of a corporation, a partner of a partnership, an unrelated independent contractor, or an entity. A service provider may also be a cash basis corporation, partnership, or personal service organization. Accrual basis service providers are not subject to Section 409A.

An independent contractor who is actively engaged in providing services to a trade or business other than as a member of the board of directors is exempt from Section 409A if the independent contractor provides "significant services" to two or more unrelated service recipients. Whether an independent contractor is providing significant services to two or more unrelated service recipients depends on the facts and circumstances. There is a safe harbor for an independent contractor whose income from a single service recipient is 70 percent or less of the independent contractor's income over the prior three years.

Citation: Treas. Reg. § 1.409A-1(f); Preamble to 2016 Proposed 409A Regulations § VIII.

Q.8 IF A BUSINESS ENGAGES AN INDIVIDUAL TO WRITE A BOOK, SONG, SOFTWARE PROGRAM, OR SIMILAR ITEM, AND THE PARTIES AGREE THAT THE BUSINESS WILL ACQUIRE OWNERSHIP OF OR DISTRIBUTION RIGHTS TO THE PROPERTY PRODUCED IN EXCHANGE FOR A MONETARY PAYMENT, DOES SECTION 409A APPLY TO THE ARRANGEMENT?

Some practitioners have taken the position that the principal purpose of this type of arrangement is acquisition of property or an interest in property and that Section 409A should not apply.

The IRS has informally taken the position that Section 409A applies in these circumstances. IRS representatives have stated that the standard for exclusion from Section 409A does not depend on whether the arrangement relates to property, but whether payment of compensation is involved. The arrangement is subject to Section 409A if it involves a legally binding right to payment of compensation in the future, unless an express exception applies (see **Q.2**). In contrast, the transaction is not subject to Section 409A if it involves the sale of property or an interest in property where the amount realized is not taxed as compensation.

Citation: 2009 ABA JCEB Questions, Q&A 20.

Q.9 ARE COMPENSATION AND BENEFIT PLANS OF TAX-EXEMPT ORGANIZATIONS SUBJECT TO SECTION 409A?

Generally, yes. The exceptions to Section 409A also apply to these plans (see **Q.2**), including plans covered by Section 457(b). Plans governed by Section 457(f), which don't qualify for favorable tax treatment under Section 457(b), are potentially subject both to Section 457(f) and Section 409A, unless an exception to Section 409A applies. For example, the short-term deferral exception will apply if the Section 457(f) plan provides for compensation subject to a substantial risk of forfeiture.

Note: Substantial risk of forfeiture is defined more strictly for purposes of Section 409A than for purposes of Section 457(f) (see **Q.291**). This could cause some Section 457(f) plan designs to violate Section 409A (see **Q.24**, **Q.291**, and **Q.295**).

Citation: I.R.C. § 409A(d); Treas. Reg. §§ 1.409A-1(a)-(b); Preamble to Treas. Reg. 1.409A-1 *et seq.*, I.R.B. 2007–19 (May 7, 2007), § II.B; Prop. Treas. Reg. § 1.457-12(e) (2016); Notice 2007–62; PLRs 9030028 and 9041026; David Boekeloo, Robert Hopkins, Louis R. Richey, *Multiple Definitions of Substantial Risk of Forfeiture Create Confusion after Section 409A, but Notice 2007–62 Is Not the Answer*, 36 TAX MGMT. COMP. PLAN. J. 396 (Jan. 2008) (discussing implications of Notice 2007–62 for § 457(f) plans).

Q.10 ARE ARRANGEMENTS INVOLVING PARTNERSHIPS SUBJECT TO SECTION 409A?

IRS guidance on the application of Section 409A to partnerships is limited. Most of the guidance that exists is in the preamble to the Section 409A regulations and IRS Notice 2005–1.

- Until further guidance is issued, the following rules apply:
  - Issuance of a profits interest in connection with performance of services that does not result in inclusion of income by the service provider at the time of issuance is not treated as the deferral of compensation for purposes of Section 409A.
  - Issuance of a capital interest in connection with performance of services is treated in the same way for purposes of Section 409A as a grant of equity-based compensation if the compensation is determined by reference to partnership equity.
  - The principles applicable to stock options and stock appreciation rights under Section 409A also apply to equivalent rights with respect to partnership interests.
  - Section 409A may apply to payments covered by Code Section 707(a)(1) (partner not acting in capacity as partner) if the payments otherwise constitute deferred compensation under a nonqualified deferred compensation plan.

- Section 409A applies to a partner's right to receive a guaranteed payment for services described in Section 707(c) in a future taxable year, unless the partner includes the payment in income by the fifteenth day of the third month following the end of the partner's taxable year in which the legally binding right to the guaranteed payment arises, or if later, the partner's taxable year in which the right to the payment becomes no longer subject to a substantial risk of forfeiture. This is equivalent to the short-term deferral rule.
- An arrangement providing for payments subject to Code Section 736 (payments to a retiring partner or a deceased partner's successor in interest) is generally not subject to Section 409A.
- Payments to a retired partner that do not constitute self-employment income under Code Section 1402(a)(10) are generally subject to Section 409A. This applies if the payments are made pursuant to a written plan on account of retirement and continue at least until the partner's death, the partner does not render services during the partnership's taxable year that ends with or within the partner's taxable year of receipt, the other partners have no obligations to the retired partner, and all of the retired partner's capital is paid out before the end of the partnership's taxable year.

The Treasury and the IRS have requested comments on the application of Section 409A to arrangements involving partnerships and partners, and the ABA Section on Taxation has made a number of suggestions.

Citation: Notice 2005–1, Q&A 7; Preamble to Final § 409A Regulations, § III.G (2007); *see also* ABA Tax Section comments at www.abanet.org/tax/pubpolicy/2005/050520eb3.pdf.

Q.11 WHAT CONSTITUTES DISABILITY PAY EXEMPT FROM SECTION 409A?

For purposes of Section 409A, the term "nonqualified deferred compensation plan" does not include a plan or a portion of a plan to the extent that the plan provides bona fide disability pay. Therefore, employer-funded or insured plans that provide benefits only in the event of disability are not subject to Section 409A. Payments under a nonqualified deferred compensation plan in the event of disability also constitute disability pay to the extent the disability benefits payable under the plan exceed the present value of the benefits otherwise payable under the nonqualified plan during the employee's lifetime. This is determined under the plan's optional form of distribution that provides the employee with the largest present value during his or her lifetime.

Example 1. An employer maintains a nonqualified defined benefit plan that provides monthly benefits to an individual commencing at age 65. A participant who becomes disabled before age 65 receives $500 per month until age 65, and at age 65 receives the monthly benefit provided for under the plan in the absence of disability. The portion of the plan providing disability benefits constitutes disability pay that is exempt from the requirements of Section 409A. The portion of the plan that provides monthly benefits at age 65 constitutes a deferred compensation plan subject to Section 409A.

Example 2. An employer maintains an account balance plan subject to a vesting schedule. In the event of a participant's disability, the participant's account balance becomes fully vested and is distributed in a lump sum. The lump sum payment on account of disability does not constitute disability pay for purposes of Section 409A because the disability benefit does not exceed the present value of the benefits that could be payable to a participant under the plan during the employee's lifetime, which is the employee's account balance. The entire plan is subject to Section 409A.

Citation: Treas. Reg. § 1.409A-1(a)(5); Treas. Reg. § 31.3121(v)(2)-1(b)(4)(iv)(C).

Q.12 WHAT CONSTITUTES A BONA FIDE DEATH BENEFIT PLAN EXEMPT FROM SECTION 409A?

A plan will be considered a bona fide death benefit plan to the extent that the total benefits payable under the plan exceed the lifetime benefits payable under the plan. For example, a so-called "death benefit only" plan that only pays benefits upon the death of a participant is not subject to Section 409A.

Citation: Prop. Treas. Reg. § 1.409A-1(a)(5) (2016).

Q.13 WHAT CONSTITUTES A BONA FIDE VACATION OR LEAVE PLAN?

There is no specific definition yet for purposes of Section 409A. The guidance issued in the context of Section 457 might be applied by analogy (see **Q.289**).

Citation: Prop. Treas. Reg. § 1.409A-1(a)(5) (2016).

Q.14 WHAT ARE THE GENERAL REQUIREMENTS FOR NONQUALIFIED DEFERRED COMPENSATION PLANS SUBJECT TO SECTION 409A?

Section 409A codifies many of the rules previously advanced by the IRS in the area of constructive receipt. In broad terms, Section 409A generally requires the following:

- An election to defer compensation must be made before the calendar year in which the compensation is earned.
- The form and time of payment of deferred compensation must be established before the compensation is earned.
- The time for payment of deferred compensation may generally not be accelerated or further deferred after the compensation is earned, with limited exceptions.
- Deferred compensation may only be paid upon a fixed date, separation from service, or certain other events.
- The deferred compensation arrangement must be documented in writing.
- As long as a plan meets these requirements in both form and operation and the plan remains unfunded (see **Q.196**), the plan will comply with Section 409A. Income tax on the amounts deferred will not occur until payment in accordance with plan provisions.

Citation: I.R.C. § 409A(a)(1)(A)(i)(I) (incorporating §§ 409A(a)(2)-(4)). For the most part, the Final Regulations clarify these major requirements.

DOCUMENTATION REQUIREMENTS

Q.15 ARE PLANS SUBJECT TO SECTION 409A REQUIRED TO BE IN WRITING?

Yes (see **Q.16**). Therefore, any undocumented arrangement that provides for deferred compensation subject to Section 409A automatically violates Section 409A.

Citation: Treas. Reg. § 1.409A-1(c)(3)(i).

Q.16 WHEN MUST A PLAN SUBJECT TO SECTION 409A BE DOCUMENTED?

A plan subject to Section 409A that allows participant elections to defer compensation must set forth in writing the conditions under which such elections may be made no later than the date the initial deferral election becomes irrevocable.

It is advisable to document any employee benefit plan before it becomes effective, but the plan may be documented as late as December 31 of the calendar year in which the legally binding right to the compensation arises. An amount that is not payable until after the next calendar year (the subsequent year) may be documented by the fifteenth day of the third month of the subsequent year.

Citation: Treas. Reg. § 1.409A-1(c)(3).

Q.17 ARE THERE SPECIFIC FEATURES PROHIBITED IN PLANS SUBJECT TO SECTION 409A THAT WERE FREQUENTLY INCLUDED IN NONQUALIFIED PLANS BEFORE ENACTMENT OF SECTION 409A?

Except for the distribution events described in the statute and regulations, event-based distributions and all discretionary distributions are prohibited in a deferred compensation plan subject to Section 409A.

Impermissible distribution events include the following:

- A plan provision permitting distribution upon admission of a participant's child to college was common before Section 409A. It is not permitted under Section 409A because it is an event-based distribution not included in the statute or regulations.
- A plan provision permitting a participant to obtain an early distribution with the consent of the board of directors of the employer or a committee was permitted before Section 409A. It is no longer permitted because Section 409A categorically prohibits discretionary acceleration of deferred compensation.
- Previously common "haircut" provisions that permitted discretionary distribution at any time if the service provider incurred a penalty, or "haircut," on the amount of the distribution are now prohibited. The authority for such distributions as a substantial limitation on the right to receive immediate payment under Treasury Regulation § 1.451-2(a) was overridden by Section 409A.
- A plan provision that permits the employer to offset any amounts a participant owes the employer against the amount due the participant under a nonqualified plan are now prohibited as impermissible accelerations, except in very narrow circumstances (see **Q.93**).

Citation: I.R.C. § 409A(a)(2); Treas. Reg. §§ 1.409A-1, 1.409A-3 (stating limits on distributions and accelerations from plans); *see also* Congressional Commentary to I.R.C. § 409A, American Jobs Creation Act of 2004, Pub. L. No. 108–357, 118 Stat. 1418 (application of Section 409A(a)(2) to event-based distributions and haircut provisions); I.R.S. CCA Memo 200935029 (Aug. 28, 2009) (offset of salary advance against deferred compensation).

Q.18 IS IT APPROPRIATE TO DOCUMENT THE PROVISIONS OF A PLAN DESIGNED TO FALL OUTSIDE THE SCOPE OF SECTION 409A?

Plans that are not subject to Section 409A, such as those that satisfy the requirements for the short-term deferral exception (see **Q.21**), are not required to be in writing. However, documentation of their provisions demonstrates that they satisfy the requirements for the exception. In particular, documenting a short-term deferral arrangement in writing may prevent a Section 409A violation if for some reason payment is not made within the short-term deferral period without a valid excuse and the arrangement inadvertently becomes subject to Section 409A.

As stated by Daniel L. Hogans, one of the architects of the Section 409A regulations, "This is a way to straddle the short-term deferral rule and the required payment deadline." In other words, if the bonus arrangement is properly documented, payments will be considered exempt from Section 409A if made by the short-term deferral deadline, and the arrangement will be considered subject to and in compliance with Section 409A if the payments are made after the short-term deferral deadline but by the end of the same year (see **Q.21**).

In addition, and very important at a practical level, the IRS has requested information regarding plans and arrangements subject to Section 409A and those exempt from Section 409A when conducting service recipient audits. Documenting any exempt plans and arrangements may make the service recipient's response quicker and easier.

Example. An employer maintains an annual bonus plan and specifies in writing that the bonus must be payable by the March 15 following the calendar year in which the bonus is earned. The employer misses the March 15 deadline with no valid excuse, but makes the bonus payment by the end of the year. Because the bonus payment is made after the March 15 deadline but within the same calendar year, the bonus payment will be considered deferred compensation subject to Section 409A. It will meet the requirements of Section 409A because the arrangement is in writing and the payment is made by the end of the calendar year in which the specified payment date occurs.

Citation: Treas. Reg. § 1.409A-1(c)(3); Annotated Final Regulations, comments by Daniel L. Hogans, following Treas. Reg. § 1.409A-1(b)(4)(ii).

Q.19 WHAT ARE THE MINIMUM DOCUMENTATION REQUIREMENTS FOR A PLAN SUBJECT TO SECTION 409A?

There is no particular format for documentation of a plan subject to Section 409A, except that it must be documented. A single document is permitted, but two or more documents may also constitute a single plan. Even e-mails or other electronic communications may be sufficient to satisfy the documentation requirements, particularly with respect to participant elections.

At a minimum, the plan must state all of the following:

- Either the amount of deferred compensation or the method or formula for determining the amount.
- The time and form of payment.
- Initial employee election procedures, if applicable.
- Definitions of key terms that comply with the requirements of Section 409A.

Practitioners drafting plans subject to Section 409A should consider including the following:

For All Plans:

Definitions with respect to distribution events, such as separation from service, leave of absence, disability, unforeseeable emergency, and change of control (see **Q.29–35**, **46**, **73**, and **82**).

- A provision for designated payment dates or payment dates measured from the separation date, such as 90 days after separation (see **Q.48**).
- A provision for grandfathering any amounts that were earned and vested on December 31, 2004 (See **Q.269**).
- An optional provision for cash-outs of small distributions.
- An optional provision for the limited available offset of the service provider's obligations to the service recipient against the amounts due the service provider under the plan (see **Q.93**).

- Optional provisions stating other desired exceptions to the prohibition against benefit accelerations. Examples include a provision permitting distribution (i) pursuant to a domestic relations order incident to a divorce or legal separation, (ii) to pay FICA taxes due on compensation deferred under the plan and any associated income taxes, or (iii) to pay taxes due on account of breach of Section 409A.
- A provision for voluntary plan termination by the service recipient (see **Q.85**).
- A provision for interpretation of all terms and provisions consistent with Section 409A, especially as to all undefined, ambiguous or incomplete definitions and provisions (see **Q.227**).
- A provision under which the employer either disclaims or accepts responsibility for any adverse tax consequences arising under Section 409A (see **Q.106**).
- A spendthrift or nonassignability provision.
- A provision that the plan constitutes an unsecured and unfunded contractual promise to pay benefits rather than a funded plan.
- Provisions designed to comply with state law employment requirements and choice of law.
- If the plan is informally funded through a rabbi trust, a provision prohibiting transfer of assets used to fund the plan to an irrevocable trust in connection with deterioration of the employer's financial health or to an offshore trust (see **Q.197**).
- If the plan is informally funded through a rabbi trust, a provision prohibiting setting aside assets in the rabbi trust during any "restricted period" with respect to a tax-qualified defined benefit pension plan of the employer that does not satisfy statutory minimum funding levels (see **Q.199**).

For Any Plan of a Publicly Held Employer:

- A provision for a six-month delay of payments due upon separation from service of a specified employee (see **Q.36**). A plan need not include a six-month delay provision with respect to a service provider who is not a specified employee, but if a non-specified

employee becomes a specified employee, the six-month delay provision must be added with respect to the service provider no later than the date the service provider first becomes a specified employee.
- A provision stating whether all payments suspended during the six-month waiting period will be paid in a single sum on expiration of the waiting period or whether, in the alternative, all individual payments due the specified employee will be delayed for six months (see **Q.36**).
- A provision stating the date for valuation of the amount due the service provider.

For Any Plan That Gives Participants the Right to Select the Time and Form of Payment (see **Q.120**)*:*

An optional provision allowing for subsequent elections changing the previously designated form and time of payment, including a provision for treating a prior election to receive payment in installments as a unitary single election or a series of individual elections for this purpose (see **Q.109**).

For an Account Balance Plan:

A provision for a reasonable rate of return or an objective measure for the rate of return, such as a stock or bond index.

For an Elective Deferral Plan:

- A provision stating the date by which elections to defer base pay, bonuses and performance-based pay must be made, both for existing participants and those who become eligible after the beginning of a year (see **Q.127**).
- If applicable, special provisions for elections to defer performance-based compensation (see **Q.121** and **Q.124**).
- A provision for treatment of a participant whose eligibility terminates and then resumes at a later time (see **Q.121**).
- A provision for automatic cancellation of a participant's deferrals on the participant's receipt of a hardship distribution from a 401(k) or 403(b) plan (see **Q.125**).

For an Employer Non-account Balance Plan:

A provision prohibiting suspension of payment on reemployment after periodic retirement distributions have begun (see **Q.70**).

Other Provisions That Are Not Permitted or Not Advisable:

- Previously used haircut provisions under which the participant could elect early distribution subject to a penalty, other conditional event-based distributions and accelerations (such as the employee's child being admitted to college), and offset provisions that do not satisfy the requirements of Section 409A must be removed from the plan (see **Q.17**).
- Blanket Section 409A savings clauses that purport to reform the document to disregard terms that violate Section 409A or to incorporate by general reference any provisions required to cause the plan to comply with Section 409A. A savings clause will not automatically disqualify a plan from meeting the requirements of Section 409A, but it will not bring a plan into compliance if the plan document includes provisions that contravene or omit requirements of Section 409A. However, a provision for application of all terms and provisions consistent with Section 409A, especially as to all undefined, ambiguous or incomplete definitions and provisions, is permissible and useful. The distinction is between reformation of a provision that is inconsistent with Section 409A and interpretation of an ambiguous provision as consistent with Section 409A. Notices 2010–6 and 2010–80, which address correction of documentation errors under Section 409A, also provide useful guidelines and checklists for documentary compliance to avoid such errors.

Citation: Treas. Reg. § 1.409A-1(c)(1)-(3); Annotated Final Regulations, comments of Daniel L. Hogans, William Schmidt and Stephen Tackney following Treas. Reg. § 1.409A-1(c)(3)(i) (savings clauses) and comments of Daniel L. Hogans following Treas. Reg. § 1.409A-1(c)(3)(iii) (electronic documentation of plan requirements); Notice 2010–6; Notice 2010–80.

SHORT-TERM DEFERRALS EXEMPT FROM SECTION 409A

Q.20 DO AMOUNTS THAT ARE PAID SHORTLY AFTER THEY ARE EARNED CONSTITUTE DEFERRED COMPENSATION SUBJECT TO SECTION 409A?

Notwithstanding the very broad general definition of the phrase "deferral of compensation" described in **Q.3**, amounts that are paid shortly after they are earned are not considered deferred compensation subject to Section 409A. This is true even if the amounts are paid after the last day of the calendar year in which the amounts are earned, provided the delay is due to the way the service recipient normally compensates service providers under its payroll system. For example, if an employee renders services to an employer during the last pay period in December but does not receive the paycheck for such services until January pursuant to the employer's standard payroll practices, the amount paid is not subject to Section 409A.

In addition, short-term deferrals—amounts paid shortly after they become vested—are not treated as deferred compensation even though payment may occur after the year in which services relating to the compensation are performed (see **Q.21**).

Citation: Treas. Reg. § 1.409A-1(b)(3) and (4).

Q.21 WHAT IS THE SHORT-TERM DEFERRAL RULE?

The short-term deferral rule is the most commonly applied exception to Section 409A. Section 409A does not apply to any payment that is not a "deferred payment," as long as the service provider actually or constructively receives the payment within 2½ months after the close of either the service provider's or service recipient's taxable year in which the payment is no longer subject to a substantial risk of forfeiture (see **Q.24**). If both the service provider and the service recipient use the calendar year as the taxable year, the deadline for payment is March 15 following the close of the calendar year in which the payment is no longer subject to a substantial risk of forfeiture. If the service recipient uses a taxable year other than the calendar year, the deadline is the later of 2½ months after the end of the calendar year or 2½ months after the end of the service recipient's taxable year in which the payment is no longer subject to a substantial risk of forfeiture.

A right to a payment that is never subject to a substantial risk of forfeiture is considered not to be subject to a substantial risk of forfeiture on the day the service provider obtains a legally binding right to the payment. For example, if an employer promises an employee a $100,000 bonus on November 15, 2017, the bonus is considered not to be subject to a substantial risk of forfeiture on November 15, 2017. If the bonus is paid by March 15, 2018, it falls within the exception for short-term deferrals under Section 409A.

A deferred payment subject to Section 409A can never constitute a short-term deferral. A payment is a deferred payment if it is made pursuant to a plan provision for payment to be made or completed on or after any date, or on or after occurrence of any event, that could occur later than the end of the applicable 2½ month period. For example, if a service provider has a legally binding right to compensation that is not subject to substantial risk of forfeiture as of November 1, 2017, and payment is scheduled to be made incident to the service provider's separation from service, then the payment is not a short-term deferral even if the service provider separates from service shortly after November 1, 2017, and receives payment on or before March 15, 2018. This is because payment would have occurred on a later date if the service provider had continued employment beyond March 15, 2018.

If a plan provides that the service provider or service recipient has the right to elect to change the payment date, schedule, or triggering event, that right is disregarded for purposes of the short-term deferral rule unless such an election is actually made. If no such election is made, whether the plan provides for a deferral subject to Section 409A is determined based on the payment date, schedule, or event that governs in the absence of an election. If the service provider or service recipient makes an election to defer a payment from the plan that would otherwise constitute a short-term deferral, whether the plan provides for a deferral subject to Section 409A is based on the payment date, schedule, or event that the service provider or service recipient elects.

How the short-term deferral rule applies to a series of installment payments depends upon whether payments are designated as a single payment or as separate payments. If a series of installment payments is designated as a single payment, then all of the installment payments are deferred compensation subject to Section 409A if any one or more of the payments is or could be made after the applicable 2½ month period. In contrast, if a series of installment payments is designated as separate payments, then the individual payments made within the applicable 2½ month period are short-term deferrals exempt from Section 409A unless payment could have occurred after the end of the applicable 2½ month period as illustrated in the example above. Designation of a series of installment payments as separate payments may be especially useful in separation agreements because it causes the short-term deferral exception to apply to the installments payable on account of separation from service by the end of the applicable 2½ month period, and these installments are not taken into account in determining the amount subject to the cap on separation pay that is exempt from Section 409A (see **Q.142**, **Q.143**, and **Q.144**).

Payments that occur within the short-term deferral period are not subject to Section 409A unless payment could have been made after the end of the applicable 2½ month period. As a result, they need not be authorized in writing for purposes of Section 409A. However, if a payment actually occurs after the short-term deferral deadline, the payment is subject to Section 409A and its documentation requirements, unless a special exception applies (see **Q.4** and **Q.23**).

Example 1. An employer with a calendar year taxable year awards a bonus to Employee A on November 1, 2017, that is not subject to a substantial risk of forfeiture. The bonus plan does not provide for a payment date or deferred payment. The bonus plan will not be considered to have provided for a deferral of compensation if the bonus is paid or made available to Employee A on or before March 15, 2018. However, if the bonus payment is not paid or made available to Employee A until a later date, the bonus arrangement will be subject to Section 409A unless one of the situations justifying delay in payment of compensation specified in **Q.23** applies.

Example 2. On November 1, 2018, an employer awards a bonus to Employee B subject to forfeiture unless Employee B continues working for the employer through December 31, 2020. Employee B has the right to make a written election not later than December 31, 2019, to receive the bonus on or after December 31, 2025, but Employee B does not make the election. Because Employee B does not make a deferral election, the bonus plan will not be considered to have provided for a deferral of compensation if the bonus is paid or made available to Employee B on or before March 15, 2021.

Example 3. On November 1, 2018, an employer awards a bonus to Employee C under which Employee C must continue to perform services through December 31, 2020, to receive the bonus. The bonus plan provides that the bonus is scheduled to be paid in a lump sum on July 1, 2021. Because the plan specifies a payment date after the applicable 2½ month period, the bonus plan provides for a deferral of compensation that does not qualify as a short-term deferral and must comply with Section 409A. This is the case even if the bonus is paid or made available on or before March 15, 2021. Moreover, payment or availability of the bonus on or before March 15, 2021 would cause an impermissible acceleration of a payment under Section 409A. Section 409A generally prohibits any acceleration of a payment more than 30 days before the scheduled payment date, which would be June 1, 2021 in this example (see **Q.48**).

Citation: Treas. Reg. § 1.409A-1(b)(4).

Q.22 WHEN IS PAYMENT CONSIDERED TO HAVE BEEN MADE FOR PURPOSES OF THE SHORT-TERM DEFERRAL RULE?

In general, when the service recipient receives actual or constructive payment of cash or property. For purposes of the short-term deferral rule, an amount is treated as paid when it is included in income under Section 457(f) whether or not an actual or constructive payment occurs. For more detail regarding the meaning of the term "payment" in the context of Section 409A generally, see **Q.49**.

Citation: Preamble to Final 409A Regulations § II.B (2007); Treas. Reg. § 1.409A-1(a)(4).

Q.23 WHAT SITUATIONS JUSTIFY DELAY IN PAYMENT OF COMPENSATION DESIGNED TO QUALIFY AS A SHORT-TERM DEFERRAL BEYOND 2½ MONTHS AFTER THE END OF THE TAXABLE YEAR IN WHICH THE COMPENSATION IS EARNED?

Compensation designed to satisfy the short-term deferral rule may be paid more than 2½ months after the end of the taxable year in which the compensation is earned and still qualify for the short-term deferral rule in the following four circumstances:

- An administrative impracticability that was not reasonably foreseeable. Payment must occur as soon as administratively practicable.
- The employer is in financial jeopardy as a going concern. Payment must occur as soon as the financial jeopardy ends.
- The employer would lose its income tax deduction under Code Section 162(m) if the payment were made on time, and, as of the date the legally binding right to the payment arose, the employer reasonably did not anticipate the application of Section 162(m) as of the date the payment becomes due. The payment must be made as soon as reasonably practical following the first date on which the service recipient anticipates or reasonably should

anticipate that the payment will no longer be restricted by the application of Section 162(m). This relief was designed to apply to mid-level employees who unexpectedly become subject to Section 162(m) at a later time. According to Daniel L. Hogans, one of the architects of the regulations, "For someone that you reasonably expect to be subject to Section 162(m), it makes more sense to just have a condition built in that to the extent that the deduction will be limited by 162(m), the amount will be deferred."

- The service recipient reasonably anticipates that making the payment on or before the end of the applicable 2½ month period would violate federal securities laws or other applicable law. The payment must be made as soon as reasonably practicable following the first date on which the employer anticipates or reasonably should anticipate that making the payment would not cause such violation. The making of a payment that would cause inclusion in gross income or the application of any penalty provision of the Code is not treated as a violation of applicable law.

Citation: Treas. Reg. § 1.409A-1(b)(4)(ii); Annotated Final Regulations, comments by Daniel L. Hogans, following Treas. Reg. § 1.409A-1(b)(4)(ii); Prop. Treas. Reg. § 1.409A-1(b)(4)(ii) (2016); Preamble to 2016 Proposed 409A Regulations § II.B.

Q.24 WHAT IS A SUBSTANTIAL RISK OF FORFEITURE, AND HOW DOES IT RELATE TO SATISFACTION OF THE SHORT-TERM DEFERRAL RULE FOR PURPOSES OF SECTION 409A?

Compensation is subject to a substantial risk of forfeiture for purposes of Section 409A if the compensation is conditioned on the performance of substantial future services or the occurrence of a condition related to a purpose of the compensation, and the possibility of forfeiture is substantial. A condition is considered related to the purpose of the compensation only if it relates to the service provider's performance or the service recipient's business activities or organizational goals, such as attainment

SHORT-TERM DEFERRALS EXEMPT FROM SECTION 409A

of a prescribed level of earnings or equity value or completion of an initial public offering.

The short-term deferral rule exempts compensation from Section 409A if payment occurs within 2½ months after the end of the taxable year in which the service provider obtains a right to the compensation that is not subject to a substantial risk of forfeiture (see **Q.21**).

In some cases, the service provider obtains a vested right to compensation in the year services are rendered, for example, with respect to base salary or wages. In those cases, the service provider has no substantial risk of forfeiture after the services are rendered and Section 409A applies if the compensation is paid more than 2½ months after the end of the taxable year in which the services are rendered.

In other cases, the compensation is made subject to a substantial risk of forfeiture. This causes the service provider's vested right to the compensation to be delayed until the substantial risk of forfeiture is satisfied. For example, a requirement that an employee remain in continuous employment with the employer for a stated period of time or until a stated age to obtain a vested right to the deferred compensation constitutes a substantial risk of forfeiture. In those cases, the substantial risk of forfeiture and the short-term deferral rule in combination permit a plan that provides for distribution within 2½ months after the end of the year in which the substantial risk of forfeiture expires to avoid becoming subject to Section 409A, even though payment is not made for many years after the compensation is earned. To receive payment, the service provider must provide additional services in the form of employment until the date provided for in the plan. If payment occurs within the short-term deferral period for the year in which the substantial risk of forfeiture lapses, the payment is exempt from Section 409A under the short-term deferral rule.

Amounts payable only upon involuntary termination are also subject to a substantial risk of forfeiture. For purposes of the short-term deferral rule and the involuntary termination exception, certain types of voluntary "good reason" termination are also considered involuntary termination (see **Q.147**).

Whether the risk of forfeiture is sufficiently substantial depends on the likelihood of its enforcement, based on the facts and circumstances.

The regulations address whether compensation is subject to a substantial risk of forfeiture under these additional circumstances:

- Voluntary salary deferrals are not subject to a substantial risk of forfeiture.
- A covenant not to compete alone does not create a substantial risk of forfeiture, even if the compensation is completely forfeitable upon breach of the covenant.
- Compensation is generally not subject to a substantial risk of forfeiture beyond the time when the recipient otherwise could have elected to receive it, unless the present value of the amount subject to a substantial risk of forfeiture is materially greater than the present value of the amount the recipient otherwise could have elected to receive in the absence of the risk of forfeiture. As a result, subsequent employee deferrals do not satisfy the requirements of Section 409A unless they satisfy the requirements for subsequent elections (see **Q.127**).
- Compensation is generally not subject to a substantial risk of forfeiture following extension of an existing substantial risk of forfeiture to a later date. As a result, rolling vesting dates usually do not create substantial risk of forfeiture. According to William Schmidt, Senior Counsel in the Office of Chief Counsel of the Executive Compensation Branch of the IRS, if compensation is subject to a substantial risk of forfeiture and the forfeiture condition is extended or modified, "as a general rule, unless there is additional consideration paid for that extension, the extension of the forfeiture period will be disregarded and the amount will be treated as vested for purposes of 409A."
- Payments contingent on attainment of a prescribed level of earnings may be subject to a substantial risk of forfeiture if the risk of not attaining that level of earnings is substantial.
- Payments contingent on completion of an initial public offering may be subject to a substantial risk of forfeiture if the risk that there will be no public offering is substantial from the outset.
- Stock options that are immediately exercisable in exchange for substantially vested stock are not subject to a substantial risk of

forfeiture even if the ability to exercise the option terminates upon separation from service.

For individuals with significant equity voting power in the entity that pays the deferred compensation, the relevant facts and circumstances for determining whether a risk of forfeiture is substantial include:

- The service provider's relationship to other equity holders and the extent of his or her control, potential control, and possible loss of control of the service recipient.
- The service provider's relationship with the service recipient and the extent to which the service provider is subordinate to other service providers.
- The service provider's relationship to the officers and directors of the service recipient.
- The person or persons who must approve the service provider's discharge.
- Past actions of the service recipient in enforcing the restrictions.

Citation: Treas. Reg. § 1.409A-1(d); Annotated Final Regulations, comments by William Schmidt, following Treas. Reg. § 1.409A-1(d)(1).

Q.25 IF A COMPENSATION ARRANGEMENT QUALIFIES AS A SHORT-TERM DEFERRAL EXEMPT FROM SECTION 409A, CAN THE PARTIES CHANGE THE FORM AND TIME OF PAYMENT UNDER THE ARRANGEMENT AFTER THE SERVICES RELATING TO THE COMPENSATION HAVE BEEN PERFORMED WITHOUT BECOMING SUBJECT TO SECTION 409A?

Yes, but only if the new payment schedule also qualifies for the short-term deferral exception. If the change includes a delay in the scheduled payment date from one taxable year to another, the constructive receipt rules may apply, independent of Section 409A (see **Q.114**).

Citation: 2009 ABA JCEB Questions, Q&A 32.

Q.26 WHAT IS THE RELATIONSHIP BETWEEN THE DEFINITIONS OF SUBSTANTIAL RISK OF FORFEITURE UNDER SECTION 409A, SECTION 83, AND SECTION 457(f)?

The definition of substantial risk of forfeiture under Section 83, which governs recognition of income on transfer of property in exchange for services, involves a facts and circumstances analysis and is broader than the definition under Section 409A. For example, forfeiture of property upon competition with a prior employer may give rise to a substantial risk of forfeiture for purposes of Section 83, but not for purposes of Section 409A.

Compensation deferred under a nonqualified deferred compensation plan maintained by a tax-exempt entity or government is generally subject to tax in the year in which there is no substantial risk of forfeiture under Section 457(f), unless the plan qualifies for favorable treatment under Section 457(b). The IRS has applied a definition of substantial risk of forfeiture that is analogous to the Section 83 definition for purposes of Section 457(f) proposed regulations issued in 2016. This is a hazard for tax-exempt and governmental employers that maintain Section 457(f) plans that employ a substantial risk of forfeiture that complies with Sections 83 and 457 but not Section 409A (see **Q.291**).

Example. A tax-exempt employer agrees to pay a hospital administrator a lump sum of $100,000 on completion of a new wing of the hospital, regardless of whether the administrator is employed by the hospital at the time the new wing is completed, as long as the hospital administrator has not engaged in competition with the hospital before completion of the new wing. At the time of the agreement, it is substantially certain that the new wing will be completed at some point in time, although the year of completion is uncertain. The parties have taken the position that the noncompetition restriction constitutes a substantial risk of forfeiture for purposes of Section 457(f), and it is assumed for purposes of this example that the noncompetition restriction constitutes a substantial risk of forfeiture for purposes of Section 457(f) under all the facts and circumstances. Even though the compensation under this arrangement would result in a deferral of taxation under Section 457(f) under existing rules, the noncompetition restriction does not constitute a substantial risk of forfeiture under Section 409A. The short-term deferral rule would not apply under Section 409A, so the arrangement would be subject to Section 409A. The arrangement would violate Section 409A because the compensation is payable upon completion of the new wing, which is an impermissible distribution event under Section 409A.

As a practical matter, designing a Section 457(f) plan for a tax-exempt entity requires consideration of both the Section 409A and Section 457(f) definitions of substantial risk of forfeiture.

Citation: I.R.C. § 409A(d); Treas. Reg. § 1.409A-1(a)(b); Preamble to Final § 409A Regulations, § II.B (2007); Prop. Treas. Reg. § 1.457-12(e) (2016); Notice 2007–62; PLRs 9030028 and 9041026; David Boekeloo, Robert Hopkins, Louis R. Richey, *Multiple Definitions of Substantial Risk of Forfeiture Create Confusion after Section 409A, but Notice 2007–62 Is Not the Answer*, 36 TAX MGMT. COMP. PLAN. J. 396 (Jan. 2008) (effect of Notice 2007–62 on plans governed by § 457(f)).

Q.27 WHAT IS A VEST AND PAY LUMP SUM SERP?

A vest and pay lump sum SERP is a nonqualified employer account balance or non-account balance deferred compensation plan that contains a substantial risk of forfeiture and requires distribution in the form of a single sum upon vesting. Benefits accrued under the plan must remain nonvested until the occurrence of a specified event, such as satisfaction of specified age and service requirements, and must be payable in a single sum within 2½ months after the end of the taxable year of vesting. If these requirements are met, the plan will be exempt from Section 409A under the short-term deferral rule (see **Q.21**).

Citation: *See* Daniel L. Hogans and Michael J. Collins, *Internal Revenue Code Section 409A: Ten Traps for the Unwary*, reprinted from PENS. & BEN. DAILY (BNA), Vol.8, No. 4 (Jan. 8, 2008), p. 2 ("vest and pay" has same meaning as "short-term deferral").

DISTRIBUTION EVENTS UNDER SECTION 409A

Q.28 WHAT ARE THE PRIMARY PERMISSIBLE DISTRIBUTION EVENTS FOR PURPOSES OF SECTION 409A?

There are seven primary permissible distribution events. Most are now defined more narrowly than under past practice. Event-based distributions are generally prohibited, except as provided in this list. The seven primary permissible distribution events are:

- Separation from service. Employees are treated differently from directors and other independent contractors for this purpose (see **Q.29** and **Q.34**). Payment must be delayed for six months from the date of separation in the case of specified employees, defined generally as a publicly traded company's key employees within the meaning of Code Section 416(i) (see **Q.36**).
- Disability. The Social Security definition applies (see **Q.46**).
- Death (see **Q.51** to **Q.55**).
- At a specified time or pursuant to a fixed schedule either stated in the plan or as elected before the deferral period begins.
- Change of control. This definition is based on the Code Section 280G golden parachute rules but is narrower (see **Q.82**).
- Unforeseeable emergency. This definition is based on the Section 457 rules (see **Q.73**).
- On plan termination (see **Q.85**). If the employer voluntarily terminates a plan, payment must be delayed for 12 months following

termination and the employer cannot implement a plan of the same type until expiration of three years after the plan termination. Immediate distribution may occur incident to plan termination on the order of a judge in a bankruptcy or reorganization proceeding.

Citation: I.R.C. § 409A(a)(2); Treas. Reg. § 1.409A-3(a).

Q.29 WHAT TYPE OF SEPARATION FROM SERVICE QUALIFIES AS A PERMISSIBLE DISTRIBUTION EVENT FOR AN EMPLOYEE UNDER SECTION 409A?

Separation from service is a permissible distribution event under Section 409A. For a specified employee of a publicly traded company, distribution cannot begin until six months after the separation (see **Q.36**).

In the case of an employee, separation from service includes death, retirement, or termination of employment, based on the facts and circumstances in each case.

Termination of Employment: Generally

The drafters of the regulation were concerned that employees would attempt to manipulate the timing of distribution by artificially extending or accelerating the date of employment termination, either by continuing on the employer's payroll after actual termination or by terminating the employment relationship and continuing as an independent contractor. To prevent such manipulation, the Section 409A regulations define termination of employment based on the level of services provided. Occurrence of termination is based on whether the facts and circumstances indicate that the employer and employee reasonably anticipate that no further services will be performed after a certain date or that the level of bona fide services the employee will perform after a certain date, either as an employee or as an independent contractor, will permanently decrease to a *de minimis* level.

Termination of Employment: Presumptions

Under the regulations, an employee is presumed to have terminated employment if the level of bona fide services performed decreases to a level equal to 20 percent or less of the average level of services performed by the employee during the immediately preceding 36-month period.

A termination of employment is presumed not to have occurred if the employee continues to provide services at an annual rate that is 50 percent or more of the services rendered, on average, during the immediately preceding 36-month period and the annual remuneration for such services is 50 percent or more of the average annual remuneration earned during the immediately preceding three full calendar years of employment (or if less, such lesser period).

There is no presumption regarding termination of employment on account of a decrease in the level of bona fide services performed to a level greater than 20 percent and less than 50 percent of the average level of bona fide services performed during the immediately preceding 36-month period. A plan may treat another level of reasonably anticipated permanent reduction in the level of bona fide services as a termination of employment if the level of reduction required is designated in writing as a specific percentage, and the reasonably anticipated reduced level of bona fide services is greater than 20 percent but less than 50 percent of the average level of bona fide services provided in the immediately preceding 36-month period. The plan document must define separation from service by the time separation from service is specified as a payment event. Once defined, any change in the definition is generally prohibited with respect to amounts previously deferred.

If the plan document does not define what constitutes a separation from service, then the default rule will apply.

Example 1. A full-time employee enters into an agreement to continue on the employer's payroll for two years subject to the requirement to provide services when requested by the employer. In practice, the employee only renders services to the employer one or two days per month. Since the employee is working at a level less than 20 percent of the average level of services performed during the immediately preceding 36-month period, it is presumed that the employee has terminated employment.

Example 2. A full-time employee enters into an arrangement to receive full compensation for a period of two years, but it is anticipated that the employer will require the employee to render services for only a few hours per week. The parties treat this arrangement as a termination of employment for purposes of Section 409A, and the employee's entire nonqualified deferred compensation plan account balance is paid to the employee pursuant to the terms of the plan. During the first month of this arrangement, the employee works only four hours each week. After a month, however, the employee's replacement unexpectedly terminates employment, and for the next two months the employee works 30 hours per week until another replacement is found. Even though the employee has worked at a level greater than 50 percent of the average level of services provided during the immediately preceding 36-month period, the presumption that the employee has not terminated employment can be rebutted by the evidence showing that the parties reasonably anticipated that the employee's level of services would permanently decrease to no more than 20 percent of the average level of services over the immediately preceding 36-month period, but unexpected circumstances caused the level of services to increase for a short period of time.

Citation: I.R.C. § 409A(a)(2)(A)(i); Treas. Reg. §§ 1.409A-1(h)(1)(i)-(ii), (h)(4), (h)(5); Preamble to Final 409A Regulations § VII.C.3.f (2007).

Q.30 WILL A SERVICE PROVIDER EXPERIENCE A SEPARATION FROM SERVICE IF HE OR SHE GOES ON A LEAVE OF ABSENCE?

No, not necessarily. The employment relationship can be treated as continuing uninterrupted during a leave of absence while the employee is on military leave, sick leave, or other bona fide leave of absence, such as temporary government service, as long as the leave does not exceed six months. The leave may be longer than six months, as long as the employee's right to reemployment with the service recipient is protected by law or contract. In any case, there must be a reasonable expectation that the employee will return to work. If the employee does not return to work before the expiration of six months or the longer period required by law or contract, the employment relationship is deemed to end on the first date immediately following expiration of the six-month or longer leave period.

If the leave of absence is due to any medically determinable physical or mental impairment that can be expected to result in death or to last for a continuous period of not less than six months and the impairment causes the employee to be unable to perform the duties of his or her employment, then a 29-month period of absence may be substituted for the six-month period described above.

Citation: Treas. Reg. § 1.409A-1(h)(1)(i).

Q.31 WILL A SERVICE PROVIDER EXPERIENCE A SEPARATION FROM SERVICE IN CONNECTION WITH AN ASSET SALE?

Only if the parties to the asset sale elect to treat the affected employees as having a Section 409A separation from service. The same-desk rule formerly used to determine whether an employee has had a separation from service under a tax-qualified 401(k) plan can be applied by the buyer and seller in a sale of assets to determine whether a separation from service has occurred. The rule must be consistently applied and the intended treatment must be specified in writing no later than the closing date of the sale of assets.

Citation: Treas. Reg. § 1.409A-1(h)(4).

Q.32 WILL A SPIN-OFF OR STOCK SALE OF A SUBSIDIARY CAUSE THE AFFECTED EMPLOYEES TO EXPERIENCE A SEPARATION FROM SERVICE?

No. A corporate spin-off or a sale of the stock of a subsidiary does not create a separation from service for purposes of Section 409A if the employee continues to work for the spun-off business or the subsidiary.

Citation: Preamble to Final 409A Regulations § VII.C.2.f (2007).

Q.33 MAY A TRANSACTION THAT IS TREATED AS A DEEMED ASSET SALE UNDER SECTION 338 BE TREATED AS AN ASSET SALE FOR PURPOSES OF THE SPECIAL SEPARATION FROM SERVICE RULES DESCRIBED IN Q.31?

No. The provision of the final regulations giving buyers and sellers in asset transactions the discretion to treat employees as separating from service is based on the recognition that, while employees formally terminate employment with the seller and immediately recommence employment with the buyer in a typical asset transaction, the employees often experience no change in the type or level of services they provide. In a deemed asset sale under Section 338, however, employees do not experience a termination of employment, formal or otherwise. Accordingly, the Treasury Department and IRS determined that it would be inconsistent with Section 409A to permit the parties to a deemed asset sale to treat service providers as having separated from service upon the occurrence of the transaction.

Citation: Prop. Treas. Reg. § 1.409A-1(h)(4) (2016); Preamble to 2016 Proposed 409A Regulations § III.A.

Q.34 WHAT CONSTITUTES A SEPARATION FROM SERVICE OF AN INDEPENDENT CONTRACTOR FOR PURPOSES OF SECTION 409A?

The definition of separation from service of an independent contractor is based on the definition of severance from employment in Treasury Regulation § 1.457-6(b)(2). An independent contractor is generally considered to have severed from employment with the eligible employer upon the expiration of the contract (or in the case of more than one contract, all contracts) under which services are performed for the eligible employer if the expiration constitutes a good faith and complete termination of the contractual relationship. An expiration of a contract does not constitute a good faith and complete termination of the contractual relationship if the eligible employer anticipates a renewal of a contractual relationship or the independent contractor becomes an employee. For this purpose, an eligible employer is considered to anticipate the renewal of the contractual relationship with an independent contractor if it intends to contract again for the services provided under the expired contract, and neither the eligible employer nor the independent contractor has eliminated the independent contractor as a possible provider of services under any such new contract. An eligible employer is considered to intend to contract again for the services provided under an expired contract if the eligible employer's doing so is conditioned only upon having a need for the services, the availability of funds, or both.

A safe harbor exists for a plan that provides for payment of deferred compensation upon a separation from service by an independent contractor. The plan must provide that (i) no deferred compensation amount will be paid to the independent contractor for at least 12 months following the date all relevant contracts expire, and (ii) if the independent contractor begins performing services again for the service recipient before the payment of any deferred compensation due upon separation from service, such deferred compensation amount will not be paid until a subsequent separation from service occurs.

Citation: Treas. Reg. § 1.409A-1(h)(2).

Q.35 HOW IS A SEPARATION OF SERVICE DEFINED WHEN A SERVICE PROVIDER PERFORMS SERVICES FOR A SERVICE RECIPIENT BOTH AS AN EMPLOYEE AND INDEPENDENT CONTRACTOR?

If a service provider simultaneously provides services both as an employee and an independent contractor of a service recipient, the service provider must separate from service both as an employee and as an independent contractor to be treated as having separated from service. However, if an employee also serves as a member of a corporate board of directors or in an analogous position for a non-corporate entity, services as a director are not taken into account in determining whether the employee has separated from service as an employee, and vice-versa.

If a service provider starts out as an employee and becomes an independent contractor, whether or not a separation from service has occurred will depend upon whether the service provider has experienced a separation from service under the standards that apply to employees. The rules for determining separation from service under the independent contractor definition do not apply.

Example 1. An employee agrees to cease performing services as an employee and become an independent contractor of the employer. It is anticipated that the service provider will provide services as an independent contractor for no more than eight hours per month. Subsequently, the service provider only performs services as an independent contractor for eight hours per month for the next two years. The service provider is considered to have separated from service under the standard applied to employees.

Example 2. An employee agrees to cease providing services as an employee and become an independent contractor of the employer. The service provider continues to receive full pay for services rendered as an independent contractor and continues to provide services at the rate of 30 hours per week for the next two years. The service provider is not considered to have terminated employment merely by virtue of moving to independent contractor status because the level of services has not permanently been reduced to a level below 20 percent of the prior level. She will experience a separation from service in the future when she has a separation from service based on the rules that apply to independent contractors.

Citation: Treas. Reg. § 1.409A-1(h)(5); Preamble to 2016 Proposed 409A Regulations § III.B; Annotated Final Regulations, comments by William Schmidt, following Treas. Reg. § 1.409A-1(h)(1)(ii), "If you start out as an employee and become an independent contractor, the employee standards still apply; you are not going to switch over to the independent contractor definition."; comments by Stephen Tackney, following Treas. Reg. § 1.409A-1(h)(5), "Regarding the limited application of the rule to the employee/independent contractor status, the regulations are talking about moving from employee to independent contractor, about the general proposition that you have not separated from service merely because you have changed status. Look at the specific rules about being an employee."

Q.36 MUST A PLAN GOVERNED BY SECTION 409A THAT IS MAINTAINED BY A PUBLICLY TRADED COMPANY REQUIRE DELAYED PAYMENTS TO SOME PLAN PARTICIPANTS, CALLED "SPECIFIED EMPLOYEES," EVEN THOUGH THERE IS A VALID SEPARATION FROM SERVICE?

Yes. Publicly traded companies must delay the distribution of Section 409A plan benefits to specified employees (see **Q.37**) for six full calendar months. A publicly traded company is one whose shares are publicly traded on an established securities market or otherwise. This includes a subsidiary whose parent company is publicly traded or an affiliate of a company that is publicly traded, either in the United States or in another country. If this issue is not identified, such as if the parent company is publicly traded in a foreign jurisdiction, Section 409A violations can result.

For this purpose, an established securities market includes:

- A national securities exchange registered under the Securities Exchange Act of 1934 (e.g., the New York Stock Exchange).
- Foreign national securities exchanges that are officially recognized by a governmental authority (e.g., Tokyo stock exchange).
- Over-the-counter markets such as NASDAQ.

The six-month delay rule applies to separation from service situations only, including small cash-out distributions. A plan required to address this rule should specify whether all payments suspended during the six-month waiting period will be paid in a single sum on expiration of the waiting period or whether all individual payments due the specified employee will be delayed for six months.

The six-month delay rule does not apply to the following situations:

i. Benefits paid due to:
   1. Death.
   2. Disability.
   3. Change in ownership or effective control.
   4. Unforeseen emergency.

ii. Accelerations of distributions due to:
   1. Domestic relations orders.
   2. Satisfying a federal, state, or local conflict of interest law.
   3. Payment of employment taxes.

Citation: Treas. Reg. § 1.409A-1(i).

Q.37 WHO ARE "SPECIFIED EMPLOYEES" OF A PUBLICLY TRADED COMPANY, ITS SUBSIDIARIES, AND ITS AFFILIATES, FOR PURPOSES OF THE SIX-MONTH DELAY RULE?

Specified employees are identified by reference to the term "key employee," as defined in Code Section 416(i) for purposes of the top-heavy plan rules. An employee is a specified employee if he or she falls within one of the following categories at any time during the 12-month period ending on the annual "specified employee identification date," for which the default is December 31:

- A 5 percent owner of the employer.
- A 1 percent owner with compensation greater than $150,000 (not indexed).
- A corporate officer with compensation greater than $175,000 (as of 2017, indexed annually). This group is generally limited to the top 10 percent of all employees. For companies with fewer than 30 employees, the number of officers included is the lesser of three or the actual number of officers. For companies with more than 500 employees, the maximum number of officers is 50.

Default Rules for Identifying Specified Employees. Unless the service recipient elects otherwise, the following rules are applied to identify specified employees:

- The individuals considered key employees under Section 416(i) at any time during the 12-month period ending on December 31

(the default specified employee identification date) are identified. For this purpose, the definition of compensation set forth in Treasury Regulation § 1.415(c)-2(a) applies.
- These individuals are specified employees for the 12-month period commencing on the next following April 1, the default specified employee effective date.

Alternative Approaches for Identifying Specified Employees. A service recipient may adopt the following rules for identifying specified employees:

- A service recipient may designate any date other than December 31 as the specified employee identification date, as long as the same specified employee identification date is used for all nonqualified deferred compensation plans of the service recipient and its entire controlled group. Any change to the specified employee identification date cannot become effective for a period of at least 12 months after it is adopted.
- A service recipient may designate any date following the specified employee identification date as the specified employee effective date, but the specified employee effective date cannot be later than the first day of the fourth month following the specified employee identification date. The same specified employee effective date must apply to all nonqualified deferred compensation plans of the service recipient and its entire controlled group. Any change to the specified employee effective date cannot become effective for a period of at least 12 months after it is adopted.
- The service recipient may elect to use any definition of compensation available under the Code Section 415 regulations, but the definition must be applied consistently to all employees of the service recipient and all members of its controlled group for purposes of identifying specified employees. Once a list of specified employees is effective, the service recipient cannot change the definition of compensation for purposes of identifying specified employees for the period during which the list is effective.

- The service recipient may elect to expand the number of individuals who will be considered specified employees using an objectively determinable standard that permits no direct or indirect election by any service provider regarding its application. The method used must result either in all service providers or not more than 200 service providers being identified as specified employees as of any date.
- A service recipient may elect not to take into account certain compensation excludable from a non-resident alien's gross income. This rule may cause a non-resident alien working outside the United States not to be included among the 50 highest-paid officers. Whether or not non-resident aliens are included among the 50 highest-paid officers, all non-resident aliens are included in the total number of employees for purposes of this test.

These elections require corporate action to make them binding for all affected nonqualified deferred compensation plans of the service recipient's controlled group (see **Q.6**). Otherwise, the election is void and the default rules apply. A board of directors' resolution of the ultimate parent of the controlled group can be used for this purpose. Including an election in one nonqualified plan document of one controlled group member may prove ineffective unless the same election provisions are included in other nonqualified plans maintained by members of the same controlled group.

A publicly traded company must provide its plan administrator with a current list of specified employees of all members of its controlled group each year to be sure that the six-month delay rule is properly enforced. The issue can be avoided if the plan provides that no distribution to any service provider will begin until six months after separation from service. If this type of provision is added to a plan by amendment, the effective date must be delayed for a period of 12 months after adoption.

Citation: Treas. Reg. §§ 1.409A-1(i) and (j).

Q.38 CAN A NONEMPLOYEE DIRECTOR CONSTITUTE A SPECIFIED EMPLOYEE OF A SERVICE RECIPIENT AS A RESULT OF THE DIRECTOR'S OWNERSHIP INTEREST IN THE SERVICE RECIPIENT?

No.

The term "specified employee" is defined by reference to the term "key employee" under the qualified retirement plan rules (see **Q.37**). A key employee is an "employee" of the service recipient who meets certain compensation and/or ownership thresholds with respect to the service recipient. Some confusion has arisen in this area because, when applying the key employee definition in the context of a partnership, a partner is considered an employee of the service recipient/partnership even though the partner is self-employed. In contrast, for purposes of the key employee definition, a nonemployee director is considered to be his or her own employer rather than an employee of the service recipient and, as a result, a nonemployee director is never considered a key employee or a specified employee of the service recipient.

This means that a deferred compensation plan for nonemployee directors need not include a provision delaying payment for six months upon separation from service.

Citation: I.R.C. §§ 401(c)(4) and 416(i). For a contrary view, see Caroline Hayday and Sasha Belinkie, Section 409A & Six Month Delay: Don't Forget Your Directors, posted on CompensationStandards.com by Broc Romanek (February 17, 2016).

Q.39 HOW ARE SPECIFIED EMPLOYEES IDENTIFIED FOLLOWING A CORPORATE TRANSACTION INVOLVING TWO PUBLIC COMPANIES?

Special default specified employee identification- and effective-date rules apply in corporate mergers and acquisitions. Generally, when one publicly traded company acquires another publicly traded company, the combined organization uses the next specified employee *identification* date and next specified employee *effective* date of the acquiring company.

In addition, the combined organization may combine the lists of specified employees of both companies as of the date of acquisition and treat the top 50 most highly compensated officers (along with certain owners) as specified employees between the date of the acquisition and the next specified employee effective date.

The regulations do not affirmatively address the identification of specified employees of the combined entities if the acquiring company's first specified employee effective date following the acquisition occurs before the acquiring company's first specified employee identification date following the acquisition. This would happen if the transaction occurs between the acquiring company's specified employee identification date and specified employee effective date. The default rules suggest that the specified employee identification date under these circumstances is the acquiring corporation's most recent specified employee identification date before the acquisition. However, it is not clear from the regulations whether only officers of the acquiring company or officers of both companies should be tested for key employee status as of that date. It appears that either position would be reasonable. On the one hand, if the specified employee identification date is taken from the acquiring company, it is reasonable to consider only the officers of the acquiring company before the acquisition. On the other hand, because the officers of the acquired company are clearly considered in determining specified employee status after the acquisition, and before the first specified employee effective date after the acquisition, it is also reasonable to consider them in this situation.

Example. Public Company A ("PC-A") acquires Public Company B ("PC-B") on January 10, 2011. PC-A uses the default dates for determining specified employees (December 31 as the specified employee identification date and April 1 as the specified employee effective date). It is clear that the post-acquisition key employee identification and effective dates will be December 31 and April 1. It is also clear that between January 10, 2011, and March 31, 2011, the default rules require combining the lists of specified employees of both PC-A and PC-B as of January 10, 2011, and deeming the top 50 highest compensated officers as the "specified employees" of the combined entity (along with certain owners) until March 31, 2011. It is reasonable to consider only the officers of PC-A, and not the officers of PC-B, in determining who was a specified employee as of December 31, 2010, because none of the officers of PC-B worked for PC-A's controlled group as of December 31, 2010. It is also reasonable to consider the officers of both PC-A and PC-B as of December 31, 2010, in determining who was a specified employee as of December 31, 2010, and to take their compensation from PC-B for 2010 into account for this purpose. If a method other than the default method is chosen, the acquiring company is required to take corporate action within 90 days of the transaction stating the method to be applied (see **Q.43**).

Citation: Treas. Reg. § 1.409A-1(i)(6)(i).

Q.40 HOW ARE SPECIFIED EMPLOYEES IDENTIFIED FOLLOWING A TRANSACTION INVOLVING A PUBLIC COMPANY AND A NONPUBLIC COMPANY?

If a public and nonpublic service recipient combine through a corporate transaction and the resulting company is a public company, the resulting company's next specified employee identification date and specified employee effective date following the corporate transaction are the specified employee identification date and specified employee effective date that the public company would have been required to use in the absence of the transaction. For the period after the acquisition and before the next specified employee effective date, the specified employees of the public company before the transaction continue to be the specified employees of the public company after the transaction, and no service providers of the acquired private company are treated as specified employees. Starting with the next specified employee effective date, all of a service provider's compensation from both companies during the 12 months ending on the next prior specified employee identification date, both before and after the acquisition, is taken into account in determining whether the service provider is a specified employee of the acquiring company.

Citation: Treas. Reg. § 1.409A-1(i)(6)(ii); 2012 ABA JCEB Questions, Q&A 20.

Q.41 HOW ARE SPECIFIED EMPLOYEES IDENTIFIED FOLLOWING A SPIN-OFF?

If as part of a corporate transaction a public company becomes two or more separate public companies, the next specified employee identification date of each of the post-transaction public companies is the specified employee identification date that the single public company would have been required to use in the absence of the transaction. For the period after the transaction and before the next specified employee effective date, the specified employees of the single public company that existed immediately before the transaction continue to be the specified employees of the two separate public companies after the transaction.

Citation: Treas. Reg. § 1.409A-1(i)(6)(iii).

Q.42 HOW ARE SPECIFIED EMPLOYEES IDENTIFIED FOLLOWING AN INITIAL PUBLIC OFFERING?

The identification date for the public company resulting from the initial public offering will be December 31, and its effective date will be April 1, effective retroactively to the December 31 and April 1 before the initial public offering. Alternatively, the service recipient may select different identification and effective dates on or before the initial public offering (subject to the requirements outlined in **Q.37 and Q.43**), in which case those dates are also applied retroactively.

Citation: Treas. Reg. § 1.409A-1(i)(6)(iv).

Q.43 ARE THERE ALTERNATIVE RULES FOR IDENTIFYING SPECIFIED EMPLOYEES FOLLOWING A CORPORATE TRANSACTION?

The final regulations permit an acquiring company to use any reasonable alternative method for identifying specified employees after a corporate transaction. The rules applicable to electing alternative methods described in the last section of **Q.37** must be followed. All corporate action necessary to carry out the method under all nonqualified deferred compensation plans of the surviving company or companies must be taken and be effective at the time of the corporate transaction. The method must be applied consistently across all nonqualified plans after the actions are taken.

Citation: Treas. Reg. §§ 1.409A-1(i)(5) and 1.409A-1(i)(6)(v).

Q.44 IS IT POSSIBLE TO COMPLY WITH THE REQUIREMENT THAT PAYMENTS TO SPECIFIED EMPLOYEES ON ACCOUNT OF SEPARATION FROM SERVICE MUST BE DELAYED FOR SIX MONTHS AFTER SEPARATION BY REQUIRING THAT PAYMENTS TO ALL SERVICE PROVIDERS ON ACCOUNT OF SEPARATION FROM SERVICE BE DELAYED FOR SIX MONTHS AFTER SEPARATION?

Yes, if this provision is included in the plan document from the beginning. If this provision is added to the plan by amendment, arguably the rules for adopting alternative approaches for identifying specified employees may be followed such that the effective date of the amendment need only be delayed for 12 months after adoption (see **Q.37**).

Citation: Treas. Reg. § 1.409A-1(i)(5).

Q.45 COULD A SPECIFIED EMPLOYEE HAVE A CLAIM FOR POST-EMPLOYMENT DISCRIMINATION OR RETALIATION AGAINST A SERVICE RECIPIENT FOR COMPLYING WITH THE SIX-MONTH DELAY REQUIREMENT UNDER SECTION 409A?

This is very unlikely in the absence of unusual circumstances. The employee would have the difficult burden of showing that the service recipient acted with discriminatory or retaliatory motives and that the motives are not related to compliance with Section 409A. Evidentiary facts on which such motives could be based would include misapplication of the rules for identifying specified employees and intentional change from one to another permissible method of identifying specified employees for the purpose of including the plaintiff as a specified employee when he otherwise would not be.

Citation: *Moran v. Davita, Inc.*, 441 F. App'x. 942 (3rd Cir. 2011).

Q.46 WHAT IS THE DEFINITION OF DISABILITY FOR PURPOSES OF SECTION 409A?

Disability is a permissible distribution event under Section 409A. To satisfy the requirements for distribution on account of disability, the service provider must either be:

- unable to engage in any substantial gainful activity by reason of a medically determinable physical or mental impairment that can be expected to result in death or can be expected to last for a continuous period of not less than 12 months (this is the Social Security definition of disability); or
- receiving income replacement benefits for a period of not less than three months under the employer's accident and health plan for employees by reason of any medically determinable physical or mental impairment that can be expected to last for a continuous period of not less than 12 months.

An inability to engage in the individual's own occupation does not satisfy the distribution standard described above. However, in the case of a request for cancellation of a current deferral election on account of disability (see **Q.125**), the Final Regulations use a less stringent "own occupation" definition of disability. Under this definition, the disability must be caused by a physical or mental impairment that can be expected to result in death or last for a period of at least six months.

Citation: I.R.C. § 409A(a)(2)(C); Treas. Reg. §§ 1.409A-3(i)(4) and 1.409A-3(j)(4)(xii).

Q.47 CAN A PLAN'S FORM AND TIME OF PAYMENT ON ACCOUNT OF DISABILITY BE DIFFERENT FROM THE PLAN'S FORM AND TIME OF PAYMENT ON ACCOUNT OF SEPARATION FROM SERVICE?

Yes, but only if the service provider is not required to separate from service on account of the disability.

Disability and separation from service are classified as separate payment events under Section 409A. If the plan provides that the form and time of payment on account of disability is determined at the time of disability, independent of separation from service, the disability is treated as a separate payment event under Section 409A. In this case, the form and time of payment on account of disability can be different from the form and time of payment on account of separation from service. In contrast, if the service recipient requires the service provider to separate from service to receive a distribution on account of the disability, then the disability cannot be treated as a separate payment event under Section 409A. The payment event must be classified as a separation from service and the time and form of payment must conform to the plan's requirements for separation from service.

Citation: 2008 ABA JCEB Questions, Q&A 40.

Q.48 ONCE A DISTRIBUTION EVENT THAT ENTITLES A PLAN PARTICIPANT TO RECEIVE PAYMENT OCCURS, WHEN MUST THE PAYMENT BE MADE?

A plan that provides for payment upon a permissible distribution event must specify that payment is made on the date of the event or another payment date that is objectively determinable and nondiscretionary at the time the event occurs. For example, a plan might provide that nonqualified deferred compensation is paid upon separation from service, or the plan might provide that nonqualified deferred compensation is paid on the 30th day after separation from service. The regulations require that payment be made as follows:

- On the payment date specified.
- On any later date within the same calendar year.
- By the fifteenth day of the third calendar month following the specified payment date, provided that the service provider is not permitted to designate the taxable year of the payment.
- No earlier than 30 days before the designated payment date, provided the service provider is not permitted to designate the taxable year of the payment.
- Death benefits have special rules (see **Q.51**).

Example. A plan provides that payment of deferred compensation will be made upon separation from service. A participant separates from service on June 1, 2010. Payment may be made as early as May 1, 2010, and as late as December 31, 2010. If instead the individual had separated from service on December 1, 2010, payment could be made as early as November 1, 2010, and as late as February 15, 2011, as long as the participant is not allowed to elect the taxable year of the payment.

Authors' Comment: It should be noted that if the conditions for distribution (e.g., requirement for a signed release to receive benefit distributions) might cross two calendar years such that the service provider might be able to select the year of inclusion, the service recipient must draft the plan in accordance with the choices offered in IRS Notice 2010-80 that results in the amounts being taxed in one of the two tax years by operation of the plan provisions rather than at the election of the service provider (see **Q.56**).

Citation: Treas. Reg. § 1.409A-3(d).

PAYMENTS

Q.49 WHEN IS A PAYMENT CONSIDERED TO HAVE BEEN MADE?

A payment is considered made when any taxable benefit is actually or constructively received. A payment includes a transfer of cash, any event that results in inclusion of an amount in income under the economic benefit doctrine, and a transfer of property includable in income under Section 83. In addition, a payment is made upon the transfer, cancellation, or reduction of an amount of deferred compensation in exchange for benefits under a welfare plan, a non-taxable fringe benefit, or any other non-taxable benefit. For example, if a service provider agrees to forgo deferred compensation in exchange for the service recipient providing a split-dollar plan, payment of the deferred compensation is considered to have been made.

Under final regulations issued on April 17, 2007, the inclusion of an amount in income under Section 457(f) was treated as a payment under Section 409A for purposes of the short-term deferral rule but was not treated as a payment for other purposes under Section 409A. Proposed regulations issued on June 22, 2016 would change this result to provide that the inclusion of an amount in income under Section 457(f) would be treated as a payment for all purposes under Section 409A. The proposed regulations will become applicable on or after the date on which they are published as final regulations in the Federal Register. For periods before this date, the existing final regulations and other applicable guidance apply, but taxpayers may rely upon the proposed regulations before they are published as final regulations, and until final regulations are published, the IRS will not assert positions that are contrary to positions in the proposed regulations. The change in the definition of payment in the proposed regulations is significant in the context of structuring nonqualified deferred compensation for tax-exempt entities. See **Q.291**, Example 2.

Citation: Preamble to Final 409A Regulations § II.B (2007); Preamble to 2016 Proposed 409A Regulations § IV; Treas. Reg. § 1.409A-1(a)(4); Prop. Treas. Reg. § 1.409A-1(q) (2016).

Q.50 IS THE TRANSFER OF PROPERTY THAT IS SUBJECT TO A SUBSTANTIAL RISK OF FORFEITURE CONSIDERED A PAYMENT UNDER SECTION 409A?

No, unless the service provider makes an election under Section 83(b) to include the fair market value of the property in income.

Citation: Prop. Treas. Reg. § 1.409A-1(q) (2016); Preamble to 2016 Proposed 409A Regulations § IV.

Q.51 IF A PAYMENT IS TO BE MADE UPON DEATH, WHEN MUST THE PAYMENT BE MADE?

At any time during the period beginning on the date of death and ending on the last day of the calendar year following the calendar year in which the death occurs.

Citation: Prop. Treas. Reg. § 1.409A-3(b) (2016); Preamble to 2016 Proposed 409A Regulations § V.A.

Q.52 IF A PAYMENT IS TO BE MADE UPON DEATH, MAY THE BENEFICIARY SELECT THE YEAR OF PAYMENT?

Yes, the beneficiary may choose to receive payment in the year death occurs or the following year without adverse consequences under Section 409A.

Citation: Prop. Treas. Reg. § 1.409A-3(b) (2016); Preamble to 2016 Proposed 409A Regulations § V.A.

Q.53 IF THE PLAN DOCUMENT SPECIFIES A MORE RESTRICTIVE PERIOD FOR PAYMENT OF DEATH BENEFITS THAN IS PERMITTED UNDER THE RULES DESCRIBED IN Q.51, MAY THE PLAN BE AMENDED TO EXPAND THE PERIOD FOR PAYMENT OF DEATH BENEFITS?

Yes. A plan providing for the payment of a death benefit at a time within the period specified in **Q.51** may be amended to provide for the payment of that amount (or the payment of that amount may be made without amending the plan) at any other time during such period (including a time determined in the discretion of a beneficiary) without failing to meet any of the Section 409A requirements, such as the general prohibition on the acceleration of payments.

Example. A plan provides for a payment to be made within 90 days after the death of a service provider. The plan may be amended to provide for the payment of the amount (or the payment may be made under the plan without such amendment) at any time during the period beginning on the date of death and ending on the last day of the calendar year following the calendar year of death.

Citation: Prop. Treas. Reg. § 1.409A-3(d)(2) (2016); Preamble to 2016 Proposed 409A Regulations § V.A.

Q.54 MUST THE PLAN DOCUMENT SPECIFY THE PERIOD DURING WHICH DEATH BENEFITS MAY BE PAID?

No. A plan may simply provide that payment will be made upon death without defining the period for payment following death in any other manner.

Citation: Prop. Treas. Reg. § 1.409A-3(d)(2) (2016); Preamble to 2016 Proposed 409A Regulations § V.A.

Q.55 DO THE RULES APPLICABLE TO PAYMENTS UPON THE DEATH OF A PARTICIPANT APPLY UPON THE DEATH OF A BENEFICIARY?

Yes. For example, if a beneficiary is receiving periodic payments as a result of the death of a deceased participant, such benefits may be accelerated upon the death of the beneficiary (see **Q.75**). Similarly, the rules regarding the timing of lump sum payments upon a participant's death (see **Q.51** and **Q.52**) apply in the same manner to the timing of lump sum payments on a beneficiary's death.

Citation: Preamble to 2016 Proposed 409A Regulations § V.A.

Q.56 CAN THE TIME OF PAYMENT DEPEND ON THE TIME THE SERVICE PROVIDER EXECUTES A RELEASE?

The timing of distribution generally cannot be affected by the timing of the service provider's execution of a claims release. Otherwise a service provider could, in some cases, control the taxable year of distribution by choosing the time to execute and deliver the release.

This rule requires careful drafting of provisions requiring release of claims as a condition to payment. The IRS has provided guidance on this topic.

Example. A plan provides that payment of deferred compensation will be made in a lump sum when a participant has both separated from service and signed a release of all claims against the employer. Under this plan, the participant could manipulate the time of payment by choosing the date to sign the release. Because the payment date is not objectively determinable and nondiscretionary at the time the separation from service occurs, the plan violates Section 409A. The arrangement could be modified to comply with Section 409A by providing that the deferred compensation will be paid 90 days after separation from service if the participant has executed a release of claims that has become irrevocable on or before that date.

Citation: Treas. Reg. §§ 1.409A-3(c) and (d); Notice 2010–80; Notice 2010–6; *see also* Andrew L. Oringer, *Release Us from Confusion Over*

Nonqualified Deferred Compensation, 36 Tax Mgmt. Comp. Plan. J. 223 (Oct. 2008) (interplay between § 409A and releases).

Q.57 CAN A PLAN PROVIDE THAT DISTRIBUTION OCCURS ON THE EARLIEST OF TWO OR MORE PERMISSIBLE EVENTS?

Yes. A plan may provide that a benefit or account will be distributed at the earliest of several permissible distribution events, such as separation from service, death, disability, change of control, or unforeseeable emergency. The plan may also provide for a different form of payment with respect to each type of distribution event.

Citation: Treas. Reg. §§ 1.409A-2(b)(2)(i) and 1.409A-3(a).

Q.58 WHAT IS THE ANTI-TOGGLING RULE AND HOW IS IT APPLIED?

In general, all times and forms of payment pursuant to a distribution event must be the same. For example, a plan cannot provide for one time and form of payment if a separation from service occurs on Monday and another time and form of payment if separation from service occurs on another day of the week. This prohibition against use of different forms of payment with respect to a type of distribution event is sometimes called the anti-toggling rule.

Notwithstanding the general rule against toggling, a plan may allow for a single toggle with respect to any type of distribution event. For example, a plan may provide that a service provider will receive a lump sum payment of the service provider's entire benefit under the plan on the first day of the month following a change of control event that occurs before the service provider attains age 55, but will receive five substantially equal annual payments commencing on the first day of the month following a change of control event that occurs on or after the service provider's attainment of age 55. The toggle is the service provider's age in relation to age 55 at the time of the change of control event. The plan cannot provide for another payment pattern based on another toggle, such as a change of control event that occurs on or after the service provider's attainment of age 65.

Special rules apply to a plan that provides for payment upon separation from service. A different time and form of payment may be designated with respect to a separation from service under each of the following conditions:

- A separation from service during a limited period of time not to exceed two years following a change of control event.
- A separation from service before or after a specified date, including attainment of a specified age, or a separation from service before or after a combination of a specified date and completion of a specified number of years of service, for example, attaining age 55 and completing 10 years of service.
- Any other separation from service.

Example. A plan provides that an individual will receive a lump sum payment of benefits upon separation from service within two years after a change of control, or payments in the form of 15 annual installments upon separation from service after attainment of age 55 and completion of ten years of service, or payments in the form of five annual installments upon separation from service at any other time. The plan provides for payment incident to three permissible payment events incident to a separation from service: change of control, a specified date, and any other separation from service. Therefore, it satisfies the anti-toggling rule.

No other toggles are permitted in connection with separation from service. For example, a plan cannot provide for different payment forms depending on whether the separation from service is voluntary or involuntary. However, in accordance with the general rule, a plan may provide for payment upon the earlier of involuntary separation from service and another permissible type of distribution event such as a fixed date.

Citation: Treas. Reg. §§ 1.409A-2(b)(2)(i) and 1.409A-3(c); 2009 ABA JCEB Questions, Q&A 18; Annotated Final Regulations, comments following Treas. Reg. § 1.409A-3(c), Stephen Tackney, "You cannot have a different form of payment based on marital status, i.e., a joint and survivor annuity if the participant is married, but a lump sum payment if the participant is single; there can be different forms of actuarially equivalent annuities, which will be treated as one time and form of payment, provided the beginning date for the payment does not change" and "I stress . . . you can't come up with a third independent toggle that isn't age and service or change of control."; Helen Morrison, "A third toggle permitting you to have a different payment for voluntary versus involuntary termination doesn't work."; Daniel L. Hogans, "There is no toggle between involuntary and voluntary termination. That is something you cannot do with deferred compensation anymore."

Q.59 CAN A PLAN PROVIDE FOR DIFFERENT FORMS OF PAYMENT DEPENDING ON WHETHER THE SERVICE PROVIDER IS MARRIED OR NOT WHEN PAYMENT BEGINS?

Generally no, because marital status is not a permissible toggle event under Section 409A. However, if all forms of payment available under the plan are annuities, as long as the payment date is the same whether the service provider is married or not, different forms of annuity can be provided for single and married participants because different forms of annuity can be treated as a single form of payment under Section 409A (see **Q.130**).

Example. A plan provides that deferred compensation will be distributed in the form of a joint and 50 percent survivor annuity if the service provider is married when payment begins, and a lump sum if the service provider is single when payment begins. This provision violates Section 409A because marital status is not a permissible distribution toggle event. A plan that provides for distribution in the form of a joint and 50 percent survivor annuity if the service provider is married when payment begins or a life annuity if the service provider is single when payment begins does not violate Section 409A because different forms of annuity can be treated as a single form of payment under Section 409A.

Citation: 2008 ABA JCEB Questions, Q&A 41.

Q.60 CAN A PLAN PROVIDE THAT DISTRIBUTION OCCURS ON THE EARLIER OF A NARROWLY DEFINED INVOLUNTARY SEPARATION FROM SERVICE AND ANOTHER PERMISSIBLE DISTRIBUTION EVENT?

Yes. For example, a plan may provide for distribution on the earlier of a fixed date or involuntary separation from service. However, the plan could not provide for a third payment form on voluntary termination of employment, because voluntary termination of employment is not a separate payment event authorized under Section 409A.

Example. A plan provides for a lump sum payment on the earliest of January 1, 2020, death, or involuntary termination of employment without cause. If employment terminates for any reason other than death or involuntary termination without cause before January 1, 2020, distribution will occur on January 1, 2020. This plan design satisfies Section 409A.

Citation: Treas. Reg. § 1.409A-3(a); Annotated Final Regulations, comments by Helen Morrison, following Treas. Reg. § 1.409A-3(a), "The definition of separation from service for payment purposes can be narrower, so that the payment may be paid on the earlier of a fixed date or involuntary separation from service."

Q.61 ARE THERE ANY SITUATIONS IN WHICH A LATE PAYMENT WILL BE EXCUSED BECAUSE OF ADMINISTRATIVE IMPRACTICABILITY?

Yes. If calculation of the amount of the payment is not administratively practicable due to events beyond the control of the service provider, the payment will be treated as made on the date specified under the plan if the payment is made during the first taxable year of the service provider in which calculation of the amount of the payment is administratively practicable. The inability of a service recipient to calculate the amount or time of a payment due to failure of a service provider to provide reasonably available information necessary to make the calculation does not constitute an event beyond the control of the service provider.

Citation: Treas. Reg. § 1.409A-3(d).

Q.62 ARE THERE ANY SITUATIONS IN WHICH A LATE PAYMENT WILL BE EXCUSED BECAUSE OF FINANCIAL DIFFICULTIES OF THE SERVICE RECIPIENT?

Yes. If making the payment on the date specified under the plan would jeopardize the ability of the service recipient to continue as a going concern, the payment will be treated as made on the date specified under the plan if the payment is made during the first taxable year of the service provider in which making the payment would not jeopardize the service recipient's ability to continue as a going concern.

Citation: Treas. Reg. § 1.409A-3(d).

Q.63 WHAT CONSTITUTES A DOWNTURN IN THE FINANCIAL HEALTH OF A SERVICE RECIPIENT?

Little guidance exists on this question. Facts and circumstances control. Certainly a going concern letter from a service recipient's independent accountant would indicate a downturn in the service recipient's financial health. Poor economic conditions alone do not constitute a downturn in the financial health of a service recipient, even if those conditions prompt the service recipient to cut expenses, including termination of its nonqualified plans, to save money. However, it is possible that a downturn in the service recipient's financial condition may occur even though insolvency or bankruptcy of the service recipient is not imminent.

Citation: 2009 ABA JCEB Questions, Q&A 19.

Q.64 MAY A SERVICE RECIPIENT DELAY MAKING A PAYMENT TO AVOID VIOLATING A LAW?

A payment may be delayed where the service recipient reasonably anticipates that making the payment will violate Federal securities laws or other applicable law. The payment must be made as soon as it will not cause such a violation. Making a payment that would cause inclusion in gross income or the application of any penalty or other provision of the Internal Revenue Code is not considered a violation of applicable law.

Citation: Treas. Reg. § 1.409A-2(b)(7)(ii).

Q.65 MAY PAYMENT BE DELAYED TO AVOID THE LOSS OF A DEDUCTION UNDER I.R.C. § 162(M)?

Yes. The service recipient must reasonably anticipate that if the payment were timely made, the service recipient would not be able to deduct it because of section 162(m), which limits a public company's deduction for compensation paid to certain employees to $1,000,000 per year. Payment must be made either during the first year the deduction will not be barred by section 162(m) or upon the service provider's separation from service (subject to the six-month delay rule applicable to specified employees, see **Q.36**). The subsequent deferral election rules (see **Q.127**) will apply to any delayed payment to a service provider under this provision unless all scheduled payments to that service provider that could be delayed in accordance with this provision are also delayed.

Citation: Treas. Reg. § 1.409A-2(b)(7)(i).

Q.66 CAN A PLAN PROVIDE THAT THE FORM OF DISTRIBUTION IS BASED ON THE VALUE OF THE SERVICE PROVIDER'S BENEFIT AT THE TIME DISTRIBUTION COMMENCES?

In general, no, except in the case of cash-outs of small amounts (see **Q.78**) and cash-outs of installment or annuity payments when the value of the participant's benefit is below an amount specified in the plan (see **Q.80**). If the form of distribution were allowed to vary based on the value of a participant's benefit, money could be credited to or debited from the participant's account balance or other benefit in order to achieve a benefit value corresponding to a specified payment schedule. In this case, the plan would afford impermissible discretion with respect to the form of payment.

Example. A plan specifies the following forms of distribution: (i) a lump sum distribution if the participant's account is less than $15,000 as of the date of the participant's separation from service; (ii) payment in five annual installments if the participant's account is between $15,000 and $50,000 as of the date of the participant's separation from service; and (iii) payment in ten annual installments if the participant's account is greater than $50,000 as of the date of the participant's separation from service. This distribution provision violates Section 409A because the form of distribution varies depending on the value of the participant's account.

Citation: 2008 ABA JCEB Questions, Q&A 25.

Q.67 IF DISTRIBUTION OF DEFERRED COMPENSATION IS SCHEDULED TO BE MADE IN CASH, CAN THE SERVICE RECIPIENT AND SERVICE PROVIDER AGREE AFTER THE SERVICES RELATED TO THE DEFERRED COMPENSATION HAVE BEEN PERFORMED THAT DISTRIBUTION WILL INSTEAD BE MADE IN THE FORM OF RESTRICTED STOCK?

No, unless the service provider elects to include the value of the restricted stock in income by making a Section 83(b) election. A distribution of property which is substantially nonvested is not treated as a payment for purposes of Section 409A if the value of such property is not currently included in income (see **Q.50**).

Citation: Prop. Treas. Reg. § 1.409A-1(q)(1)(2016); Preamble to 2016 Proposed 409A Regulations, Section entitled "Proposed Effective Dates." Prior to the issuance of the 2016 proposed regulations, the IRS and Treasury had indicated there was no answer to this question and it was under study. See 2009 ABA JCEB Questions, Q&A 22.

Q.68 MAY A DISTRIBUTION OF DEFERRED COMPENSATION BE MADE IN THE FORM OF A STOCK OPTION?

No, unless the option will be includible in income because it has a readily ascertainable fair market value. A distribution of an option is not treated as a payment for purposes of Section 409A if the option has no readily ascertainable fair market value.

Citation: Prop. Treas. Reg. § 1.409A-1(q)(2) (2016); Preamble to 2016 Proposed 409A Regulations, Section entitled "Proposed Effective Dates."

Q.69 MAY A SERVICE PROVIDER AND SERVICE RECIPIENT AGREE TO CANCEL A DEFERRED COMPENSATION ARRANGEMENT AND REPLACE IT WITH A SPLIT-DOLLAR ARRANGEMENT?

No. The split-dollar arrangement is considered a substitution for, and payment of, the deferred compensation that is relinquished (see **Q.49**, **Q.90** and **Q.92**). Accordingly, such a relinquishment and substitution agreement, often referred to as a "SERP swap," results in an impermissible acceleration of the payment of the deferred compensation.

Citation: I.R.C. § 409A(a)(3); Treas. Reg. § 1.409A-3(f); Prop. Treas. Reg. § 1.409A-1(q) (2016).

Q.70 CAN DISTRIBUTIONS SCHEDULED ON ACCOUNT OF SEPARATION FROM SERVICE UNDER A DEFERRED COMPENSATION PLAN SUBJECT TO SECTION 409A BE SUSPENDED IF THE EMPLOYEE IS REHIRED AND RESUMES ELIGIBILITY UNDER THE PLAN?

There is no provision in the statute or regulations that permits such a suspension. The suspension would constitute a subsequent deferral that does not satisfy the waiting period requirements for subsequent deferrals (see **Q.127**).

This rule applies even if the date scheduled for distribution has not yet occurred when the employee resumes employment, such as in the case of a six-month delay for a specified employee or a plan provision or participant election that requires passage of a period of time before distribution.

Authors' Comment: In practice, the employee could defer additional compensation earned after employment resumes, use the distributions of previously deferred compensation for current expenses, and achieve a roughly equivalent result.

Citation: Treas. Reg. §§ 1.401A-1(h)(1)(i), 1.409A-2(b), 1.409A-3(a), (i)(2)(i), (j)(1), (j)(4); *see also* PLRs 201221033 and 201147038.

Q.71 DOES A 409A VIOLATION ALWAYS OCCUR IF THE SERVICE RECIPIENT REFUSES OR INADVERTENTLY FAILS TO MAKE A PAYMENT OF DEFERRED COMPENSATION WHEN DUE?

No. If a service recipient refuses or inadvertently fails to pay deferred compensation when due, the payment generally will be treated as made in a timely manner if the service provider makes reasonable good faith efforts to collect the payment.

The service provider must give notice to the service recipient within 90 days after the last date on which the payment could have been timely made under the terms of the plan and the Section 409A regulations (the "timely payment date"). If still not paid, the service provider must take further measures to enforce the payment within 180 days after the timely payment date. Otherwise, the service provider's efforts to collect the payment are deemed not to be reasonable good faith efforts.

In any case, there can be no collaboration between the service provider and service recipient with respect to the delay.

Citation: Treas. Reg. § 1.409A-3(g).

ACCELERATION OF BENEFITS

Q.72 MAY DEFERRED COMPENSATION DISTRIBUTIONS BE ACCELERATED?

Generally, no. Acceleration is permitted only in limited circumstances, as follows:

- By Statute:
  - Unforeseeable emergency (see **Q.73**).
  - Change of control (see **Q.82**).
  - Disability (see **Q.46**).
  - Death.
- By Regulation:
  - Plan termination (see **Q.85**).
  - Domestic relations order (see **Q.83**).
  - Compliance with conflict of interest laws (see **Q.77**).
  - To fund employment and state, federal and foreign withholding taxes, including those due on vesting under a Section 457(f) plan (see **Q.95**).
  - To fund taxes due on account of income inclusion upon failure to comply with Section 409A (see **Q.96**).
  - Cash-outs (limited to the Code Section 402(g)(1)(b) elective deferral maximum for the year of distribution, $18,000 in 2017) (see **Q.78**).
  - To avoid imposition of the excise taxes imposed under Code Section 409(p). This tax may be imposed if synthetic equity (which includes deferred compensation) and employer stock held under an ESOP sponsored by an S corporation become overly concentrated

in certain individuals who, with their family members, own a majority of the S corporation (see **Q.97**).

Citation: I.R.C. § 409A(a)(2)(A)(i)-(vi); Treas. Reg. §§ 1.409A-3(i)(4)(ii)-(vii) and (ix)-(xi).

Q.73 WHAT IS AN UNFORESEEABLE EMERGENCY FOR PURPOSES OF SECTION 409A?

For purposes of Section 409A, an unforeseeable emergency includes the following:

- A severe financial hardship of the service provider resulting from an illness or accident of the service provider or the service provider's spouse or dependent within the meaning of Code Section 152(a).
- Loss of the service provider's property due to a casualty.
- Other similar extraordinary and unforeseeable circumstances arising as a result of events beyond the control of the service provider.

In all events, the facts and circumstances control.

A distribution on account of a qualifying unforeseeable emergency cannot exceed the amount necessary to satisfy the emergency plus the taxes reasonably anticipated as a result of the distribution. The distribution must also take into account the extent to which the emergency need is or may be relieved by reimbursement or compensation from insurance or otherwise, or by the liquidation of the participant's assets, except to the extent that such liquidation itself would cause a severe financial hardship. The participant is not required to apply for or obtain a hardship distribution from the participant's 401(k) or 403(b) account.

The IRS has taken the position that the same criteria apply in determining what constitutes an unforeseeable emergency for purposes of Sections 409A and 457.

These standards are different from and generally narrower than those governing hardship distributions from 401(k) and 403(b) plans. Requests for hardship distributions from 401(k) and 403(b) plans and requests for distribution on account of unforeseeable emergency under 409A and 457 plans must be evaluated independently.

For purposes of unforeseeable emergency distributions under Sections 409A and 457, the IRS has expressly approved reasonably anticipated federal and state income taxes (including penalties), casualty losses from a natural disaster, pending home foreclosure or eviction, medical expenses (including prescription drug costs) and funeral expenses of the participant's spouse or dependent, the cost of repairing a participant's principal residence following a severe water leak, and funeral expenses of a non-dependent adult child. The IRS has expressly disapproved college expenses, home purchase, and payment of accumulated credit card debt, because they are deemed foreseeable in nature and not otherwise authorized by statute. In all cases, the facts and circumstances prevailed and documentation of actual expenses or reliable estimates was required.

A plan's administrative procedures should include a process sufficient to demonstrate operational compliance with Section 409A and be absent of intent to circumvent the requirements of Section 409A by use of plan provisions for distribution on account of unforeseeable emergency.

Citation: I.R.C. § 409A(a)(2)(B)(ii); Treas. Reg. §§ 1.409A-3(i)(3)(i)-(iii); Rev. Rul. 2010–27; Rev. Rul. 2004–56.

Q.74 WHEN CAN A PLAN BE AMENDED TO PROVIDE FOR ACCELERATION OF DISTRIBUTION INCIDENT TO UNFORESEEABLE EMERGENCY, DEATH, OR DISABILITY?

This can be done at any time, even after the service provider's unforeseeable emergency, death, or disability has occurred. Amendment of a plan to add unforeseeable emergency, death, or disability as a potential earlier alternative payment event that applies to an amount previously deferred will not be treated as an impermissible acceleration of payment. Formal documentation of provisions for distribution by reason of unforeseeable emergency, death, or disability can be provided at any time before payment begins.

Citation: Treas. Reg. § 1.409A-3(j)(2); 2010 ABA JCEB Questions, Q&A 27.

Q.75 IF A DESIGNATED BENEFICIARY HAS BECOME ENTITLED TO PAYMENTS UPON THE DEATH OF THE PARTICIPANT, ARE THERE ANY SITUATIONS IN WHICH THE PAYMENTS DUE TO THE BENEFICIARY MAY BE ACCELERATED?

Yes, upon death, disability, or unforeseeable emergency of the beneficiary.

Citation: Prop. Treas. Reg. § 1.409A-3(j) (2016); Preamble to 2016 Proposed 409A Regulations § VI.A.

Q.76 MAY A SERVICE PROVIDER WHO HAS ELECTED TO RECEIVE BENEFITS IN THE FORM OF A PERIODIC BENEFIT MEASURED BY JOINT LIFE EXPECTANCIES CHANGE BENEFICIARIES WITHOUT CAUSING AN ACCELERATION OF BENEFITS?

Yes, subject to the following requirements:

- If the change in beneficiaries occurs after benefits have commenced, the change must not result in a change in the time and form of payments.
- If the beneficiary change occurs before the commencement of benefits, a change in the identity of a beneficiary will not constitute an acceleration of a payment provided (i) the benefit commencement date does not change and (ii) any change in the time of payments stems solely from the different life expectancy of the new beneficiary.

Example. A service provider elects to receive her deferred compensation benefit in the form of annual payments measured over the joint lives of her and her husband. Her husband predeceases her, and she wishes to change her beneficiary to her daughter. If benefits have already commenced, the form and time of payments must not change following the husband's death (in other words, the daughter's life expectancy may not be used to determine the amount of each future payment). If benefits have not commenced, annual payments may be made over the joint lives of the service provider and her daughter, provided the scheduled commencement date of the annual benefit does not change.

Citation: Treas. Reg. § 1.409A-3(j)(3).

Q.77 MAY BENEFITS BE ACCELERATED TO COMPLY WITH CONFLICT OF INTEREST OR FOREIGN ETHICS LAWS?

Yes, if the acceleration is reasonably necessary to comply with a bona fide foreign ethics or conflicts of interest law.

Citation: Prop. Treas. Reg. § 1.409A-3(j)(4)(iii)(B) (2016); Preamble to 2016 Proposed 409A Regulations § VI.

Q.78 WHAT CONSTITUTES A CASH-OUT THAT CAN BE ACCELERATED AND PAID IN A LUMP SUM WITHOUT VIOLATING SECTION 409A?

A service recipient can exercise discretion to cash out a service provider's entire accumulated deferral amount under a plan at any time if the service provider's entire accumulated deferred amount under the plan and all plans of the same type under the special aggregation rule required under Section 409A (see **Q.107**) is less than the applicable dollar amount under Section 402(g)(1)(B) in effect for the calendar year of distribution ($18,000 in 2017).

A service recipient can make a cash-out distribution under this rule whether or not the service provider has separated from service and whether or not the plan expressly provides that the service recipient has this discretion.

Example. A service provider who participates in only one nonqualified plan maintained by the service recipient is scheduled to receive payment in five installments incident to separation from service. The first installment is payable 30 days after separation from service and the remaining four installments are payable on the first day of each of the next four calendar years.

The service provider separates from service on August 31, 2018. On September 30, 2018, the service provider has an account balance of

$20,000 and the plan pays the service provider 20 percent of that amount, or $4,000, which reduces the service provider's account balance to $16,000. The plan may disregard the remaining portion of the five-year installment schedule and distribute the entire remaining balance of the service provider's account at any time after the first distribution.

Citation: Treas. Reg. §§ 1.409A-3(j)(4)(i) and (v); Preamble to Final § 409A Regulations, § VIII.H (2007); 2010 ABA JCEB Questions, Q&A 32 and 33.

Q.79 MAY A CASH-OUT OF SMALL BENEFITS BE CONDITIONED ON THE ELECTION OR CONSENT OF THE SERVICE PROVIDER?

No. The service provider cannot be given any direct or indirect election with respect to the cash-out of small benefits. Whether such an election has been offered is based upon all the facts and circumstances, including whether similarly situated service providers have been treated the same or differently.

Citation: Treas. Reg. §§ 1.409A-3(j)(4)(i).

Q.80 MAY A PLAN PROVIDE THAT INSTALLMENT OR ANNUITY PAYMENTS WILL BE CASHED OUT IN A SINGLE SUM IF THE PRESENT VALUE OF THE SERVICE PROVIDER'S REMAINING BENEFIT FALLS BELOW A SPECIFIED LEVEL SET FORTH IN THE PLAN?

Yes. This is expressly authorized in the Section 409A regulations and other guidance, and it is independent of the general rule permitting cash-outs of small benefits (see Q. 78).

The plan can provide either that such a cash-out can occur only at the time payments are scheduled to begin, or at any time the present value of the service provider's remaining benefit falls below the specified level. In either event, the cash-out amount must be specified in the plan at the time of deferral.

Unlike the rule for small cash-outs (see **Q.78**), the service recipient cannot exercise discretion in this matter. If the plan authorizes cash-out at any time the present value of the service provider's benefit falls below the specified level, the service recipient has to track the value of the participant's remaining benefit every time an installment or annuity payment is made to determine whether the threshold for a cash-out distribution has been reached.

Citation: Treas. Reg. §§ 1.409A-2(b)(2)(ii) and (iii); 2008 ABA JCEB Questions, Q&A 25.

Q.81 MAY A PLAN PROVIDE FOR A DISTRIBUTION OF BENEFITS UPON A CHANGE OF CONTROL?

A plan may provide for plan termination and distribution of all benefits or simply permit the commencement of benefits upon the occurrence of a change in ownership or effective control of a corporation or a change in ownership of a substantial portion of a corporation's assets (see **Q.82**). The rules for terminating a plan upon a change of control are described in **Q.85** and **Q.86**. If service providers are afforded an election to commence payments upon a change of control, the election must be made at the time of deferral in accordance with the rules described in **Q.121**. It may only be changed in accordance with the rules described in **Q.127**.

Citation: I.R.C. § 409A(a)(2)(A)(v); Treas. Reg. § 1.409A-3(i)(5).

Q.82 HOW IS A CHANGE IN OWNERSHIP OR EFFECTIVE CONTROL DEFINED FOR PURPOSES OF SECTION 409A?

The definition of change in ownership or effective control for this purpose is unique to Section 409A. In general:

- A change in ownership requires a transfer of stock which results in a person (or persons acting as a group) owning more than 50 percent of the total fair market value or voting power of a corporation.

- A change in effective control requires a 30 percent or more acquisition of voting power or a hostile election of a majority of directors over a 12-month period.
- A change in ownership of a substantial portion of assets requires acquisition of 40 percent or more of a corporation's assets during a 12-month period.

Acquisition of an equity position by the federal government or another entity pursuant to the Emergency Economic Stabilization Act of 2008 on or after June 4, 2009, is not treated as a change in ownership or effective control for this purpose (think automobile industry bailout).

Under this definition, a very small acquisition of stock could result in a change in ownership or effective control for this purpose. For example, if an individual who has a 49.9 percent voting interest in a corporation acquires an additional 0.2 percent voting interest in the corporation, a change in ownership or effective control occurs under this definition.

Authors' Comment: Section 409A allows a plan to adopt a more restrictive definition of change in ownership or effective control to avert unintended consequences of the broad definition set forth in the regulations. Hence the plan designer can adopt a definition that trips or does not readily trip a distribution of benefits.

Citation: I.R.C. § 409A(a)(2)(A)(v); Treas. Reg. § 1.409A-3(i)(5).

Q.83 WHAT ARE THE REQUIREMENTS FOR ENFORCEABILITY OF A DOMESTIC RELATIONS ORDER DIRECTING ACCELERATION OF DISTRIBUTION OF AMOUNTS DEFERRED BY A PARTICIPANT UNDER A PLAN GOVERNED BY SECTION 409A?

The regulations under Section 409A permit splitting or accelerating a nonqualified plan benefit pursuant to a "domestic relations order" (DRO) as defined in Section 414(p)(1)(B). A domestic relations order includes any judgment, decree, or order (including approval of a property settlement agreement) that relates to child support, alimony or marital rights to a spouse, former spouse, child, or other dependent pursuant to a state domestic relations order. This is different from a Section 414(p)(1)(A) "qualified domestic relations order" (QDRO) since a QDRO presumes a qualified plan trust holding qualified "plan assets" to which the QDRO attaches. A typical unfunded, nonqualified, deferred compensation plan has no (and should have no) plan assets. In fact, it is possible that the plan sponsor will not even informally fund a nonqualified plan by investing in assets which mirror the nonqualified plan's liabilities, especially in the case of an employer-paid supplemental plan.

Therefore, a DRO for Section 409A purposes is and must be fundamentally different than a QDRO in its content. A DRO on a 409A-covered nonqualified deferred compensation plan actually directs the service recipient to either: (i) split the unfunded promise to pay on the books until such time as it is due to be paid under the terms of the plan or (ii) to accelerate actual payment of the current value of the participant spouse's portion of the unsecured plan benefit promise. A DRO that is valid for purposes of Section 409A is exempt from both the Section 409A prohibition against accelerations and the subsequent election rule. In general, Section 409A permits a DRO on a Section 409A-covered plan, but does not require the service recipient to acknowledge and honor a DRO.

Authors' Comment: The application of DROs to nonqualified deferred compensation plans was confusing prior to enactment of Section 409A and remains so today. As an initial matter, plan sponsors do not like to be caught in divorce litigation between a participant and spouse with regard to their plan. Second, the federal and state taxation with respect to a division of nonqualified benefits is different than with respect to a qualified plan. It currently appears that the imposition of federal income taxes may follow the property division. However, employment taxes clearly do not, and state income taxation is in question, especially where the spouse is resident where the plan benefit would not be income taxable for state purposes, and the participant is a resident in a state where the benefit would be taxable. That state may seek to tax all the benefit to the participant who earned the benefit regardless of the division of benefits pursuant to a DRO.

In general, the practice (even after Section 409A) seems to be for the plan sponsor that receives such a DRO to consult with the participant to point out and discuss the tax issues and recommend the participant consult with his or her own attorney to change the property settlement provisions to resolve the request without the DRO. This change would usually afford the nonparticipant spouse a different interest in other marital property (e.g., give the nonparticipant spouse a larger share of the participant's 401(k) or a personal mutual fund account to reflect the participant's retention of the 409A-covered plan benefit).

Citation: Treas. Reg. §§ 1.409A-3(j)(4)(ii) and 1.409A-2. For a more detailed discussion of splitting and distributing nonqualified deferred compensation unfunded and unsecured benefits using DROs in divorce situations, see Richey, Baier & Phelan, *The Advisor's Guide to Nonqualified Deferred Compensation*, 2014 Edition, ALM NUCO at pages 283–285; *see also* the Specimen DRO for Section 409A-Covered Plans in the Appendix.

Q.84 IS A DEFERRED COMPENSATION PLAN SUBJECT TO SECTION 409A REQUIRED TO ACCELERATE DISTRIBUTION OF AMOUNTS DEFERRED BY A PARTICIPANT OR TO DIVIDE THE PARTICIPANT'S ACCOUNT IN FAVOR OF THE ADVERSE PARTY NAMED IN A DOMESTIC RELATIONS ORDER THAT SATISFIES THE REQUIREMENTS FOR ENFORCEABILITY UNDER SECTION 409A?

No. A plan is permitted, but not required, to accelerate distribution or divide the bookkeeping account pursuant to a domestic relations order that meets the requirements of Section 409A. A grandfathered plan that does not contain a specific provision regarding distribution pursuant to a domestic relations order, especially one that contains an express provision against assignment of a participant's rights, must be amended to accelerate distribution or divide the participant's account pursuant to a domestic relations order. Such an amendment would not constitute a material modification to the plan that would jeopardize the plan's grandfathered status (see **Q.270**).

Citation: Treas. Reg. §§ 1.409A-3(j)(4)(ii) (permitted but not required) and 1.409A-6(a)(4)(i)(C) (permitted but not required for grandfathered plans).

Q.85 IN WHAT CIRCUMSTANCES MAY AN EMPLOYER TERMINATE OR LIQUIDATE A PLAN THAT IS SUBJECT TO SECTION 409A?

Before the effective date of Section 409A, employers could terminate and liquidate plans without limitations other than those contained in the plan. The Section 409A regulations permit termination in only three situations, including:

1. Employer voluntary termination, subject to the following:
   - All plans of the same type under the special aggregation rule required under Section 409A (see **Q.107**) must also be terminated with respect to all participants (e.g., all elective deferral account balance plans, all employer account balance plans).
   - A new plan of the same type may not be established for at least three years from the date the service recipient takes all necessary action to terminate the plan.
   - No payments other than those otherwise payable under the terms of the plan can be made during the 12 months following the date of plan termination.
   - All payments must be made within 24 months following the date of plan termination.
   - Termination cannot occur proximate to a downturn in the financial health of the service recipient.
2. Termination in connection with a change of control of the employer. All plans of the same Section 409A type (see **Q.107**) that are maintained by the service recipient immediately after the change of control must be terminated with respect to each participant that experienced the change of control. Action to terminate all plans of the same type that must be aggregated under the special aggregation rule required under Section 409A must be taken during the period beginning 30 days before and ending 12 months after the change of

control (see **Q.82**), and distribution must be completed within 12 months after the action to terminate is taken. As a consequence,
- An employer could take action exactly 12 months after a change of control to terminate a plan, and full distribution under the plan would have to occur no later than 12 months thereafter (conceivably up to 24 months after the change of control).
- An employer could take action to terminate a plan 30 days or less before a change of control, with full distribution under the plan occurring no later than 12 months thereafter. This is useful if the acquired company wants to pay out all nonqualified benefits before the change of control to provide certainty to participants that their benefits will be paid. Such payouts are typically made on the day before or the day of the change of control when it is virtually certain that the change of control will be consummated. If distributions are made in anticipation of a change of control that does not occur, a Section 409A violation results.
- Any executive covered by a nonqualified plan that is terminated incident to a change of control is not allowed to participate in any nonqualified plans of the same 409A type maintained by the buyer, even if the termination occurs immediately before the change of control. In contrast, termination of a qualified 401(k) plan is prohibited if more than two percent of the participants in the plan participate in an alternative defined contribution plan maintained by the employer. When a company is acquired, its 401(k) plan is sometimes terminated immediately before the closing and its participants are allowed to participate in the buyer's 401(k) program. The two percent rule is satisfied because the buyer is not in the same controlled group as the seller when the plan is terminated; therefore, its plan is not an alternative defined contribution plan maintained by the employer for this purpose.
3. Termination in connection with corporate dissolution taxed under Code Section 331 or with the approval of a bankruptcy court. The amounts deferred under the plan must be included in the participants' gross income by the end of the calendar year in which the

plan termination occurs, the end of the calendar year in which the deferred amount is no longer subject to a substantial risk of forfeiture, or the end of the first calendar year in which the payment is administratively practicable, whichever is last.

Citation: Voluntary Plan Termination—Treas. Reg. §§ 1.401(k)-1(d)(4) and 1.409A-3(j)(4)(ix)(A); Change of Control—Treas. Reg. § 1.409A-3(j)(4)(ix)(B); Corporate Dissolution—Treas. Reg. § 1.409A-3(j)(4)(ix)(C).

Q.86 CAN AN EXISTING PLAN WITHOUT A PROVISION FOR TERMINATION BE AMENDED TO PROVIDE FOR PLAN TERMINATION?

Yes. A provision for plan termination permitted under Section 409A (see **Q.85**) may be added by plan amendment at any time. Participant consent to the amendment cannot be required. This is because a service provider cannot be given any direct or indirect election with respect to termination of a plan, and a service provider's ability to withhold consent to a plan amendment authorizing plan termination is treated as an impermissible election.

Citation: Treas. Reg. §§ 1.409A-3(j)(4)(i) and (ix); 2010 ABA JCEB Questions, Q&A 26.

Q.87 CAN A SERVICE RECIPIENT VOLUNTARILY TERMINATE A PLAN WITH RESPECT TO ONE OR MORE, BUT NOT ALL, SERVICE RECIPIENTS PARTICIPATING IN THE PLAN?

No. To terminate a plan voluntarily, the service recipient must terminate and liquidate all plans of the same type under the special aggregation rule required under Section 409A (see **Q.107**) with respect to all service recipients participating in all such plans.

Example. A service recipient maintains a nonqualified defined benefit plan for ten executives. The plan is documented in a series of ten separate individual agreements with a different level of defined benefit for each.

The employer decides that it does not wish to continue the plan for the six junior employees but wishes to retain it for four senior employees. The company cannot terminate the plan for the six junior employees without also terminating the plan for the four senior employees since the agreements for all ten are categorized as a single non-account balance plan under the aggregation rule, even though documented separately. The employer also cannot implement this same plan type for a period of three years following the termination of the existing plan.

Authors' Comment: However, note that this employer could terminate the employer non-account balance plans of all the employees but then immediately create and implement an employer account balance plan for the four senior employees since an employer account balance plan is a different plan type from a non-account balance plan. Another solution is to terminate and then install a plan or plans that are excepted from 409A coverage under the short-term deferral exception if that is possible.

Citation: Treas. Reg. § 1.409A-3(j)(4)(ix); 2010 ABA JCEB Questions, Q&A 25. IRS representatives have stated informally that this is among the most frequently asked questions they receive. Clarifying guidance has been issued in the proposed regulations. Prop. Treas. Reg. § 1.409A-3(j)(4)(ix)(C)(2) (2016); Preamble to 2016 Proposed 409A Regulations § VI.C.

Q.88 MUST A SPECIFIED EMPLOYEE OF A PUBLIC COMPANY WAIT AT LEAST SIX MONTHS TO RECEIVE DISTRIBUTION DUE UPON A PLAN TERMINATION?

No. The six-month-delay rule applies only if distribution is due on account of separation from service.

Example. A specified employee separates from service on June 30, 2028. On July 1, 2028, the service recipient experiences a change of control and provides for immediate distribution of all nonqualified benefits pursuant to a plan termination. Although the specified employee would have been required to wait six months to receive her benefits absent the plan termination, she may now receive payment immediately in accordance with the plan termination provisions.

Citation: Treas. Reg. § 1.409A-3(j)(4)(ix).

Q.89 DOES ACCELERATION OF VESTING OF DEFERRED COMPENSATION ALONE CAUSE A PROBLEM UNDER SECTION 409A?

No, as long as acceleration of vesting does not result in acceleration of the time scheduled for distribution. However, acceleration of vesting could constitute a material modification of a grandfathered plan in existence on or before October 3, 2004, and could cause such a plan to lose its grandfathered status (see **Q.270**).

Citation: Treas. Reg. § 1.409A-3(a); Notice 2005–1, Q&A 15.

Q.90 WHAT IS THE SUBSTITUTION RULE?

The distribution of an amount as a substitute for a deferred compensation payment is generally treated as payment of the deferred compensation and, accordingly, an impermissible acceleration of benefits. The potential application of this rule is not always obvious. Even if no explicit reduction or offset to deferred compensation is documented, the payment of an amount or creation of a new right to a payment proximate to a reduction in deferred compensation is presumed to be a substitute for the deferred compensation. The presumption is rebuttable by a showing that the compensation paid would have been received regardless of such reduction. Factors indicating that a payment would have been received regardless of a reduction in deferred compensation include that the amount paid is materially less than the amount of the reduction or consists of a type of payment customarily made in the ordinary course of business of the service recipient to service providers whose deferred compensation has not been reduced.

Citation: Treas. Reg. § 1.409A-3(f).

Q.91 MAY A SERVICE PROVIDER BORROW MONEY FROM HIS OR HER NONQUALIFIED PLAN OR PLEDGE NONQUALIFIED PLAN BENEFITS AS SECURITY FOR A LOAN OR OTHER AMOUNT DUE CREDITORS?

No. A loan from the service recipient that is secured by, or subject to offset against, the service provider's right to deferred compensation constitutes a substitute payment (see **Q.90**), which will typically result in a prohibited acceleration of such deferred compensation. In addition, if a service provider's right to deferred compensation is made subject to anticipation, alienation, sale, transfer, assignment, pledge, encumbrance, attachment, or garnishment by creditors of the service provider or the service provider's beneficiary, the deferred compensation is treated as having been paid.

Authors' Comment: Section 409A is additive to pre-409A theories of income inclusion. The IRS may continue to apply constructive receipt, assignment of income, economic benefit, and cash equivalency principles to transactions involving deferred compensation in order to impose current income inclusion with respect to a right to receive future nonqualified deferred compensation payments. Before enactment of Section 409A, loans or other amounts due creditors that were secured by nonqualified deferred compensation benefits resulted in current income inclusion under these principles. Accordingly, pre-409A nonqualified deferred compensation plan documents routinely contained (or should have contained) a provision prohibiting anticipation, alienation, sale, transfer, assignment, pledge, encumbrance, attachment, or garnishment by creditors of the service provider or the service provider's beneficiary. Post-409A plan documents should continue to include such a provision.

Citation: Treas. Reg. § 1.409A-3(f).

Q.92 DOES SECTION 409A PROHIBIT FORFEITURE, REDUCTION, OR VOLUNTARY RELINQUISHMENT OF DEFERRED COMPENSATION?

No. Forfeiture or voluntary relinquishment of deferred compensation alone is not treated as a distribution of the amount forfeited or relinquished under Section 409A. However, if the service provider receives or acquires the right to receive a different form of compensation in connection with the forfeiture or relinquishment, the series of transactions may be treated as a distribution under Section 409A. For example, if a service provider forfeits a right to receive deferred compensation due in a future year and simultaneously receives the right to current compensation roughly equal to the value of the amount forfeited, the IRS views this combination of events as a substitution and impermissible acceleration of payment of the deferred compensation in violation of Section 409A.

Citation: I.R.C. § 409A(a)(3); Treas. Reg. § 1.409A-3(f).

Q.93 DOES SECTION 409A PERMIT OFFSET OF THE AMOUNT DUE THE SERVICE PROVIDER ON DISTRIBUTION BY THE AMOUNT THE SERVICE PROVIDER OWES THE SERVICE RECIPIENT?

Generally, no. If a deferred compensation plan contains a provision that any amount due the service provider under the plan will be offset by amounts the service provider owes the service recipient, such as a salary advance, the plan violates Section 409A because it authorizes an impermissible acceleration. Only a very limited provision for offset is permitted. The service provider's debt must have been incurred in the ordinary course of the service relationship, the amount offset cannot exceed $5,000 in any taxable year, and the offset must be taken at the same time and in the same amount as payment of the debt would otherwise have been due.

Authors' Comment: It was previously common for plans to include generic offset provisions that would not now satisfy the requirements of Section 409A. Such provisions could have been eliminated or revised as late as 2010 under IRS Notice 2010-80 to comply with the requirements of Section 409A without penalty.

Citation: I.R.C. § 409A(a)(3); Treas. Reg. §§ 1.409A-3(f) and 1.409A-3(j)(4)(xiii); I.R.S. Chief Counsel Advice 200935029 (Sept. 28, 2009).

Q.94 DOES SECTION 409A PERMIT OFFSETS OF DEFERRED COMPENSATION TO COMPLY WITH FEDERAL DEBT COLLECTION LAWS?

Yes, to the extent reasonably necessary to comply with federal laws relating to debt collection.

Citation: Prop. Treas. Reg. § 1.409A-1(j)(13)(B) (2016); Preamble to 2016 Proposed 409A Regulations § VI.D.

Q.95 MAY DEFERRED COMPENSATION BE REDUCED TO REFLECT REQUIRED TAX WITHHOLDING AMOUNTS RELATING TO SUCH DEFERRED COMPENSATION?

Yes. A plan may provide for the acceleration of deferred compensation to pay any Federal Insurance Contributions Act (FICA), Railroad Retirement Act (RRTA), state, local, or foreign taxes due with respect to compensation deferred under the plan. Additionally, a plan may provide for the acceleration of deferred compensation to pay the federal and other taxes due with respect to those wages that arise from the payment of the taxes described in the preceding sentence and to pay the additional withholding amounts attributable to the pyramiding of wages and taxes. The total payment under this acceleration provision must not exceed the aggregate tax withholding required by the applicable taxing authorities.

Citation: Treas. Reg. §§ 1.409A-3(j)(4)(vi) and 1.409A-3(j)(4)(xi).

Q.96 MAY PAYMENT OF DEFERRED COMPENSATION BE ACCELERATED IF THE PLAN VIOLATES THE REQUIREMENTS OF SECTION 409A?

Yes. A plan may provide for the acceleration of the payment of deferred compensation at any time the plan fails to meet the requirements of Section 409A. The accelerated payment may not exceed the amount required to be included in income as a result of the failure to comply with the requirements of Section 409A.

Citation: Treas. Reg. § 1.409A-3(j)(4)(vii).

Q.97 MAY PAYMENT OF DEFERRED COMPENSATION BE ACCELERATED TO PREVENT A NONALLOCATION YEAR UNDER I.R.C. SECTION 409(P)?

Yes.

Section 409(p) sets forth anti-abuse rules for employee stock ownership plans (ESOPs) that are maintained by S corporations. No assets of an ESOP may be allocated for the benefit of certain substantial owners of an S corporation (referred to as "Disqualified Persons") if, at any time during the plan year (a "nonallocation year"), Disqualified Persons, in the aggregate, own 50 percent or more of the equity of the S corporation. Synthetic equity, including nonqualified plan interests, is taken into consideration when performing the somewhat complex calculations necessary to determine whether a nonallocation year has occurred.

A plan may provide for the acceleration of a nonqualified deferred compensation payment to prevent the occurrence of a nonallocation year in the plan year of an ESOP next following the plan year in which such payment is made. The amount distributed may not exceed 125 percent of the minimum amount necessary to avoid the occurrence of a nonallocation year.

Citation: Treas. Reg. § 1.409A-3(j)(4)(x).

Q.98 MAY PAYMENT OF DEFERRED COMPENSATION BE ACCELERATED PURSUANT TO THE SETTLEMENT OF A DISPUTE REGARDING THE SERVICE PROVIDER'S ENTITLEMENT TO RECEIVE SUCH DEFERRED COMPENSATION?

Yes, provided the acceleration is due to an arm's length settlement of a bona fide dispute regarding the service provider's right to the deferred amount.

Whether a payment qualifies for this exception is based on all relevant facts and circumstances. A payment will be presumed not to meet this exception unless the payment is subject to a substantial reduction in value. A reduction that is less than 25 percent of the present value of the deferred amount in dispute generally is not a substantial reduction.

A payment will be presumed not to meet this exception if the payment is made proximate to a downturn in the financial health of the service recipient.

Example. A corporation maintains a nonqualified defined benefit plan that provides an executive with a lifetime monthly benefit beginning at age 65. The benefit is forfeited if the executive is terminated for cause. When the executive is age 50, the corporation fires him, allegedly for cause, when the present value of his benefit is $1,000,000. The corporation advises the executive that his monthly retirement benefit has been forfeited. The executive disputes that cause exists for his termination and files a lawsuit against the corporation seeking to have his monthly benefit reinstated. The parties agree to settle the dispute for a lump sum payment from the corporation to the executive of $400,000. At the time of settlement, the corporation's financial condition is sound. The payment is not considered an impermissible acceleration of deferred compensation because it constitutes an arm's length settlement of a bona fide dispute regarding the executive's right to the deferred amount.

Citation: Treas. Reg. § 1.409A-3(j)(4)(xiv).

Q.99 IS AN ELECTION CHANGE UNDER A CAFETERIA PLAN THAT RESULTS IN AN ACCELERATION OF DEFERRED COMPENSATION PROBLEMATIC?

No, provided that any such acceleration arises solely because the election change under the cafeteria plan causes a change in the amount eligible to be treated as compensation under the deferred compensation plan. Such change must apply in the same manner as any other increase or decrease in compensation.

A similar rule applies in determining whether an impermissible change in a deferral election results from a change in a cafeteria plan election.

Citation: Treas. Reg. §§ 1.409A-2(a)(1) and 1.409A-3(j)(6).

Q.100 IF A SERVICE RECIPIENT DETERMINES THAT A SERVICE PROVIDER WHO IS A MEMBER OF A TOP HAT PLAN IS NO LONGER A MEMBER OF A SELECT GROUP OF MANAGEMENT OR HIGHLY COMPENSATED EMPLOYEES, MAY THE SERVICE RECIPIENT CANCEL THE SERVICE PROVIDER'S DEFERRAL ELECTIONS AND IMMEDIATELY DISTRIBUTE HIS OR HER PLAN BENEFITS?

No, not at this time. The Preamble to the Final 409A regulations states that an exception to the anti-acceleration provisions in this circumstance is not feasible because of the current lack of clarity with respect to (i) the scope of coverage of the top hat plan rules and (ii) the actions required when a plan participant no longer satisfies the requirements to qualify for top hat plan participation.

In January 2020, at the request of three United States Senators, the United States Government Accountability Office (GAO) published a report on top hat plans that recommended that the Department of Labor (DOL) determine whether specific instructions should be issued for companies to follow to correct eligibility errors that occur when rank-and-file employees are found to be participating in top hat plans. The GAO recommended that the DOL create a method of correction for a top hat plan that inadvertently covers an employee who is not a member of a "select group of management or highly compensated employees." In response, the DOL directed the GAO to a 2015 amicus brief it filed that suggested that plans could be modified to exclude ineligible rank-and-file employees, awarding them the full vesting and other protections afforded under ERISA and distributing their benefits from the plan while maintaining the plan's status as a top hat plan for those executives who do qualify. The amicus brief further suggested that this approach would avoid providing a windfall gain to the management and highly-compensated employees who could properly have been included in a top-hat plan.

The DOL brief does not address the issue of whether a distribution as a result of ineligibility would run afoul of Section 409A's prohibition on accelerated distributions. When the IRS was presented with the scenario in the DOL amicus brief, the IRS responded that removing employees from the plan and awarding them full and immediate vesting and payout of benefits could constitute an impermissible acceleration of nonqualified deferred compensation. The IRS said it was willing to work with the DOL to create an exception to the accelerated payment rule for plans that seek to remove ineligible rank-and-file employees from a top hat plan, but the DOL would first need to better define a top-hat employee and then decide the proper approach for removing ineligible rank-and-file employees from a plan.

Citation: Preamble to Final Section 409A Regulations § VIII(F) (2007); GAO-20-70 (Jan. 2020); Advisory Council on Employee Welfare and Pension Benefit Plans, Report to the Honorable Eugene Scalia, United States Secretary of Labor, Examining Top Hat Plan Participation and Reporting at pp. 5 & 38; Brief for the DOL as Amicus Curiae, p. 24, Bond v. Marriott International, Inc., No. 15-1160 (4th Cir. 2016).

TAX CONSEQUENCES

Q.101 WHAT CONSTITUTES A VIOLATION OF SECTION 409A THAT CAUSES A SERVICE PROVIDER TO INCUR TAX LIABILITY UNDER SECTION 409A?

Section 409A requires compliance in both form and operation with its restrictions on elections, distributions, and accelerations. Any violation must be corrected in accordance with the guidance provided in IRS Notice 2008–113 for operational errors (see **Q.240** through **Q.255**) or Notice 2010–6 for documentation errors (see **Q.224** through **Q.239**). If a violation is not corrected, as prescribed, the additional taxes imposed in connection with violation of Section 409A will apply with respect to vested amounts (see **Q.103**).

Citation: I.R.C. § 409A(a)(1)(A); Prop. Treas. Reg. § 1.409A-4, I.R.B. 2008–51 (Dec. 22, 2008); Notice 2010–80; Notice 2010–6; Notice 2008–113.

Q.102 WHAT IS THE GENERAL FEDERAL INCOME TAX SCHEME FOR PLANS SUBJECT TO SECTION 409A?

Section 409A is characterized as a clarification of the federal income tax doctrine of constructive receipt, not as a replacement of that doctrine. In the absence of a breach of the requirements of Section 409A, federal income tax is imposed on nonqualified deferred compensation offered by a taxable entity in the taxable year in which payment is actually or constructively received. Payments are taxable as ordinary income at then current rates. Special timing rules apply to taxation of certain deferred compensation payable by tax-exempt entities pursuant to Code Section 457(b) (see **Q.2**).

There are three negative tax consequences in the event of a breach of the requirements of Section 409A:

- The entire amount of the participant's vested account balance in the case of an individual account balance plan (see **Q.117**), or the present value of the participant's vested benefit in the case of a non-account balance plan (see **Q.119**), as of the end of the tax year in which the breach occurs under all plans of the same type (see **Q.107**) is treated as ordinary income for the year of breach, whether or not distributed in that year. It is possible that non-vested benefits would also be treated as ordinary income for the year if, based on the facts and circumstances, there is an attempt to evade Section 409A.
- An additional income tax is imposed on the participant equal to 20 percent of the amount treated as ordinary income.
- The income tax imposed is increased by a premium interest tax. This tax is equal to the amount of interest at the underpayment rate (determined under Code Section 6621) plus one percentage point applied to the underpayments that would have occurred had the deferred compensation been includible in income for the taxable year in which first deferred or, if later, the first taxable year in which the deferred compensation is not subject to a substantial risk of forfeiture.

The following steps are required to determine the income tax due on account of the breach:

- Allocate the amount required to be taken into income to the respective calendar years in which it was first deferred or became vested.
- Recalculate the income tax for each affected year including the additional deferred compensation as income.

- Determine the hypothetical underpayment of taxes that would have resulted had the deferred amounts been includible in income when first deferred or vested.
- Determine the interest that would have been due upon the hypothetical underpayment based upon the premium interest rate.

Citation: I.R.C. § 409A(a)(1); *see also* Prop. Treas. Reg. § 1.409A-4, I.R.B. 2008–51 (Dec. 22, 2008).

Q.103 WHAT ARE THE FEDERAL INCOME TAX CONSEQUENCES OF A BREACH OF SECTION 409A?

Vested amounts not previously taxed. Under proposed regulations, the adverse tax consequences due to failure to comply with Section 409A with respect to amounts deferred under a plan apply to the year in which noncompliance with Section 409A occurs and all previous taxable years. All amounts that are not subject to a substantial risk of forfeiture and were not previously included in income are taken into account for this purpose.

Nonvested amounts. If any of a service provider's deferred amounts under a plan are nonvested on the last day of the year in which a Section 409A violation occurs, the nonvested deferred amounts generally are not includible in income under Section 409A for the year of violation. If the violation is corrected before the service provider's taxable year in which the deferred amounts are no longer subject to a substantial risk of forfeiture, no adverse tax consequences arise under Section 409A with respect to those amounts, subject to the anti-abuse rule in **Q.104**.

Subsequent deferrals. Failure to meet the requirements of Section 409A during a year generally does not affect taxation of amounts deferred under the plan for a subsequent year during which the plan complies with Section 409A in form and operation.

Citation: I.R.C. §§ 409A(a)(1)(A)(i)(II) and (B); Prop. Treas. Reg. § 1.409A-4, I.R.B. 2008–51 (Dec. 22, 2008).

Q.104 ARE THERE SITUATIONS IN WHICH A SUBSTANTIAL RISK OF FORFEITURE WILL BE DISREGARDED FOR PURPOSES OF DETERMINING WHETHER AN AMOUNT IS INCLUDIBLE IN INCOME UNDER Q.103?

Yes, if the correction of a Section 409A violation with respect to nonvested amounts does not meet the following anti-abuse requirements:

- The nonvested amounts must be non-compliant with Section 409A before any correction (i.e., the correction must not create the non-compliance);
- The service recipient must not have a prior history of making and correcting similar failures;
- The employer must make corrections in a consistent manner; and
- Any corrections must be made in accordance with applicable IRS guidance on plan corrections.

Citation: Prop. Treas. Reg. § 1.409A-4(a)(1)(ii)(B) (2016); Preamble to 2016 Proposed 409A Regulations § VII.

Q.105 WHO IS RESPONSIBLE FOR PAYMENT OF THE TAXES IMPOSED ON ACCOUNT OF A BREACH OF SECTION 409A?

Even though the service recipient is generally responsible for documentation and operation of the plan, the service provider is responsible for payment of these taxes. The service recipient does not lose its expense deduction incident to the taxable deemed distribution arising from a Section 409A violation.

The adverse tax consequences associated with noncompliance could be shifted from the service provider to the service recipient by an indemnity or other contractual provision in the plan document (see **Q.106**).

Authors' Comment: Plan provisions will sometimes specifically state that the employer is not liable for Section 409A taxes and penalties against any participant.

Citation: I.R.C. § 409A(a)(1)(A)(ii); *see* Prop. Treas. Reg. § 1.409A-4, I.R.B. 2008–51 (Dec. 22, 2008); *Wilson v. Safelite Group, Inc.,*

930 F. 3rd 429 (6th Cir. 2019) (action by terminated executive against his employer for failure to administer its nonqualified plan in compliance with 409A is preempted by ERISA); *see also, Davidson v. Henkel*, 12-CV-14103, 2015 WL 74257 (E.D. Mich. Jan. 5, 2015) for a case addressing employer liability for failure to withhold and pay FICA taxes on vested benefits prior to distribution.

Q.106 IS AN EMPLOYER REQUIRED TO INDEMNIFY PLAN PARTICIPANTS AGAINST THE TAXES IMPOSED BY SECTION 409A IF THE RELATED VIOLATION OF SECTION 409A IS DUE TO THE EMPLOYER'S OWN ACTION OR INACTION?

No. The plan document may include express acceptance or disclaimer of responsibility not only for the taxes due, but also for the service provider's costs of audit and litigation, depending on the intention of the parties.

Citation: Treas. Reg. § 1.409A-3(i)(1)(v).

Q.107 WHAT IS THE AGGREGATION RULE, AND HOW DOES IT APPLY TO DETERMINE FEDERAL INCOME TAX LIABILITY ON ACCOUNT OF A VIOLATION OF SECTION 409A?

In the event of an operational violation of Section 409A, a service provider's vested amounts under all plans of the same type as the plan under which the breach occurred are aggregated for purposes of determining the federal income tax consequences of the breach, including the amount subject to ordinary income tax for the year of the breach and the amount of the additional taxes imposed by Section 409A.

If the service provider participates in several plans of the same type, including plans maintained by any member of the controlled group of businesses that includes the service recipient, they are all aggregated for this purpose. If the service provider participates in two or more different types of plans, then the different plan types are not aggregated for this purpose.

There are nine plan types for this purpose:

- Participant elective deferral account balance plans (e.g., voluntary elective salary and bonus deferral plans).
- Employer account balance plans (e.g., employer matching contributions under a defined contribution plan, phantom stock plans, and cash balance plans to the extent they are treated as account balance plans under the FICA tax withholding rules set forth in Treasury Regulation § 31.3121(v)(2)-1(c)(1)(iii)(C), even though they are treated as defined benefit plans under the tax-qualified plan rules).
- Employer non-account balance plans (e.g., defined benefit supplemental executive retirement plans and cash balance plans to the extent they are treated as non-account balance plans under the FICA tax withholding rules under Treasury Regulation § 31.3121(v)(2)-1(c)(2)(i)).
- Stock equity plans (including stock appreciation rights and non-qualified stock option plans).
- Severance/separation pay plans payable solely on an involuntary separation from service or as a result of participation in a window program.
- Split-dollar life insurance plans.
- Foreign plans.
- Reimbursement/fringe benefit plans.
- Other miscellaneous types of plans.

Plans for employees are not aggregated with plans of the same type for outside directors of the employer or other independent contractors. Plans of the same type for independent directors and other independent contractors are aggregated with each other.

These plan aggregation rules do not apply to the requirement that a plan be documented in writing. Deferrals under an arrangement that fails to meet the documentation requirement are subject to the income tax for breach of Section 409A, but deferrals under other plans that satisfy the plan documentation requirement are not subject to income tax on account of this breach, even if they are of the same type as the plan in breach.

Citation: Treas. Reg. §§ 1.409A-1(c)(2) and 1.409A-1(c)(3)(viii); Annotated Final Regulations, comments by Daniel L. Hogans, following Treas. Reg. § 1.409A-1(c)(2)(i)(C)(2): "Cash balance plans are account balance plans consistent with 3121(v)."

Q.108 DO THE PLAN AGGREGATION RULES APPLY FOR OTHER PURPOSES UNDER SECTION 409A?

The aggregation rules also apply in the context of other aspects of Section 409A, including elections to defer (see **Q.121**) and distributions on plan termination (see **Q.85**).

Citation: I.R.C. § 409A(a)(1)(A)(ii); Treas. Reg. §§ 1.409A-1(c)(2) (aggregation rule generally and by plan type); 1.409A-2(a)(7) (elections); 1.409A-3(j)(4)(ix) (plan termination and liquidation).

Q.109 WHAT IS A DOCUMENTARY VIOLATION OF SECTION 409A?

A documentary violation occurs when the plan document does not comply with the requirements of Section 409A, such as a plan that contains a "haircut" provision that permits the service provider to accelerate distribution with a penalty (see **Q.17**).

Citation: Treas. Reg. § 1.409A-1(c)(3).

Q.110 WHAT IS THE EFFECT OF A DOCUMENTARY VIOLATION OF SECTION 409A?

All vested deferred compensation of all service providers accrued under the plan as of the effective date of the noncomplying provision and thereafter is subject to the taxes imposed by Section 409A, but all plans of the same type are *not* aggregated for this purpose (see **Q.107**).

Citation: I.R.C. § 409A(a)(1)(A)(ii); Treas. Reg. § 1.409A-1(c)(3)(viii).

Q.111 WHAT IS AN OPERATIONAL VIOLATION OF SECTION 409A?

An operational violation occurs when the plan provisions comply with Section 409A, but the plan is administered otherwise, such as if the plan provides for distribution to a service provider in one taxable year and by inadvertence, the distribution occurs in an earlier or later taxable year.

Citation: Notice 2008–113.

Q.112 WHAT IS THE EFFECT OF AN OPERATIONAL VIOLATION OF SECTION 409A?

An operational violation of Section 409A causes adverse tax consequences only with respect to the individuals affected by the violation, not the entire plan. An operational violation will affect the federal income tax treatment of all vested interests of that individual under all plans of the same type (see **Q.107**). The existence of nine plan types and the disaggregation of plans for employees and plans for independent contractors limit the amounts at risk in connection with a particular operational violation of Section 409A. For example, if an employer maintains two employer non-account balance plans for an employee, the employee's interests under both plans are taken into account in determining the employee's federal income tax liability if either plan violates Section 409A in operation. If an employer maintains an employer account balance plan and an employer non-account balance plan for the same employee, then if one plan violates Section 409A but the other does not, only the employee's interest under the plan that violates Section 409A is taken into account in determining the employee's federal income tax liability in connection with the violation.

Citation: I.R.C. § 409A(a)(1)(A)(ii); Treas. Reg. § 1.409A-1(c)(2).

Q.113 IF A PLAN FAILS TO COMPLY WITH SECTION 409A IN ONE YEAR BUT DEFERRALS CONTINUE UNDER THE PLAN IN SUBSEQUENT YEARS DURING WHICH THE PLAN OTHERWISE FULLY COMPLIES WITH SECTION 409A BOTH IN FORM AND OPERATION, DOES THE 409A FAILURE ADVERSELY IMPACT THE SUBSEQUENT DEFERRALS?

No. Although the IRS believes that the statutory language could reasonably be construed to provide that a 409A failure is treated as continuing during taxable years beyond the year in which the initial failure occurred, the agency declined to adopt this interpretation because of the harsh results and administrative complexity that would ensue. Instead, the adverse tax consequences that result from a failure to comply with 409A apply only with respect to untaxed vested amounts deferred under a plan in the year in which such noncompliance occurs and all previous taxable years. As a result, a failure to meet the requirements of Section 409A during a service provider's taxable year generally would not affect the taxation of amounts deferred under the plan for a subsequent taxable year during which the plan complies with Section 409A in form and operation.

Citation: Preamble to 2008 Proposed 409A Regulations § II; Prop. Treas. Reg. § 1.409A-4(a)(1)(ii)(A).

Q.114 DOES SECTION 409A REPLACE ALL PRIOR LAW GOVERNING FEDERAL INCOME TAXATION OF UNFUNDED DEFERRED COMPENSATION ARRANGEMENTS?

No. The requirements and doctrines of prior federal income tax law, such as the economic benefit, constructive receipt and nonassignability rules, remain applicable to plans subject to Section 409A except to the extent that Section 409A changed the prior law. The legislative history is clear that Section 409A is intended to be additive and only to clarify the constructive receipt rules. The prior income tax law also continues to govern plans not subject to Section 409A, such as grandfathered plans, plans that satisfy the short-term deferral rule, and plans of tax-exempt entities governed by Section 457(b) (see **Q.2**). Correction of operational or documentary errors in plans exempt or excepted from Section 409A are subject to these prior principles.

Citation: I.R.C. § 409A(c); Ways and Means Committee Report on H.R. 4520, 2004 TNT 118–7, page 276 (June 16, 2004).

Q.115 HAVE ANY STATES IMPOSED A PERSONAL INCOME TAX THAT PARALLELS SECTION 409A?

Yes, one state currently. California's rate is 5 percent effective for taxable years beginning on or after January 1, 2013, and is applicable to amounts subject to a violation of Section 409A. As originally enacted, California applied a 20 percent state excise tax. The premium late interest penalty of the federal law has never been applied by the state. Even so, the combination of federal and state ordinary income tax, the federal and state excise taxes, the federal Social Security and Medicare taxes, and the interest penalty under Section 409A impose extreme tax consequences in the event of a violation of Section 409A for a California taxpayer.

Citation: Cal. Rev. Tax Code § 17501 as amended by AB 1173, signed into law Oct. 10, 2013; *California Franchise Tax Board Statement,* Tax News (May, 2008) *available at* https://www.ftb.ca.gov./professionals/taxnews/2008/May/0508.pdf (California's adoption of § 409A correction procedures, and Form 540 Instructions, Line 33).

Q.116 CAN THE NEGATIVE INCOME TAX CONSEQUENCES OF A BREACH OF SECTION 409A BE MEDIATED?

Yes, on prompt identification and correction of a breach in either form or operation under Notice 2008–113 (for operational errors) (see **Q.240** through **Q.255**), Notice 2010–6 (for form errors) (see **Q.224** through **Q.239**), or both. California has adopted parallel correction procedures, but does not impose parallel reporting requirements (see **Q.115**).

DEFERRED COMPENSATION PLANS SUBJECT TO 409A

Q.117 HOW ARE PARTICIPANT ACCOUNT BALANCE PLANS TREATED FOR PURPOSES OF SECTION 409A?

Participant account balance plans are a separate plan type for purposes of Section 409A (see **Q.107**). These plans require voluntary service provider elections to defer compensation earned and otherwise payable in the current year, such as salary, fees, bonus and commissions, so the amounts deferred and any appreciation and earnings are typically 100 percent vested at all times and are not subject to a substantial risk of forfeiture or the short-term deferral rule (see **Q.21** through **Q.24**). If the plan complies with Section 409A and other law governing constructive receipt in both form and operation, federal income tax will be deferred until distribution as provided for under the plan.

Citation: I.R.C. § 409A(a); Treas. Reg. §§ 1.409A-1–3.

Q.118 HOW ARE EMPLOYER ACCOUNT BALANCE PLANS TREATED FOR PURPOSES OF SECTION 409A?

Employer account balance plans are a separate plan type for purposes of Section 409A (see **Q.107**). Typical employer account balance plans are based on the employer's promise to make future payments to supplement the employer's contributions under a tax-qualified defined contribution retirement plan. If the plan includes vesting requirements or other substantial risks of forfeiture, it can be designed to satisfy the short-term deferral rule (see **Q.21**). If the plan complies with Section 409A and other law governing constructive receipt in both form and operation, federal income tax will be deferred until actual or constructive receipt of deferred amounts as provided for under the plan.

Citation: I.R.C. § 409A(a); Treas. Reg. §§ 1.409A-1–3.

Q.119 HOW ARE EMPLOYER NON-ACCOUNT BALANCE PLANS TREATED FOR PURPOSES OF SECTION 409A?

Employer non-account balance plans are a separate plan type for purposes of Section 409A (see **Q.107**). Typical employer non-account balance plans are nonqualified defined benefit pension plans that promise the employee monthly periodic payments for life or a specified period of time, rather than the amount accrued in an individual account. If the plan includes vesting requirements or other substantial risks of forfeiture, it can be designed to satisfy the short-term deferral rule (see **Q.21**). If the plan complies with Section 409A and other law governing constructive receipt in both form and operation, federal income tax will be deferred until actual or constructive receipt of deferred amounts as provided for under the plan.

Citation: I.R.C. § 409A(a); Treas. Reg. §§ 1.409A-1–3.

SERVICE PROVIDER ELECTIONS

Q.120 WHAT TYPES OF SERVICE PROVIDER ELECTIONS ARE TYPICALLY PROVIDED FOR UNDER DEFERRED COMPENSATION PLANS SUBJECT TO SECTION 409A?

In an elective deferral account balance plan, the service provider must make a threshold election to defer the compensation rather than receive it on a current basis. This type of election is not appropriate for plans consisting solely of employer-provided benefits, because the amounts accrued under such plans do not depend on the service provider's deferral of compensation.

In addition, elective deferral account balance plans typically provide for service provider elections respecting the time and form of payment. Plans consisting solely of employer-provided benefits may also provide for such elections. Vest and pay plans do not provide for this type of election (see **Q.27**). If a plan provides for service provider elections, Section 409A imposes strict limits on the time of the initial election and subsequent changes (see **Q.121** and **Q.127**).

Citation: Treas. Reg. § 1.409A-2(a).

Q.121 WHEN MUST INITIAL ELECTIONS TO DEFER AND TO DESIGNATE THE TIME AND FORM OF PAYMENT BE MADE UNDER SECTION 409A?

In general, the service provider's initial election to defer compensation, including the amount deferred or the method of determining the amount deferred and the time and form of payment, must occur and must be irrevocable before the beginning of the taxable year of the service provider in which the services relating to the compensation are to be rendered. The service recipient generally cannot retain any right to override these elections once they become irrevocable. Because almost all individuals are required to use the calendar year as the taxable year, the deadline is generally December 31 preceding the beginning of the calendar year of deferral.

The following exceptions and limitations apply:

- *30-Day Rule for Newly Eligible Participants:* A service provider who becomes eligible for deferred compensation for the first time after the general deadline for making elections with respect to a taxable year may make an initial election to defer within 30 days following the date of initial eligibility. The election must apply only to compensation earned after the date of the election. The controlled group and plan aggregation rules apply to determine a participant's first date of eligibility.

- *Deferral of Bonuses in the Case of a Mid-Year Start (Pro Rata Rule):* In the case of a newly eligible participant with a mid-year start, the deferred amount of any compensation based on a specified performance period, such as an annual bonus, cannot exceed a pro rata portion of such compensation based on the time remaining in the performance period after the start date unless the compensation qualifies as performance-based compensation. For example, if an initial deferral election becomes effective on October 1, a participant may defer a maximum of 92/365ths or 25.2 percent of the participant's annual bonus for the taxable year.

- *Previously Eligible Participants (Retirees and Transferees):* A service provider who has not been an active participant in any Section 409A

plan at the same type for at least 24 months is subject to the initial eligibility rules. For this purpose, a service provider is an active participant in a plan if, under the plan's terms and without further amendment or action by the service recipient, the service provider is eligible to elect to defer compensation or otherwise accrue benefits (other than earnings on prior deferrals) under the plan.
- *Performance-Based Compensation:* Special rules apply to elections to defer performance-based compensation (see **Q.124**).
- *Fiscal Year Plans:* If compensation is payable on the basis of one or more of the service recipient's fiscal years and if no part of the compensation is payable during the fiscal year, the initial elections may be made not later than the close of the service recipient's prior fiscal year. For example, this includes an annual bonus arrangement based on the employer's performance during its fiscal year, as long as no part of the bonus is payable until after the end of the fiscal year.
- *Sales Commissions:* For *bona fide* sales or renewal sales commissions, elections must be made before January 1 of the calendar year in which the customer remits payment for the services or product or, if applied consistently to all similarly situated service providers, the January 1 in which the sale occurs.
- *Investment Commissions:* For investment commissions based on the value of financial products, the services are deemed to be performed over the 12 months before the date on which the investment commission is determined, so the election must be made before January 1 of the calendar year in which the 12-month measuring period begins.
- *Annualized Recurring Part-year Compensation (Educator Compensation):* For recurring part-year compensation of educators who have the right to elect to annualize their compensation over a 12-month period rather than the shorter period during which they render services (typically nine months), the arrangement will not be subject to Section 409A if the participant elects to annualize the recurring part-year compensation over a period not to exceed 13 months and the election is made before the first day of the employment period (see **Q.126**).

- *Evergreen Elections:* An evergreen election that remains in effect until terminated or modified is permitted if it meets the Section 409A test for irrevocability each calendar year. For example, a plan could provide that a service provider's deferral election will remain in effect until changed or revoked, but that as of each December 31 the election will become irrevocable with respect to compensation earned in the following calendar year.

Authors' Comment: Evergreen elections should be implemented carefully since there can be situations where the evergreen election cannot be executed. For example, an evergreen election to defer compensation to a fixed date cannot be executed once the fixed date calendar year is reached.

- *Excess Benefit Plans:* For excess benefit plans, the sole purpose of which is to fund benefits in excess of the limits imposed on tax-qualified retirement plans under the Code, the initial election must be made not later than 30 days after the employee becomes eligible to participate. For this purpose, eligibility to participate occurs on the first day of the year immediately following the year in which the employee first accrues a benefit under the plan. The initial election will apply to all benefits accrued under the plan before and after the election until an appropriate subsequent election is made (see **Q.127**).

  Because of the changing variable elements that apply in determining accruals under defined benefit excess benefit plans, it is possible that an employee would accrue a benefit in one year, have that benefit reduced to zero in a later year, and increased again after that. In this case, the initial elections must be made when the employee first accrues a benefit, and all subsequent accruals under the plan are subject to that election until a proper subsequent election is made (see **Q.127**).

  Former participants who lose eligibility or terminate employment and subsequently regain eligibility to participate are also governed by this rule (see **Q.135**).

- *Linked Plans:* For nonqualified deferred compensation plans under which the amount deferred is determined in whole or in part by the benefits to be provided under a qualified pension plan, the following

changes will not be treated as impermissible Section 409A elections or accelerations:
- An increase or decrease in amounts deferred under the nonqualified deferred compensation plan that results directly from changes in the qualified plan limits imposed by the Code, such as the limit on qualified plan compensation imposed by Code Section 401(a)(17).
- The participant's actions or inactions under the qualified plan as to pre-tax elective deferrals that do not result in an increase or decrease in the amount deferred under the nonqualified deferred compensation plan by more than the Section 402(g)(1)(b) limits ($18,000 in 2017) in any calendar year.
- The participant's actions or inactions under the qualified plan as to pre-tax and after-tax elective deferrals that affect employer matching amounts or other contingent amounts credited under the nonqualified plan that do not exceed 100 percent of the matching or contingent amounts that would have been credited under the qualified plan in the absence of the qualified plan limitation.
- *Elections of Time and Form of Payment with respect to Employer Plans:* If a plan does not permit a participant to elect to defer current compensation, which is typical of employer non-account balance plans, the plan may permit a participant to elect the time and form of payment by the latest date that the participant could have made a deferral election if such an election were available under the plan or the date that the service recipient grants a legally binding right to the compensation, whichever is later.
- *Compensation Subject to Forfeiture:* If a participant's right to a payment under a plan is conditioned on continued future services for at least 12 months, the plan may permit the participant to elect to defer receipt of the payment within 30 days after the participant acquires a legally binding right to the payment.
- *Deferral of Short-Term Deferral Awards Prior to Vesting:* If a participant's right to a payment under the plan is subject to a substantial risk of forfeiture, the plan may permit the participant to elect to defer the payment if the election to defer is made at least 12 months before the date the substantial risk of forfeiture is scheduled to

lapse and the date for payment specified in the election to defer is at least five years after the date scheduled for lapse. For example, an employer grants an employee a bonus on January 1, 2018, payable on January 1, 2020, provided that the employee continues to be employed through January 1, 2020. The employee may elect to defer the compensation on or before January 1, 2019, as long as the election delays payment to January 1, 2025, or later (five years from the date the substantial risk of forfeiture was scheduled to lapse).

- *Plan Aggregation:* All plans of a controlled group that are of the same type for purposes of Section 409A are treated as a single plan for this purpose (see **Q.107**), so all initial elections under all plans of the same type must occur within the same time period. Some employers limit eligibility to participate and make initial elections under all plans maintained by the controlled group that are of the same type for this purpose to one or two 30-day window periods per year, such as June and December, to be sure that this requirement is satisfied.

Citation: Treas. Reg. §§ 1.409A-1(c) and 1.409A-2(a).

Q.122 MUST THE METHOD FOR CALCULATING INSTALLMENT PAYMENTS UNDER A NONQUALIFIED PLAN BE SPECIFIED IN WRITING AT THE TIME OF AN INITIAL DEFERRAL ELECTION?

Yes. All deferred payments elected by a service provider must be objectively determinable under a nondiscretionary formula. If the calculation method is not specified in the plan document, it must be set forth in other written instruments that detail the material terms of the plan, such as an administrative manual or similar documentation. If a service provider has a choice regarding different installment option calculation methods, this choice must be made at the time of the initial deferral election.

Authors' Comment: If more than one installment option calculation method is offered, the plan should provide for a default method in the event the service provider fails to elect one of the available options.

Citation: Treas. Reg. § 1.409A-1(c)(3); Treas. Reg. § 1.409A-2(b)(2)(i).

Q.123 WHICH YEAR'S DEFERRAL ELECTION APPLIES TO BASE PAY EARNED DURING THE FINAL PAYROLL PERIOD OF ONE YEAR AND PAID ON THE FIRST PAY DATE OF THE NEXT YEAR IN ACCORDANCE WITH THE SERVICE RECIPIENT'S STANDARD PAYROLL PRACTICE?

Unless the plan provides otherwise, the cash basis rule applies and the deferral election for the subsequent year applies, even though the services related to the pay were performed in the prior year. If a plan is amended to provide that the deferral election for the year in which the pay is earned applies, the plan amendment cannot be effective until 12 months after the amendment is adopted.

Example. In December 2017, a service provider elects to defer 25 percent of her base salary for 2018. In December 2018, the service provider elects to defer zero percent of her base salary for 2019. The service provider performs services during the last two weeks of 2018 and, in accordance with the service recipient's standard payroll practice, receives her base pay for those services in January 2019. The service provider's zero percent deferral election for 2019 applies to this payment unless the plan provides otherwise.

Citation: Treas. Reg. § 1.409A-2(a)(13).

Q.124 HOW IS PERFORMANCE-BASED COMPENSATION DEFINED FOR PURPOSES OF SECTION 409A?

The Section 409A regulations set forth the following principles for determining whether an amount constitutes performance-based compensation:

- The performance goals may be based upon individual or organizational criteria.
- The performance period must be at least 12 consecutive calendar months. Quarterly bonuses would not qualify.
- The participant must perform services continuously from the beginning of the performance period or the date the performance

criteria are established, whichever is later, through the date of the election to defer.
- The performance goals must be communicated to the participant in writing within 90 days from the beginning of the performance period.
- Any performance-based compensation must be separately identified or designated under the plan.
- Compensation will not fail to constitute performance-based compensation merely because of a provision for automatic payment in the event of death, disability or a change of control.
- Compensation fails to qualify as performance-based compensation if the plan contains a provision for automatic payment in the event of termination of employment irrespective of performance.

Elections to defer performance-based compensation must be made by the earlier of six calendar months before the end of the performance period (for example, by June 30 in the case of a calendar year bonus performance period) or the date the performance-based compensation has become readily ascertainable. For this purpose, compensation is readily ascertainable to the extent it is certain to be paid.

These requirements are similar, but not identical, to the requirements for performance-based compensation for purposes of Code Section 162(m). For example, neither board nor shareholder approval is required for compensation to qualify as performance-based compensation under Section 409A.

Citation: Treas. Reg. § 1.409A-2(a)(8).

Q.125 IS A BONUS DEFERRAL ELECTION THAT IS SUBJECT TO SECTION 409A CANCELED IF THE SERVICE PROVIDER SEPARATES FROM SERVICE AFTER THE ELECTION IS MADE OR BECOMES FINAL, BUT BEFORE THE DATE THE BONUS AMOUNT IS CREDITED TO THE SERVICE PROVIDER'S ACCOUNT?

No. There is no exception to the general rule for this, so cancellation is equivalent to an impermissible subsequent change in deferral election (see **Q.127**). If the plan contains a provision for distribution of the deferred amount on separation from service, then the deferred amount should be distributed when it is credited to the service provider's account, unless the service provider is a specified employee of a publicly held service recipient. In that case, distribution should occur on the later of the date the deferred amount is credited to the service provider's account or six months after separation from service.

Citation: Treas. Reg. § 1.409A-2(b) (requirements for subsequent elections); 2009 ABA JCEB Questions, Q&A 21.

Q.126 DOES A SERVICE PROVIDER'S ABILITY TO ELECT THAT COMPENSATION EARNED IN A NINE- OR TEN-MONTH PERIOD, TYPICALLY AN ACADEMIC YEAR, BE PAID OVER A TWELVE-MONTH PERIOD SPANNING TWO TAXABLE YEARS CREATE NONQUALIFIED DEFERRED COMPENSATION SUBJECT TO SECTION 409A?

In principle, yes. This pattern, typical to employees of academic institutions, is called recurring part-year compensation. For example, a school year starts August 1, 2010, and ends May 31, 2011 (10 months), and a teacher earns $5,400 per month ($54,000 per year). If the teacher were paid over 10 months, the teacher would receive $27,000 in 2010 for the five months of August through December, and $27,000 in 2011 for the following five months of January through May. If the teacher were paid over 12 months, the teacher would receive $4,500 per month, totaling $22,500 in 2010 for the five months of August through December and $31,500 in 2011 for the following seven months of January through July. As a result, $4,500 that the teacher earned in 2010 would be paid in 2011, so this amount would constitute nonqualified deferred compensation subject to Section 409A.

Is There an Exception to the General Rule of Section 409A Coverage?

Yes. A service provider receiving regular recurring part-year compensation is excepted from compliance with both Section 409A and Section 457 if the compensation is not deferred beyond the last day of the 13th month following the beginning of the work period (for example, if the first day of work for the school year is September 1, the latest date for payment is October 31 of the following year), and the amount of the service's provider's compensation does not exceed the annual compensation limit under Section 401(a)(17) ($270,000 for 2017).

What Does Section 409A Require If an Election Is Offered?

The IRS has excepted regular recurring part-year compensation from the requirements of Section 409A. If this exception is not available, the general rules for elections to defer compensation under Section 409A apply as follows:

- The employee must make an election that notifies the employer that the employee wants to spread payment of the compensation over the longer period.
- The election must be made before the beginning of the work period. For example, it must be made before the first day of the school year for which the employee is entitled to payment, which may be before the first day students arrive for class.
- The election must be irrevocable. It cannot be changed after the work period begins.
- The election must state how the compensation is to be paid, such as ratably over the 12 months starting with the beginning of the school year.

No particular form is necessary for this election, and it does not have to be filed with the IRS.

What If an Employee Does Not Submit an Election or Misses the Deadline?

If an employee does not submit an election or submits an election after the deadline, the employee must be paid in the same way as other employees who do not make an election.

If a School District Provides for an Election, Must the Election Requirements Be Made in Writing?

Yes, but Section 409A does not require any specific type of documentation. For example, it is sufficient if an employee signs and delivers an election form with the required information. In addition, an election may be made electronically, such as by e-mail. Other rules, such as the inability to change the election and the deadlines for the election, can be provided in any other document, such as an employee handbook or school board rules and regulations.

Is an Employee Required to Make This Election Every Year?

No. A procedure may provide that a pre-existing election remain in place until the participant elects to change it. For example, an employee may elect to receive salary over 12 months, and the election will remain in effect indefinitely until the employee changes it. However, any change in such an evergreen election must be made before the beginning of the school year to which the change applies. A change in the method of payment in the middle of a school year is not allowed.

Does Section 409A Require That an Employee Be Provided an Election?

No. For example, a school district may provide that all teachers will have their pay spread over 12 months, without providing any election to the teachers. In this case, employee elections are inappropriate.

Did the IRS Impose Any Additional Taxes If a School District and Its Employees Failed to Meet These Requirements for Any School Year Beginning before 2008?

No. The IRS will not impose additional taxes for failure to meet the deferral election timing and written plan requirements with respect to the annualization of compensation for work periods or school years beginning before January 1, 2008. This relief applies only to compensation that qualifies for the timing rule in the regulations applicable to elections to annualize recurring part-year compensation, and only to the extent the compensation is paid on or before December 31, 2008.

Citation: Treas. Reg. § 1.409A-2(a)(14); Notice 2008–62; IR 2007–142; Preamble to 2016 Proposed 409A Regulations § II.F; Prop. Treas. Reg. § 1.409A-1(b)(13) (2016).

Q.127 CAN A PARTICIPANT MAKE A SUBSEQUENT ELECTION TO CHANGE THE TIME OR FORM OF PAYMENT SPECIFIED IN AN EARLIER ELECTION?

Yes. The plan document must authorize the subsequent elections and the following requirements must be satisfied:

- The plan must provide that a subsequent election cannot take effect for at least 12 months after it is made.
  Example 1. An employee changes his election to receive a death benefit from 30 days after death to two years after death. If the employee dies within 12 months after the election, the election is void. Otherwise, it is effective.
- If the event triggering distribution is separation from service, change of control, a specified time, or pursuant to a fixed schedule elected at the time of deferral, the plan must provide that payment be delayed for a period of at least five years from the date the payment would otherwise have occurred. This restriction does not apply to distributions triggered by disability, death, or unforeseeable emergency.
  Example 2. An employee entitled to a single sum payable 30 days after separation from service elects to delay payment for a period of five years after separation from service. The election is invalid. If the employee elects to delay payment for a period of five years and 30 days after separation from service, the election is valid, provided the employee does not separate from service within 12 months.
- The plan must provide that an election changing a specified time or fixed schedule elected at the time of deferral must be made at least 12 months before the date previously scheduled for the first payment.

Authors' Comment: This creates a "pend" period in which the old form of payment is retained and effective until a period of 12 months has passed and the revised subsequent election timing and form become effective. This rule is designed to prevent a service provider from manipulating the subsequent election rule to change the form of the distribution shortly before separating from service.

Example 3. An employee elected that compensation deferred during a year be paid in 10 individual annual installments commencing on the employee's 60th birthday. At age 59½, the employee makes a new election to delay commencement of payment for five years, when he attains age 65. Because the new election is made less than 12 months before the employee's 60th birthday, the payment scheduled for his 60th birthday cannot be delayed, even though it complies with the requirement that the period of delay be at least five years. If the plan provides that each installment in a series of installments is treated as a separate payment for this purpose, the remaining installments can be delayed in accordance with the new election because they would not have been payable within 12 months of the new election. If the plan provides that all installments in a series of installments are treated as a single payment for this purpose, the new election is void and cannot be enforced.

Authors' Comment: The first and third requirements appear to overlap. The IRS has not provided guidance on how they relate to each other. The first requirement (a subsequent election cannot take effect for at least 12 months after it is made) by its terms applies to all subsequent elections, whatever the triggering event. It makes the election void if the triggering event occurs within the 12-month "pend" period following the subsequent election. The third requirement (an election must be made at least 12 months before the date previously scheduled for the first payment), applies only to an election changing a specified date or fixed schedule elected at the time of deferral. Unlike the other events that can trigger distribution, there is no uncertainty about the time or possibility of occurrence of a specified time or fixed schedule. If the plan provides that a series of payments is treated as a string of separate payments for this purpose, because each payment is subject to its own election, then the third requirement applies to installments scheduled to be paid more than 12 months from the date of the new election but not to installments scheduled to be paid less than 12 months from the date of the new election (see **Q.133**).

Note: A mere change of form of payment from one type of annuity to another actuarially equivalent annuity (using reasonable assumptions) commencing at the same time is not subject to these requirements (see **Q.130**).

Citation: Treas. Reg. § 1.409A-2(b), specifically § 1.409A-2(b)(2) (on definition of "payment"); *see* Treas. Reg. § 1.409A-2(b)(2)(ii) (on elections to change the form of annuity payment).

Q.128 MAY A PARTICIPANT REVOKE A SUBSEQUENT ELECTION TO CHANGE THE TIME OR FORM OF PAYMENT SPECIFIED IN AN EARLIER ELECTION?

Yes, if the plan document permits this and the subsequent election has not become irrevocable. A subsequent deferral election is not considered made until the election becomes irrevocable under the terms of the plan. The plan may permit a subsequent deferral election to be changed at any time up until the last permissible date for making such a subsequent election (see **Q.127**).

Citation: Treas. Reg. § 1.409A-2(b)(1).

Q.129 IF A PLAN DOES NOT INCLUDE A PROVISION PERMITTING A PARTICIPANT TO MAKE A SUBSEQUENT ELECTION TO CHANGE THE TIME OR FORM OF PAYMENT SPECIFIED IN AN EARLIER ELECTION, MAY THE PLAN BE AMENDED TO ADD SUCH A PROVISION?

Yes. The plan sponsor may amend the plan to add a subsequent election provision, but it must be done promptly if a participant request is imminent.

Authors' Comment: The authors strongly recommend that any such amendment be adopted and become effective before the participant makes the subsequent election, although the Final 409A Regulations would appear to allow the amendment to be adopted and become effective as late as the date on which the subsequent election becomes irrevocable (see **Q.128**).

Citation: Treas. Reg. §§ 1.409A-1(c)(3)(i) and (iii).

Q.130 IS A CHANGE OF FORM OF PAYMENT FROM ONE TYPE OF ANNUITY TO ANOTHER ACTUARIALLY EQUIVALENT ANNUITY COMMENCING AT THE SAME TIME SUBJECT TO THE REQUIREMENTS THAT APPLY TO SUBSEQUENT ELECTIONS?

No. All types of annuity are treated as a single form of payment under Section 409A. This permits a service provider to make consistent changes regarding the form of payment under a tax-qualified pension plan and a nonqualified excess plan without encumbrance of the delays generally required under nonqualified plans. This rule permits a change in the form of annuity payment but it does not permit a change in the time when payment begins.

Citation: Treas. Reg. § 1.409A-2(b)(2)(ii).

Q.131 MAY A SERVICE RECIPIENT AMEND A PLAN TO CHANGE ACTUARIAL ASSUMPTIONS APPLICABLE TO ANNUITY PAYMENT FORMS AVAILABLE UNDER THE PLAN WITHOUT TRIGGERING THE SUBSEQUENT ELECTION RULES OR OTHERWISE VIOLATING SECTION 409A?

Yes. There is no requirement that the same actuarial methods and assumptions be used over the term of a service provider's participation in a plan. Accordingly, a service recipient may change the actuarial assumptions and methods used to determine annuity payments due to to any service provider whose benefits have not commenced, provided that all of the actuarial assumptions and methods are reasonable.

Authors' Comment: Whether the service recipient has the legal ability to amend a nonqualified plan to change actuarial assumptions requires an analysis of the governing plan documents, communications to service providers, and state contract law.

Citation: Treas. Reg. § 1.409A-2(b)(2)(ii)(D).

Q.132 CAN A PARTICIPANT MAKE A SUBSEQUENT ELECTION TO DEFER ONLY A PORTION OF AN AMOUNT PREVIOUSLY DEFERRED?

Yes. A subsequent election may apply to all or a specified portion of the amount subject to the earlier election. For example, a participant could make a subsequent election to further defer 50 percent of an account balance subject to an existing election for payment of the account in a lump sum. The participant could also elect that the amount further deferred be paid in installments over a specified period of time rather than a lump sum.

Citation: Treas. Reg. § 1.409A-2(b)(2)(i).

Q.133 CAN A PARTICIPANT MAKE A SUBSEQUENT ELECTION TO DEFER PERIODIC INSTALLMENTS AFTER DISTRIBUTION HAS BEGUN?

Yes, subject to the following:

- The plan must provide for subsequent elections to defer payments previously deferred pursuant to a fixed schedule and the three required conditions described in **Q.127** must be satisfied.
- The plan must provide that each installment payable pursuant to a fixed schedule is treated as a separate and independent deferral amount.

If both of these requirements are satisfied, a participant may make a subsequent deferral election with respect to installments due at least 12 months after the subsequent election, but not with respect to the installments due in the intervening period. The period of delay must be at least five years from the previously scheduled distribution date for each installment.

If the plan does not provide that each installment payable pursuant to a fixed schedule is treated as a separate and independent deferral amount, then the entire series of payments is treated as a single deferral amount for which distribution has already begun and further deferral of any portion is not possible.

Authors' Comment: A subsequent election on an installment can become very complex to administer, especially when elections are by class year and installments are treated as individual elections for purposes of the subsequent election rule. The ability of plan providers to take full advantage of this rule is usually dependent on the recordkeeper's ability to administer it properly. The service recipient should investigate the flexibility of the recordkeeper in advance to handle such subsequent elections when individual installment payments will be subsequently deferred if this ability is considered important to the plan.

Citation: Treas. Reg. § 1.409A-2(b)(2)(iii).

Q.134 CAN A PARTICIPANT MAKE A SUBSEQUENT ELECTION TO CHANGE THE FORM OF PAYMENT FROM PERIODIC INSTALLMENTS TO A SINGLE SUM?

Yes, if all of the requirements for subsequent deferral elections are satisfied (see **Q.127**), the series of payments is treated as a single deferral amount, the subsequent deferral election is made at least 12 months before payment is scheduled to begin, and payment is delayed for at least five years from the date previously scheduled for the first distribution.

Citation: Treas. Reg. § 1.409A-2(b)(2)(iii) and (5).

Q.135 CAN A PARTICIPANT CANCEL AN ELECTION TO DEFER COMPENSATION DURING THE PLAN YEAR IN WHICH THE COMPENSATION WOULD OTHERWISE HAVE BEEN PAID IN THE ABSENCE OF THE ELECTION?

Generally, no. The following exceptions apply:

- A plan may allow a service provider to cancel a deferral election for the rest of the year if the service provider becomes disabled (see **Q.46**), takes an unforeseeable emergency distribution from the plan (see **Q.73**), or takes a hardship withdrawal from a 401(k) plan.
- A plan may require cancellation of a deferral election for the rest of the year upon the occurrence of any of the events set forth in the previous paragraph. If a 401(k) plan is designed to satisfy the safe harbor hardship withdrawal requirements, suspension of elective deferrals under a nonqualified plan upon a hardship withdrawal must be mandatory.
- An election may be changed or terminated if the election pertains to performance-based compensation (see **Q.124**) and the deadline for making the election has not yet occurred.

Cancellation or change in a deferral election with respect to a service provider's taxable year is not otherwise permitted, even if the service provider separates from service and then resumes service during the same taxable year.

Citation: I.R.C. § 409A(a)(4)(B)(iii) (performance-based compensation); Treas. Reg. §§ 1.401(k)-1(d)(3)(iv)(E) and (F) (suspension of contributions to nonqualified plan on account of 401(k) hardship distribution); 1.409A-2(a)(1) (initial elections generally) and (8) (performance-based compensation); 1.409A-3(a) (permissible payments generally), (j)(4) (permitted cancellations of deferrals); Preamble to Final 409A Regulations, § VI.D (2007) (prohibition of change in a deferral election with respect to a service provider's taxable year).

Q.136 CAN A PLAN PERMIT A SERVICE PROVIDER TO ELECT MULTIPLE FORMS OF PAYMENT WITH RESPECT TO VARIOUS PORTIONS OF A DEFERRED AMOUNT?

Yes. If a plan permits this, it can create multiple subaccounts for a service provider and each subaccount can be governed by a separate election with respect to the time and form of distribution. The amount subject to each distribution form must clearly be identified either as a percentage of the value of the account or subaccount or as a specified dollar amount as of the time of the election. The distribution rules apply separately to each subaccount.

Providing this level of flexibility requires complicated record keeping by the plan administrator.

Citation: Treas. Reg. § 1.409A-2(b)(2)(i).

Q.137 IF A SERVICE PROVIDER IS ALLOWED TO ELECT DIFFERENT DEFERRAL PERCENTAGES FOR DIFFERENT TYPES OF COMPENSATION DURING A YEAR, SUCH AS BASE PAY, ANNUAL BONUS AND LONG-TERM BONUS, WILL A SECTION 409A VIOLATION OCCUR IF THE MIX OF THE SERVICE PROVIDER'S COMPENSATION CHANGES MID-YEAR?

There is no definitive answer to this question. The IRS has indicated that the answer will depend on the facts and circumstances of each case. An important factor is whether the amount to which the deferral election applied was objectively determinable and whether the deferral election was irrevocable. Any evidence of collusion between the service provider and service recipient in changing the mix of compensation to change the effect of the initial deferral election would clearly be a problem, but evidence of collusion is not the only possible evidence of a problem. According to informal statements on the topic by IRS representatives, other facts could be sufficient to support an IRS determination that a deferral election was in effect revocable at the discretion of the parties through changes in the service provider's compensation package.

Example. A plan allows a service provider to make separate deferral elections with respect to the service provider's base pay and annual bonus. In December 2017, at a time when 60 percent of the service provider's compensation is paid as base pay and 40 percent as annual bonus, the service provider elects to defer 0 percent of her base pay for 2018 and 50 percent of her annual bonus earned in 2018. The service recipient decides in February 2018 to change the mix of the service provider's compensation to 80 percent base pay and 20 percent bonus. Whether this change in the compensation mix is treated as an impermissible change in the service provider's deferral election will be based on all of the facts and circumstances. In this case, relevant facts might include how other similarly situated service providers' compensation was adjusted and the rationale for the adjustment.

Citation: 2009 ABA JCEB Questions, Q&A 25.

Q.138 CAN THE SUBSEQUENT ELECTION RULE BE USED TO INCREASE PARTICIPANT FLEXIBILITY IN A PLAN WITH MULTIPLE ANNUAL ELECTION OPTIONS?

Yes, if the plan provides for subsequent elections to delay distribution to a specified date, a participant can elect to defer compensation to a specified date in anticipation of a need for cash, such as in anticipation of a child's expected college expenses. If the participant finds that the distribution is not needed, the participant can make a subsequent election at least 12 months before the specified distribution date to delay distribution for an additional five years or more.

Authors' Comment: Providing this level of flexibility requires complicated record-keeping by the plan administrator, so the capabilities of the recordkeeper are important if this feature will be added to a plan.

Citation: Treas. Reg. § 1.409A-2(b)(1).

Q.139 CAN THE SUBSEQUENT ELECTION RULE AND THE SINGLE OR MULTIPLE PAYMENT ELECTION BE USED IN COMBINATION TO INCREASE THE SECURITY OF BENEFITS ACCRUED UNDER A PARTICIPANT INDIVIDUAL ACCOUNT PLAN BENEFIT?

Yes, if the plan provides for distribution in installments on a fixed date, treatment of each installment in a series as an individual payment, and subsequent elections to delay distribution. A participant can then elect before the beginning of each year to defer compensation earned during the year for two years, payable in the form of five annual installments (see **Chart 1**). At the end of year one and each subsequent year, the participant can make a subsequent election to defer distribution of the next scheduled installment payment for an additional five years or more (see **Chart 2**). If the participant determines for any reason that additional deferrals are not appropriate, the participant can stop all new elections to defer future compensation and all subsequent elections to further defer previously deferred amounts. In this case, distribution begins one year after termination of new deferrals and distribution is complete five years later.

Providing this level of flexibility requires complicated record-keeping by the plan administrator.

Chart 1: Participant elects a two-year fixed date deferral to be paid in five annual installments.

TAX YEAR	ELECTED DEFERRAL AMOUNT	SCHEDULED DISTRIBUTION AMOUNT	DISTRIBUTION DATE
2017	$50,000	$0	
2018		$0	JAN. 8
2019		$10,000	JAN. 8
2020		$10,000	JAN. 8
2021		$10,000	JAN. 8
2022		$10,000	JAN. 8
2023		$10,000	JAN. 8

Chart 2: Participant subsequently elects to push back the first installment five years to the end of the previously scheduled sequence of installments. This subsequent election is repeated every year as desired.

TAX YEAR	PRIOR ELECTED DISTRIBUTION SCHEDULE	5-YEAR REDEFEREAL	REVISED DISTRIBUTION SCHEDULE
2018			
2019	$10,000		
2020	$10,000		$10,000
2021	$10,000		$10,000
2022	$10,000		$10,000
2023	$10,000		$10,000
2024		$10,000	$10,000

Citation: Treas. Reg. §§ 1.409A-2(b)(1) and 1.409A-2(b)(2)(i) (single or multiple "payments" and definitions of payments generally).

Q.140 WHAT IS A ROLLING RISK OF FORFEITURE, AND HOW DO THE 409A RULES APPLY TO A ROLLING RISK OF FORFEITURE?

A rolling risk of forfeiture is an election by a service provider to defer payment of compensation subject to a substantial risk of forfeiture to a future date, subject to the continued application of the substantial risk of forfeiture until the date the compensation is paid.

Rolling risks of forfeiture are expressly disregarded under Section 409A unless the present value of the amount subject to the extended substantial risk of forfeiture is "materially greater" than the amount which would have otherwise been paid upon lapse of the original substantial risk of forfeiture.

Citation: Preamble to Final 409A Regulations § V.B (2007); Treas. Reg. § 1.409A-1(d)(1).

Q.141 HOW IS THE TERM "MATERIALLY GREATER" DEFINED FOR PURPOSES OF SECTION 409A IN THE CONTEXT OF ROLLING RISKS OF FORFEITURE?

There is not yet a specific definition for this term under Section 409A, but there is for purposes of Section 457. Under Section 457, an amount is considered "materially greater" in this context if the present value of the amount to be paid upon the extended lapse of the substantial risk of forfeiture, measured as of the date the substantial risk of forfeiture would have lapsed without regard to the extension, is more than 125 percent of the amount the service provider otherwise would have received on such date in the absence of the extension.

Although the preamble to the Section 457 proposed regulations specifically provides that no inference is intended that the 125 percent standard would apply in the Section 409A context, it is reasonable to apply this standard in the 409A context until specific IRS guidance to the contrary is issued.

Example 1. A service recipient and service provider agree that the service provider will be paid $100,000 on December 31, 2020 if the service provider continues to provide substantial services to the service recipient until that date. On September 1, 2020, the parties agree that the $100,000 payment will be deferred until December 31, 2022 provided that the service provider continues to provide substantial services to the service recipient until that date. The extended substantial risk of forfeiture is disregarded for purposes of Section 409A, and the service provider has made an impermissible deferral action under Section 409A. The $100,000 deferred payment is subject to immediate taxation on December 31, 2020. In addition, the Section 409A 20 percent additional tax applies to the $100,000 payment.

Example 2. Assume the same facts as in Example 1, except that the service recipient agrees to pay the service provider an additional $50,000 (for a total of $150,000) on December 31, 2022 provided the service provider continues to provide substantial services to the service recipient until that date. The present value of the amount subject to the extended substantial risk of forfeiture should be considered "materially greater" than the amount which would have otherwise been paid on December 31, 2020, and, accordingly, the extended risk of forfeiture should not be disregarded. The $150,000 payment on December 31, 2022 should qualify as a short-term deferral, which will be subject to tax when paid.

Citation: Preamble to 2016 Proposed 457 Regulations § IV.E.

SEVERANCE PLANS

Q.142 WHAT SEVERANCE PAYMENTS ARE EXEMPT FROM SECTION 409A?

Severance payments solely on account of involuntary termination of employment or termination for good reason (see **Q.146**) that are paid in their entirety within the short-term deferral period are exempt from Section 409A under the short-term deferral rule.

Severance payments that do not qualify as short-term deferrals are exempt from Section 409A if they satisfy all of the following requirements:

- The severance payments must occur only on involuntary separation from service, voluntary separation for good reason (see **Q.147**), or pursuant to a window program (see **Q.152**).
- The severance payments cannot exceed the lesser of two times the participant's annualized compensation for the year before the separation or two times the maximum limit on compensation taken into account under a tax-qualified retirement plan pursuant to Section 401(a)(17) for the year of separation (for 2017, the Section 401(a)(17) limit is $270,000, and two times this amount is $540,000).
- Payment must be complete by the end of the second calendar year following the year the participant separates from service.

Citation: Treas. Reg. §§ 1.409A-1(b)(4) and 1.409A-1(b)(9).

Q.143 MAY THE SEVERANCE PLAN EXEMPTION APPLY TO SERVICE PROVIDERS WHOSE EMPLOYMENT BEGINS AND ENDS IN THE SAME YEAR?

Yes. In this circumstance, since the service provider has no compensation from the service recipient in the taxable year preceding the year in which the service provider separates from service, the service provider's annualized compensation for the taxable year in which the service provider separates from service is used for purposes of the "two times annualized compensation" limit on severance pay.

Citation: Prop. Treas. Reg. § 1.409A-1(b)(9)(iii)(A)(1) (2016); Preamble to 2016 Proposed 409A Regulations § II.D.

Q.144 MUST THE DESIGN OF A SEVERANCE PAY PROGRAM USE ONLY THE SHORT-TERM DEFERRAL RULE OR ONLY THE SEVERANCE PLAN RULES, OR CAN THE TWO RULES BE USED IN COMBINATION?

The two rules can be used in combination to maximize the amounts exempt from Section 409A if the documentation is drafted appropriately. To accomplish this, each payment in a series of severance payments must be designated in writing as a separate payment for purposes of Section 409A. Then the payments made within the short-term deferral period will fall outside the scope of Section 409A under the short-term deferral rule (see **Q.21**), and the remaining payments will qualify as involuntary separation pay to the extent such payments satisfy the limits on the amount and time of payment.

Example. An executive with base compensation of $30,000 per month has an employment agreement that promises two years of salary continuation payments following the executive's involuntary termination of employment without cause. The executive's employment is involuntarily terminated without cause on June 30, 2017, and severance payments begin on July 1, 2017, in the amount of $30,000 per month. If the executive's employment agreement provides that each monthly severance payment is considered a separate payment for purposes of Section 409A, then the first nine severance payments (from July 1, 2017, through March 1, 2018) will be exempt from Section 409A under the short-term deferral rule because they will be made within 2½ months after the close of the calendar year of severance. The remaining 15 monthly severance payments, totaling $450,000, are exempt from Section 409A under the severance pay rules because the total amount is less than two times the Section 401(a)(17) limit for 2017 and all payments are completed by the end of the second calendar year following the year of termination.

If the plan provided for treating all installments as a single payment rather than providing that each installment is treated as a separate payment, the results would be as follows:

- The entire benefit would be treated as one payment.
- The payment would not be subject to the short-term deferral exception because payment could not have been completed within 2½ months after the year of termination.
- The exempt amount would have been limited to two times the Section 401(a)(17) limit for 2017, or $540,000.
- Payments in excess of that amount, or $180,000, would have been subject to Section 409A.

Citation: Treas. Reg. §§ 1.409A-1(b)(4)(i)(F) and (9)(v)(D).

Q.145 IS THERE ANY OTHER EXEMPTION THAT COULD APPLY TO SEVERANCE PAYMENTS UNDER SECTION 409A?

In addition to the exclusions from Section 409A under the short-term deferral and severance pay rules, the limited payment rule permits the parties to a separation pay arrangement to treat the right to payment that does not exceed the applicable dollar limitation under Section 402(g)(1)(B) ($18,000 for 2017) as beyond the scope of Section 409A for the year of separation from service. This exception can be used in combination with the short-term deferral rule and the separation pay rules.

Citation: Treas. Reg. §§ 1.409A-1(b)(4)(i)(F) and (9)(v)(D).

Q.146 CAN SEVERANCE AMOUNTS PAYABLE ON ACCOUNT OF VOLUNTARY TERMINATION OR TERMINATION FOR GOOD REASON QUALIFY AS SEVERANCE PAY OR SHORT-TERM DEFERRALS FOR PURPOSES OF SECTION 409A?

Severance pay that is available incident to voluntary termination of employment generally does not qualify for the severance pay exemption from Section 409A, even if the service provider has an involuntary severance. Also, because it is not subject to a substantial risk of forfeiture, it does not qualify for the short-term deferral exception to Section 409A.

However, a plan can provide that an employee's voluntary decision to terminate employment for good reason (see **Q.147**) based on the employer's negative treatment of the employee can be treated as if it were an involuntary severance for purposes of the short-term deferral rule and severance pay deferral rules.

Citation: Treas. Reg. §§ 1.409A-1(b)(9)(iii) and (n).

Q.147 WHEN IS TERMINATION FOR GOOD REASON CONSIDERED EQUIVALENT TO INVOLUNTARY SEVERANCE?

The regulations include a safe harbor definition of good reason that a plan may use for this purpose. The safe harbor requires the following:

- The separation from service must occur during a pre-determined period of time not to exceed two years following the initial existence of one or more of the following conditions arising without the consent of the participant:
  - A material diminution in the participant's base compensation.
  - A material diminution in the participant's authority duties, or responsibilities.
  - A material diminution in the authority, duties, or responsibilities of the supervisor to whom the participant is required to report, including a requirement that the participant report to a corporate

officer or employee instead of reporting directly to the board of directors of a corporation.
- A material diminution in the budget over which the participant retains authority.
- A material change in the geographic location at which the participant must perform the services.
- Any other action or inaction that constitutes a material breach by the employer of the agreement under which the participant provides services.
- The amount, time, and form of payment upon separation from service must be substantially identical to the amount, time, and form of payment payable due to an involuntary separation from service, to the extent such a right exists.
- The participant must be required to provide notice to the employer of the existence of a condition giving rise to good reason no later than 90 days after the initial existence of the condition, and the employer must be provided a cure period of at least 30 days.

This is a safe harbor. Other good reason definitions may be treated as equivalent to involuntary severance based on all of the facts and circumstances. The facts and circumstances must include employer actions resulting in a material negative change to the employee in the employer-employee relationship, such as the duties to be performed, the conditions under which the duties are to be performed, or the compensation to be received for performing the services. Other factors include the extent to which the payments are in the same amount and are to be made at the same time and in the same form as payments available upon involuntary severance, whether the employee is required to give the employer notice of the existence of the condition that would result in treatment as a separation from service for good reason, and whether the employer has a reasonable right to cure.

Citation: Treas. Reg. § 1.409A-1(n)(2).

Q.148 IF A SEVERANCE ARRANGEMENT IS EXEMPT FROM SECTION 409A, CAN THE PARTIES MODIFY THE FORM AND TIME OF PAYMENT UNDER THE ARRANGEMENT WITHOUT MAKING THE ARRANGEMENT SUBJECT TO SECTION 409A?

Yes, but only if payments under the new schedule also qualify for the severance plan exemption from Section 409A. If the new schedule provides for shifting any payments from an earlier taxable year to a later taxable year, the constructive receipt rules may apply independent of Section 409A (see **Q.114**).

Citation: 2009 ABA JCEB Questions, Q&A 32 (analogous question on short-term deferrals).

Q.149 IS A MITIGATION PROVISION PERMITTED IN A SEVERANCE AGREEMENT THAT IS SUBJECT TO SECTION 409A?

Yes. Some severance arrangements provide that if the service provider receives compensation for services from another employer during the period when payments are due under the severance arrangement, the payments due under the severance arrangement will be reduced by the compensation the service provider receives from the other employer. The IRS treats this as a forfeiture permissible under Section 409A, rather than an impermissible offset.

Citation: 2008 ABA JCEB Questions, Q&A 27.

Q.150 IF ALL PAYMENTS DUE UNDER A SEVERANCE ARRANGEMENT DO NOT MEET THE SHORT-TERM DEFERRAL EXCEPTION, THE SEPARATION PAY EXCEPTION, OR THE SMALL DISTRIBUTION EXCEPTION, DOES THE ARRANGEMENT VIOLATE SECTION 409A?

If all or a portion of severance pay does not fit within any of these exceptions, it is subject to Section 409A but is not necessarily in breach of Section 409A. If the plan meets all of the requirements of Section 409A in both form and operation, there is no breach. This requires that the arrangement clearly specify the form and time of payment and that the form and time of payment not be changed after the schedule is established. In the case of a public company, any payments to specified employees must be delayed for at least six months following separation.

Citation: I.R.C. § 409A(a)(1)(a)(i); Treas. Reg. § 1.409–1(c)(1)-(3).

Q.151 CAN SEVERANCE PAYMENTS SUBSTITUTE FOR NONQUALIFIED DEFERRED COMPENSATION PAYMENTS THAT ARE BEING FORFEITED?

No. Any payment or benefit, including severance pay, that is a substitute for or replacement of amounts deferred under a separate nonqualified deferred compensation plan is treated as payment of the compensation deferred under the separate nonqualified deferred compensation plan (see **Q.90**). If an employee receives a severance payment at separation from service and also has a legally binding but forfeitable right to deferred compensation payable at a future date that is forfeited on account of the separation from service, whether or not the severance payment is treated as a substitute for the amount forfeited is based on the facts and circumstances. If the separation from service is voluntary, it is presumed that the severance payment is a substitute for the forfeited amount in breach of Section 409A. The presumption may be rebutted by a demonstration that the employee would have obtained the severance payment regardless of the forfeiture.

Example. An executive is terminated before age 65 and as a result forfeits the right to receive a nonqualified pension payment commencing at age 65. If the executive receives a lump sum severance payment equal to the present value of the forfeited benefit, the severance payment is presumed to be an accelerated payment of the forfeited benefit in violation of Section 409A.

Citation: Treas. Reg. § 1.409A-1(b)(9)(i).

Q.152 WHAT IS A WINDOW PROGRAM FOR PURPOSES OF THE SEVERANCE PAY EXCEPTION TO SECTION 409A?

A window program is a program established by an employer to provide severance for a period not in excess of 12 months under which the employer pays special severance pay to employees who separate from service during the window period. A program will not be considered a window program if the employer establishes a pattern of repeatedly providing for similar separation pay in similar circumstances for substantially consecutive periods.

Citation: Treas. Reg. § 1.409A-1(b)(9)(vi).

Q.153 DO COLLECTIVELY BARGAINED SEVERANCE PLANS AND FOREIGN SEVERANCE PLANS REQUIRED BY LOCAL LAW GET SPECIAL TREATMENT?

Yes. They are generally exempt from Section 409A. To meet the requirements for exemption, a collectively bargained severance plan must provide benefits only on involuntary separation, pursuant to a window program, or it must cover employees of multiple employers.

Citation: Treas. Reg. §§ 1.409A-1(b)(9)(ii)-(iv), (h)(6), (m), (n).

STOCK-BASED COMPENSATION

Q.154 DOES SECTION 409A APPLY TO INCENTIVE STOCK OPTIONS OR TO OPTIONS ISSUED UNDER A STATUTORY EMPLOYEE STOCK PURCHASE PLAN?

Incentive stock options under Code Section 422 and options granted under an employee stock purchase plan described in Code Section 423 are generally exempt from Section 409A. This exemption does not apply to a modification, extension, or renewal of a statutory option treated as the grant of a new nonqualified option under Section 422 or 423. In that case, the option is treated as if it had been a nonqualified option from the date of the original grant for purposes of Section 409A.

Citation: Treas. Reg. § 1.409A-1(b)(5)(ii).

Q.155 DOES SECTION 409A APPLY TO NONSTATUTORY STOCK OPTIONS AND STOCK APPRECIATION RIGHTS (SARS)?

Nonqualified stock options and SARs are within the scope of Section 409A because they provide the service provider with a legally binding right to compensation that will be realized in a later taxable year. However, the final regulations provide that nonqualified stock options and SARs can be structured to avoid Section 409A treatment.

Nonqualified stock options can be structured as follows:

- The stock subject to the option must constitute "service recipient stock" (see **Q.157**).
- The option exercise price cannot be less than the fair market value of the underlying stock on the date the option is granted.

- The number of shares subject to the option must be fixed on the date of grant.
- The transfer or exercise of the option must be subject to taxation under Section 83 and Treasury Regulation § 1.83–7.
- The option cannot include any feature for deferral of compensation other than the deferral of recognition of income until the date of exercise or disposition, whichever is later, or the date the stock acquired pursuant to the option exercise first becomes substantially vested.

Stock appreciation rights can be structured as follows:

- The stock subject to the SAR must constitute "service recipient stock" (see **Q.157**).
- The SAR exercise price cannot be less than the fair market value of the underlying stock on the date of grant.
- The number of shares subject to the SAR must be fixed on the date of grant.
- The compensation payable under the SAR cannot be greater than the excess of the fair market value of the stock on the date the SAR is exercised over an amount specified in the SAR documents on the date of grant.
- The SAR must not include any feature for the deferral of compensation other than the deferral of recognition of income until the SAR is exercised.

For example, a nonstatutory option or SAR that permits the service provider to elect to defer receipt of the compensation payable on exercise until termination of employment would not satisfy these requirements and would cause the option or SAR to be subject to Section 409A.

Citation: Treas. Reg. § 1.409A-1(b)(5).

Q.156 HOW ARE A SERVICE PROVIDER'S RIGHTS TO RECEIVE NONVESTED STOCK ON THE EXERCISE OF A STOCK RIGHT AND TO PAY THE EXERCISE PRICE WITH PREVIOUSLY ACQUIRED SHARES TREATED UNDER SECTION 409A?

Neither of these rights is treated as a deferral of compensation for purposes of Section 409A.

Citation: Treas. Reg. § 1.409A-1(b)(5)(i)(D).

Q.157 WHAT CONSTITUTES SERVICE RECIPIENT STOCK FOR PURPOSES OF THE STOCK-BASED COMPENSATION EXCEPTION TO SECTION 409A?

Service recipient stock generally means common stock of a corporation that employs a service provider (subject to the discussion in **Q.158**) or a direct or indirect parent of the employer, looking at the line of ownership only in an upward direction. Liquidation preferences are permitted, but dividend preferences are not. The minimum ownership requirement for each parent and subsidiary in the chain of ownership is generally 50 percent. If justified by legitimate business criteria, ownership can be as little as 20 percent.

Example. An employee works for Corporation C, which is 50 percent owned by Corporation A and 50 percent owned by Corporation B. Corporation A and Corporation B are not related to each other. The common stock of any of the three companies is service recipient stock with respect to the employee.

For this purpose, whether or not criteria are legitimate business criteria is based on all the facts and circumstances. There must be a sufficient nexus between the service provider and the issuer of the option or SAR such that the grant serves a legitimate non-tax business purpose. Avoidance of Section 409A is not a sufficient nexus. For example, stock options of a corporation that owns an interest in a joint venture that is an operating business granted to service providers of the joint venture who formerly were employees of the issuer, or who the issuer reasonably expects will become employees of the issuer in the future, generally constitutes use of service recipient stock based on legitimate business criteria, as long as the issuer owns at least 20 percent of the joint venture. However, if a service provider has no business nexus with an owner, which generally happens when the owner is a passive investor in a joint venture that employs the service provider, an option or SAR issued to the service provider with respect to the stock of the passive investor generally is not based on legitimate business criteria.

Except as provided in **Q.159**, service recipient stock does not qualify for this exception if it is subject to a mandatory repurchase obligation (other than a right of first refusal) or a put or call right that is not a lapse restriction as defined in Treasury Regulation § 1.83-3(i) if the purchase price is based on a measure other than the fair market value of the issuer's stock. For example, if an option is issued with an exercise price equal to fair market value of the issuer's stock on the date of grant, but the service provider must sell the stock received on exercise at a formula price equal to two times the issuer's book value on the date of sale, the price is determined independent of its relationship to fair market value. This option does not satisfy this requirement and it is subject to Section 409A.

Citation: Treas. Reg. § 1.409A-1(b)(5)(iii).

Q.158 MAY A SERVICE RECIPIENT GRANT STOCK RIGHTS TO AN INDIVIDUAL BEFORE THE INDIVIDUAL BECOMES A SERVICE PROVIDER AND STILL HAVE THE UNDERLYING STOCK QUALIFY AS SERVICE RECIPIENT STOCK?

Yes, if it is reasonably anticipated that (i) the individual will begin providing services to the service recipient within 12 months after the date of grant of a stock right, and (ii) either the person actually begins providing services to the service recipient within 12 months after the date of grant or, if services do not begin within that period, the stock right is forfeited.

Citation: Prop. Treas. Reg. § 1.409A-1(b)(5)(iii)(E)(1) (2016); Preamble to 2016 Proposed 409A Regulations § II.C.2.

Q.159 CAN STOCK WHICH IS SUBJECT TO A MANDATORY REPURCHASE OBLIGATION UPON A SERVICE RECIPIENT'S TERMINATION FOR CAUSE OR VIOLATION OF A RESTRICTIVE COVENANT QUALIFY AS SERVICE RECIPIENT STOCK?

Yes, even if the repurchase obligation is based on a measure other than fair market value. This is an exception to the general rule that mandatory repurchase obligations below fair market value disqualify stock from being considered service recipient stock (see **Q.157**).

Citation: Prop. Treas. Reg. § 1.409A-1(b)(5)(iii)(A) (2016); Preamble to 2016 Proposed 409A Regulations § II.C.1.

Q.160 HOW IS FAIR MARKET VALUE OF SERVICE RECIPIENT STOCK CALCULATED FOR PURPOSES OF DETERMINING THE EXERCISE PRICE OF AN OPTION OR SAR?

For stock that is readily tradable on an established securities market, the fair market value of the stock is based on market price. Fair market value may be based on the last sale before or the first sale after the grant, the closing price on the trading day before the trading day of the grant, the average of the high and low prices on the trading day before or the trading day of the grant, or any other reasonable method using actual transactions with respect to such stock as reported by the established securities market. An average selling price may be used if the employer designates the recipient of the stock right and the number and class of shares of stock that are subject to the stock right, and the method for determining the exercise price, including the period over which the averaging will occur, before the beginning of the specified averaging period. The averaging period cannot exceed 30 days before or after the grant date.

For stock that is not readily tradable on an established securities market, fair market value can be determined by reasonable application of a reasonable valuation method, based on all the facts and circumstances. The facts and circumstances may include the value of the company's tangible and intangible assets, the present value of its anticipated future cash flows, the market value of stock or equity interests in similar businesses, recent arm's-length sales or transfer of the stock, control premiums or discounts for lack of marketability, and whether the valuation method is used for other purposes that have a material economic effect on the employer, its stockholders, or its creditors. The use of a valuation method is not reasonable if it fails to take into consideration all available material information. For example, the use of a prior valuation that does not take into account information that became available at a later time and may materially affect the value of the company, such as resolution of material litigation or issuance of a patent, is not reasonable. A valuation as of a date more than 12 months before the grant date is not reasonable. The employer's consistent use of a valuation method for other purposes unrelated to compensation of service providers tends to support its reasonableness.

Any of the following valuation methods is presumed reasonable, subject to rebuttal by the IRS upon a showing that either the valuation method or its application was grossly unreasonable:

- A valuation determined by an independent appraisal as of a date not more than 12 months before the grant date.
- A formula valuation that satisfies the requirements of Treasury Regulation § 1.83–5, if the same method is used for purposes of any transfer of shares of the same class or a substantially similar class to the company or the owner of more than 10 percent of the total combined voting power of all classes of stock of the company, other than an arm's-length transaction involving the sale of all or substantially all of the outstanding stock, provided the valuation method is used consistently for all purposes.
- A valuation made reasonably, in good faith, and evidenced by a written report that takes into account the relevant factors with respect to illiquid stock of a start-up corporation. For this purpose, a start-up corporation means a corporation that has conducted business for less than 10 years and has no stock that is readily tradable on an established security market. This methodology is not available if the service recipient or service provider may reasonably anticipate,

as of the time of the grant, that the service recipient will undergo a change of control event within the 90 days following the grant date or make a public offering of securities within 180 days following the grant date. A valuation will not be considered made reasonably and in good faith unless the valuation is performed by a person or persons that the corporation reasonably determines is qualified to perform such a valuation based on the person's or persons' significant knowledge, experience, education, or training. For this purpose, significant experience generally means at least five years of relevant experience in business valuation or appraisal, financial accounting, investment banking, private equity, secured lending, or other comparable experience in the line of business or industry in which the service recipient operates.

A different valuation method may be used for each grant, but a single valuation method must be used for each separate action and cannot be changed retroactively. For example, one valuation method may be used to establish the exercise price of the stock option and a different valuation method may be used to determine the value at the date of the repurchase of stock pursuant to a put or call right, but once established, the exercise price or amount to be paid cannot be changed by retroactive application of another valuation method.

Representatives of the IRS and the Treasury have stated that the government will not use hindsight to judge a valuation method. Taking all relevant facts into account, the IRS will be evaluating the taxpayer on its application of the method, not whether the taxpayer "got the number exactly right."

Citation: Treas. Reg. § 1.409A-1(b)(5)(iv); Annotated Final Regulations, comments by Daniel L. Hogans, following Treas. Reg. §§ 1.409A-1(b)(5)(iv)(B)(2) and 1.409A-1(b)(5)(iv)(B)(2)(iii).

Q.161 WHAT IS THE RELATIONSHIP BETWEEN SECTION 409A AND ASC 718?

Both Section 409A and ASC 718 require valuation of a company's stock, but they have different purposes. Section 409A requires valuation for purposes of determining income tax incidence and ASC 718 for purposes of corporate accounting by public companies. The prescribed valuation techniques are similar but not identical.

For purposes of Section 409A, the strike price of the stock on the date of grant must equal or exceed the stock's fair market value on that date to satisfy the exception from Section 409A for stock options and stock appreciation rights. The valuation rules developed under Section 83 apply for this purpose.

Public companies must use ASC 718 (formerly FAS 123R) to determine fair value of their stock for accounting purposes. Private companies anticipating a possible future public offering also use this method of determining fair value.

The AICPA has developed a practice aid for use in conducting ASC 718 valuations of private companies under current rules, entitled *Valuation of Privately Held Company Equity Securities Issued as Compensation*. It can be purchased at www.AICPA.org under the Practice Aids tab. Independent accounting firms and other independent appraisers commonly use this practice aid in determining fair market value of the stock of privately held companies for purposes of both ASC 718 and Section 409A.

Citation: Treas. Reg. § 1.409A-1(b)(5)(iv); www.AICPA.org.

Q.162 CAN THE EXERCISE PERIOD BE EXTENDED OR THE OPTION OR SAR MODIFIED WITHOUT CAUSING LOSS OF THE EXCEPTION FROM SECTION 409A COVERAGE?

A change in the terms of a stock right is generally treated as a grant of a new stock right. The new stock right may or may not constitute a deferral of compensation based on the facts and circumstances as of the deemed grant date of the new stock right. For this purpose, a change in terms of a stock right includes any change in the terms of the stock right itself and any change in the terms of the plan pursuant to which the stock right was granted or in the terms of any other agreement governing the stock right that may directly or indirectly reduce the exercise price, regardless of whether the holder actually benefits from the change in terms.

Extension of the exercise period is generally treated as an additional deferral feature that causes the option to be treated as an arrangement providing for the deferral of compensation from the original grant date, causing a violation of Section 409A. This rule does not apply if the exercise price equals or exceeds the fair market value of underlying stock at the time of the extension or if the stock right is extended to the earlier of the date the original exercise period could have expired or the tenth anniversary of the original grant date.

The following are not treated as changes for this purpose:

- A change shortening the exercise period.
- Addition of a provision enabling tender of previously acquired stock for the stock available under the stock right.
- Addition of a provision enabling use of shares to facilitate payment of the exercise price, employment taxes or required withholding taxes resulting from the exercise.

Citation: Treas. Reg. § 1.409A-1(b)(5)(v).

Q.163 HOW CAN A NONQUALIFIED STOCK OPTION OR SAR BECOME SUBJECT TO SECTION 409A?

A nonqualified stock option or SAR can become subject to Section 409A for a number of reasons, including the following:

- Issuance with an exercise price below fair market value of the underlying stock on the date of grant.
- Extension of the exercise period at a time when the exercise price is below the fair market value of the underlying stock.

If the option or SAR allows the recipient to choose the exercise date, as is common, the option or SAR will not meet the requirement under Section 409A that the form and time of payment of deferred compensation be established before the services relating to the deferred compensation are performed. However, it is possible to structure a nonqualified option or SAR to comply with Section 409A.

Citation: Treas. Reg. § 1.409A-1(b)(5)(i).

Q.164 IF A NONQUALIFIED STOCK OPTION OR SAR IS INTENDED TO BE EXEMPT FROM SECTION 409A, MAY THE OPTION OR SAR INCLUDE DIVIDEND EQUIVALENT RIGHTS WHICH ARE CONTINGENT UPON EXERCISE?

No. If upon exercise of a stock right a service provider has the right, directly or indirectly, to receive an amount equal to all or part of the dividends or other distributions paid on the shares underlying a stock right between the date of grant and the date of exercise of the stock right, this benefit constitutes an offset to the exercise price of the stock option or an increase in the amount payable under the stock appreciation right. This generally will cause such stock right to be subject to Section 409A (see **Q.163**).

This rule does not prevent the adjustment of a stock right to reflect the payment of stock dividends between the date of grant and the date of exercise (see **Q.166**).

Citation: Treas. Reg. § 1.409A-1(b)(5)(i)(E).

Q.165 IF A NONQUALIFIED STOCK OPTION OR SAR IS INTENDED TO BE EXEMPT FROM SECTION 409A, MAY THE OPTION OR SAR INCLUDE DIVIDEND EQUIVALENT RIGHTS THAT EXPIRE UPON EXERCISE?

Published IRS guidance has not directly addressed this question. If dividend equivalent rights expire upon exercise of a stock right, they could be considered as payments that (i) are contingent upon the exercise of the stock right, and therefore (ii) indirectly reduce the exercise price, causing the stock right to be subject to Section 409A from inception. The more conservative approach would be to only provide dividend equivalent rights that are in no way dependent on the exercise of the stock right. For example, dividend equivalent rights could permissibly be provided during the period when a stock right is nonvested, with payment of the dividend equivalents made upon vesting of the stock right.

Citation: Treas. Reg. § 1.409A-1(b)(5)(i)(E).

Q.166 IF A NONQUALIFIED STOCK OPTION OR SAR IS INTENDED TO BE EXEMPT FROM SECTION 409A, MAY THE OPTION OR SAR BE ADJUSTED TO REFLECT A STOCK SPLIT OR STOCK DIVIDEND?

Yes, if the only effect of the stock split or stock dividend is to increase (or decrease) on a pro rata basis the number of shares owned by each shareholder of the class of stock subject to the stock right. The exercise price and number of shares subject to the stock right must be proportionally adjusted to reflect the stock split or stock dividend, and the aggregate exercise price of the stock right following the adjustment must not be less than the aggregate exercise price before the stock split or stock dividend.

Citation: Treas. Reg. § 1.409A-1(b)(5)(v)(H).

Q.167 HOW CAN A NONQUALIFIED STOCK OPTION OR SAR BE STRUCTURED TO COMPLY WITH SECTION 409A?

There has been no guidance from the IRS on this matter. Section 409A generally requires the following:

- The form and time of payment of deferred compensation must be established in advance.
- The form and time of payment generally cannot be changed after the period for earning the compensation begins.
- The time of payment must be tied to a fixed date or a Section 409A qualifying event—separation from service, death, disability, change of control, or unforeseeable emergency.

A typical option or SAR will not comply with these requirements because the recipient retains the right to determine the exercise date. To comply with the Section 409A requirements, the time when the option or SAR will be exercised must be set in advance based on a fixed date or other Section 409A qualifying event. The time for exercise cannot be changed after the option or SAR has been issued.

Citation: Treas. Reg. § 1.409A-1(b)(5)(i).

Q.168 DOES SECTION 409A APPLY TO RESTRICTED STOCK, RESTRICTED STOCK UNITS, OR PHANTOM STOCK UNITS?

Restricted stock is stock issued subject to a substantial risk of forfeiture. Because the issuance of restricted stock by a service recipient to a service provider involves a transfer of property, it is subject to Section 83, not Section 409A.

A restricted stock unit is a bookkeeping entry representing the value of one share of stock and is typically subject to vesting requirements. A restricted stock unit is typically settled in cash at the time of vesting or shortly thereafter. If settlement occurs within 2½ months after the close of the year in which vesting occurs, the restricted stock unit is a short-term deferral beyond the scope of Section 409A (see **Q.21**). If settlement occurs more than 2½ months after the close of the year in which vesting occurs, such as at termination of employment, then the restricted stock unit is subject to Section 409A and must be structured to comply with Section 409A.

A phantom stock unit is a bookkeeping entry representing the value of one share of stock similar to a restricted stock unit, but a phantom stock unit may or may not have a vesting requirement. A phantom stock unit subject to a vesting requirement is treated the same as a restricted stock unit for purposes of Section 409A. If a phantom stock unit is fully vested when issued, the short-term deferral rule does not apply unless the unit is structured so that settlement occurs no later than 2½ months following the close of the year of grant. Otherwise, a vested phantom stock unit is subject to Section 409A and must be structured to comply with Section 409A.

Citation: Treas. Reg. § 1.409A-1(b)(6)(i); *see* Treas. Reg. §§ 1.83-3(e) and 1.409A-1(b)(4) and (l).

Q.169 IS A DEFERRED COMPENSATION PLAN SUBJECT TO SECTION 409A REQUIRED TO SPECIFY A VALUATION DATE FOR RESTRICTED STOCK UNITS GRANTED UNDER THE PLAN?

This is not required to satisfy Section 409A. However specifying a valuation date in the plan document or the plan procedures will avoid disputes in situations where the valuation may change substantially between the date of vesting and the date of distribution, such as in the case of a six-month delay in distribution after separation from service of a specified employee of a publicly traded corporation.

Citation: *Graphic Packaging Holding Co., Inc. v. Humphrey*, 2010 U.S. App, LEXIS 23718, 50 E.B.C. 1289 (11th Cir. 2010).

Q.170 CAN DIVIDEND-EQUIVALENT DISTRIBUTIONS ON PHANTOM OR RESTRICTED STOCK UNITS QUALIFY AS CURRENT COMPENSATION OR SHORT-TERM DEFERRALS?

Yes. Dividend equivalents distributed currently can qualify as current compensation or short-term deferrals even if the underlying units are subject to Section 409A, as long as the dividend-equivalent arrangement meets the requirements for current compensation or the short-term deferral exception (see **Q.21**). Dividend-equivalent distributions are analogous to notional earnings, which must be payable at least once a year to qualify as current compensation or short-term deferrals.

Example. A service provider is credited with fully vested phantom stock units which are settled on separation from service. Dividend equivalents with respect to the underlying units are distributed to the service provider on each dividend payment date, but only if the service provider is employed on the dividend payment date. The phantom stock unit arrangement is subject to Section 409A. The dividend equivalents are exempt from Section 409A because they are subject to a substantial risk of forfeiture requiring continuing employment, and therefore they constitute short-term deferrals.

Citation: Treas. Reg. § 1.409A-3(e); 2008 ABA JCEB Questions, Q&A 35.

Q.171 WHAT ARE TRANSACTION-BASED COMPENSATION PAYMENTS?

The phrase "transaction-based compensation payments" refers to payments related to a change of control in one of the following circumstances:

- A service recipient purchases stock held by a service provider; or
- A service recipient or a third party purchases a stock right held by a service provider; or
- The payments are calculated by reference to the value of stock of the service recipient.

Citation: Preamble to 2016 Proposed 409A Regulations § V.B; Treas. Reg. § 1.409A-3(i)(5)(iv)(A).

Q.172 WHAT SPECIAL PAYMENT RULES APPLY TO TRANSACTION-BASED COMPENSATION?

Transaction-based compensation may be treated as paid on a designated date or pursuant to a payment schedule that complies with the Section 409A requirements if the transaction-based compensation is paid on the same schedule and under the same terms and conditions as applied to payments to shareholders generally with respect to stock of the service recipient in connection with a change of control. If payments meet the requirements set forth in the preceding sentence, such payments will not violate the initial or subsequent deferral election requirements provided they are paid not later than five years after the change of control.

Citation: Treas. Reg. § 1.409A-3(i)(5)(iv)(A).

Q.173 HOW DO THE TRANSACTION-BASED COMPENSATION RULES APPLY TO STOCK OPTIONS OR STOCK APPRECIATION RIGHTS THAT WERE EXEMPT FROM SECTION 409A WHEN ISSUED?

The purchase of a stock option or a stock appreciation right in a manner consistent with the transaction-based rules described in **Q.172** will not cause the stock option or stock appreciation right to be subject to Section 409A.

Citation: Preamble to 2016 Proposed 409A regulations § V.B; Prop. Treas. Reg. § 1.409A-3(i)(5)(i)(A) (2016).

EMPLOYMENT AGREEMENTS

Q.174 WHICH COMMON PROVISIONS OF AN EMPLOYMENT AGREEMENT MIGHT CREATE ISSUES UNDER SECTION 409A?

Employment agreements present subtle issues under Section 409A. Affected provisions may include the following:

- Severance (see **Q.142–153**).
- Equity awards (see **Q.154–173**).
- Nonqualified deferred compensation arrangements.
- Tax gross-up payments (see **Q.177**).
- Offset of the employer's obligation to make payments due the employee by amounts the employee owes the employer (see **Q.93**).
- Continued coverage under self-insured medical plans following termination (see **Q.175**).
- In-kind or other reimbursement arrangements that continue after termination, such as continued use of a corporate jet or entitlement to reimbursement for financial planning services (see **Q.175**).
- Bonus provisions.
- Releases (see **Q.56**).

Citation: Treas. Reg. §§ 1.409A-1(b)(4) and (9).

Q.175 WHAT ISSUES DO FRINGE BENEFIT ARRANGEMENTS POSE UNDER SECTION 409A?

Section 409A potentially applies to any taxable payment made in a year following the year in which the legally binding right to receive the payment arises. Section 409A is not limited to cash payments. It can include in-kind benefits such as the right to use a company car or plane.

Nontaxable benefits. Nontaxable benefits generally are exempt from Section 409A.

Health care. The following health care reimbursements and in-kind benefits are not subject to Section 409A:

- Insured post-employment health benefits.
- Self-funded reimbursed medical expenses during the COBRA coverage period that are allowable as a deduction under Code Section 213, disregarding the requirement that expenses exceed 7.5 percent of adjusted gross income. Expenses must be incurred during the coverage period provided for in the plan or agreement, which cannot be longer than the maximum COBRA coverage period.

Any other post-employment medical reimbursement is subject to Section 409A.

Other exempt reimbursements. Reasonable outplacement services and reimbursements taxable to a service provider after separation from service and deductible by the service recipient are exempt from Section 409A if they are incurred not later than the end of the second taxable year following separation and reimbursed not later than the end of the third taxable year following separation. This exemption applies even if the service provider is entitled to additional reimbursements for the same types of expenses incurred after the exempt period ends.

Fringe benefits and reimbursement arrangements not exempt from Section 409A. Other fringe benefit and reimbursement arrangements are generally subject to Section 409A. They are deemed to comply with Section 409A if the following requirements are met:

- For cash reimbursements of covered expenses, the arrangement must be in writing and must provide for reimbursement of expenses incurred during an objectively prescribed period.
- The amount of reimbursable expenses incurred or in-kind benefits available in one taxable year cannot affect the amount of reimbursable expenses or in-kind benefits available in a different taxable

year. For example, an employment agreement provision that the employee can be reimbursed for up to $30,000 in financial planning expenses during the first three years following separation from service would violate Section 409A because the use of the benefits in one calendar year would reduce the availability of the benefits in a different calendar year.
- The reimbursement arrangement must specify that payment must be made by no later than the end of participant's taxable year following the taxable year in which the expense is incurred.
- The right to reimbursement or in-kind benefits cannot be subject to liquidation or exchange for another benefit.

Citation: Treas. Reg. §§ 1.409A-1(b)(9)(v) and 1.409A-3(i)(1)(iv).

Q.176 IF A FORMER HIGHLY PAID SERVICE PROVIDER IS ALLOWED TO CONTINUE SELF-INSURED MEDICAL COVERAGE FOR LIFE BY PAYING THE FULL COST OF COVERAGE, IS THE ARRANGEMENT SUBJECT TO SECTION 409A?

No. If the former service provider pays the full cost of coverage, benefits payable under the plan are excludable from the service provider's income. If benefits are non-taxable because the cost of coverage is paid for in its entirety by the service provider, the benefits are not subject to Section 409A.

Citation: I.R.C. § 104(a)(3); Treas. Reg. § 1.104–1(d); 2007 ABA JCEB Questions, Q&A 1.

Q.177 IS A PROVISION IN AN EMPLOYMENT AGREEMENT FOR A TAX GROSS-UP PAYMENT, SUCH AS TO COMPENSATE AN EXECUTIVE FOR GOLDEN PARACHUTE TAXES, PERMITTED UNDER SECTION 409A?

Yes, if the agreement provides that the gross-up payment must be made by the end of the calendar year following the year in which the participant remits the related taxes to the government. A right to reimbursement for expenses associated with a tax audit or litigation addressing the existence or amount of a tax liability is permitted if the agreement requires that payment be made and payment is in fact made by the end of the calendar year following the calendar year in which the taxes subject to the audit or litigation are remitted to the government. If no taxes are due as a consequence of the audit or litigation, payment must be made by the end of the calendar year following the calendar year in which the audit is completed or there is a final and non-appealable settlement or other resolution of the litigation.

Citation: Treas. Reg. § 1.409A-3(i)(1)(v).

Q.178 ARE PAYMENTS MADE PURSUANT TO A SETTLEMENT WITH AN EMPLOYER, PAYMENTS MADE UNDER INDEMNIFICATION AGREEMENTS, OR PAYMENTS MADE TO ACQUIRE DIRECTORS' AND OFFICERS' INSURANCE TREATED AS NONQUALIFIED DEFERRED COMPENSATION SUBJECT TO SECTION 409A?

No.

Legal Settlements: Section 409A generally does not apply to an employer's payment of settlement or award amounts that result from the resolution of a bona fide legal claim based on a wrongful termination, employment discrimination, the Fair Labor Standards Act, or workers' compensation laws. This is true whether the claim arose under federal, state, local, or foreign laws, and whether or not the settlement or award amounts are treated as compensation for federal income tax purposes.

This exception applies only to bona fide claims. It does not apply to payment of pre-existing deferred compensation subject to Section 409A that is restructured as part of a legal settlement or award resolving the dispute. It does not apply to payments in exchange for a waiver and release of claims unless the amounts paid relate to an actual bona fide claim for damages under applicable law.

Indemnification Payments: Section 409A does not apply to indemnification or directors' and officers' insurance payments for damages or expenses incurred in connection with bona fide legal claims against the service provider in connection with the service provider's rendition of services, to the extent the right to indemnification is permissible under applicable law.

Citation: Treas. Reg. § 1.409A-1(b)(10)-(11).

Q.179 ARE PAYMENTS OF EMPLOYMENT-RELATED LEGAL FEES AND EXPENSES DEFERRED COMPENSATION SUBJECT TO SECTION 409A?

No. An arrangement does not provide for a deferral of compensation to the extent that it provides for the payment or reimbursement of a service provider's reasonable attorneys' fees and other expenses incurred to enforce a claim by the service provider against the service recipient with respect to the service relationship.

Citation: Prop. Treas. Reg. § 1.409A-1(b)(11) (2016); Preamble to 2016 Proposed 409A Regulations § II.E.

SPLIT-DOLLAR AND OTHER LIFE INSURANCE ARRANGEMENTS

Q.180 WHICH SPLIT-DOLLAR LIFE INSURANCE ARRANGEMENTS ARE SUBJECT TO OR EXEMPT FROM SECTION 409A COVERAGE?

A split-dollar arrangement is any arrangement between an owner and non-owner of a life insurance contract under which:

- Either party to the arrangement pays, either directly or indirectly, all or any portion of the premiums on a life insurance contract, including a payment by means of a loan to the other party that is secured by the life insurance contract.
- At least one of the parties to the arrangement paying premiums is entitled to recover (either conditionally or unconditionally) all or any portion of those premiums from the proceeds of the life insurance contract.
- The arrangement is not a part of a group term life insurance plan described in Code Section 79.

Only two types of split-dollar life insurance arrangements are exempt from Section 409A:

- Employer-owned endorsement split-dollar policies that provide only an interest in the policy's death proceeds to the non-owner employee, because they are bona fide death benefit plans.

- Loan split-dollar policies, because a loan does not involve deferral of compensation for purposes of Section 409A. To demonstrate the economic reality of the loan, required minimum interest rates must be charged and paid by the owner-employee.

Citation: Notice 2007–34; *see also* Treas. Reg. §§ 1.61–22 and 1.7872–15.

Q.181 ARE SPLIT-DOLLAR LIFE INSURANCE PROGRAMS SUBJECT TO GRANDFATHERING UNDER SECTION 409A?

Yes. If a split-dollar arrangement was entered into on or before October 3, 2004, contributions before January 1, 2005, and cash value attributable to those contributions, are not subject to Section 409A unless the plan is materially modified after October 3, 2004.

The grandfathered portion can be calculated by use of any reasonable method that allocates increases in cash value attributable to premiums earned and vested on or before December 31, 2004.

Allocation based on the percentage of grandfathered and non-grandfathered premiums paid is deemed reasonable. For this purpose, grandfathered premiums generally include premiums that were earned, vested, and actually paid on or before December 31, 2004.

A method that disproportionately allocates costs and expenses to the non-grandfathered portion will not be deemed reasonable.

Citation: Notice 2007–34.

Q.182 WHAT IS A BONUS LIFE INSURANCE OR ANNUITY PLAN, AND HOW CAN IT BE USED AS A SUBSTITUTE FOR A NONQUALIFIED DEFERRED COMPENSATION PLAN SUBJECT TO SECTION 409A?

A bonus life insurance or annuity plan uses a life insurance policy or annuity contract owned by the service provider to receive annual current bonus compensation contributions from the service recipient as a substitute for an unsecured and unfunded deferred compensation plan subject to Section 409A. This type of plan is commonly used in place of an employer-paid SERP by closely held businesses and tax-exempt entities.

This type of plan has the following advantages:

- Increases in cash value are not subject to federal income tax until distribution to the employee-owner.
- The employee-owner can take pre-death distributions of cash value accumulated under the life insurance policy free of income tax to the extent of premiums paid.
- The employee-owner can borrow against the cash value free of income tax if the policy is maintained in force until the death of the insured.
- Proceeds payable on death are not subject to income tax and with appropriate planning can also be made exempt from federal estate tax.
- Distributions from an annuity after the annuity starting date are treated as pro rata from contributions and income. The part treated as contributions is not subject to income tax on receipt, and the part treated as income is subject to income tax at ordinary rates.
- It is possible that annuities and life insurance can be protected from the creditors of the service recipient if the policy is not owned by the service recipient. The laws of the service provider's state of residence govern this issue.
- Bonus payments are deductible by the service recipient in the year paid or accrued because they are current compensation, not deferred compensation.

This type of arrangement has the following disadvantages:

- Proceeds of surrender before the annuity starting date are treated as income first and subject to tax at ordinary rates.
- On death of the annuitant under an annuity policy, proceeds of the annuity are treated as income in respect of a decedent for federal income tax purposes.

- The service provider is required to recognize income for the taxable year in which the bonus is paid. To make the service provider's tax cost roughly equivalent to that of a deferred compensation plan, the service recipient could gross up the bonus to include the time value of the tax from the date of the bonus through the expected future date of distribution to the service provider under a deferred compensation plan. The cost of the gross up would be partially offset by the immediate income tax deduction the service recipient would realize at the time of the bonus, rather than waiting for the deduction until the expected future date of distribution under a deferred compensation plan.
- Because the service recipient does not own the life insurance or annuity policy, the service recipient does not have the advantage of the golden handcuffs that a nonqualified deferred compensation plan typically provides.
- There are two parts of a bonus life insurance transaction:
  - The bonus; and
  - The personally owned life insurance or annuity.
- The service recipient bonus element could be subject to Section 409A, unless carefully crafted.
- A binding agreement to make annual bonus payments for a period of years into a life insurance or annuity policy, a common practice before the effective date of Section 409A, constitutes a nonqualified deferred compensation plan that would be subject to Section 409A.
- Even an annual bonus can be subject to Section 409A if it is not a short-term deferral paid within 2½ months after the end of the appropriate taxable year.
- The arrangement will be subject to Section 409A if the service recipient continues or promises to pay annual contributions into the policy after the service provider's separation from service, since post-employment payments are generally treated as deferred compensation for past services for purposes of Section 409A.

Authors' Comment: A wholly discretionary annual bonus that terminates at the earlier of termination or retirement will assure that the bonus portion of the arrangement will not be subject to Section 409A.

Citation: *Consider* I.R.C. § 409A(d); Treas. Reg. §§ 1.409A-1(a) and (b) as to covered and Section 409A exempted/excepted plans. *Also review Mozingo v. Trend Personnel*, No. 15-11263 (5th Cir. App. Ct. Aug. 31, 2016) for a recent case defining the characteristics of a properly structured bonus life or annuity insurance plan for ERISA and tax purposes.

Q.183 IS A KEY PERSON LIFE INSURANCE POLICY OWNED BY THE SERVICE RECIPIENT SUBJECT TO SECTION 409A?

No. If a life insurance policy on the life of a service provider is owned and payable only to the service recipient upon the death of the insured service provider, the policy is not subject to Section 409A. Such an arrangement is a way for the service recipient to fund various potential costs and losses incident to the death of the insured service provider or to fund a buy-out of the service provider's ownership interest in the business, rather than a deferred compensation plan.

Citation: Treas. Reg. §§ 1.409A-1(a)(1), (b), (c); (no suggestion that a key person life insurance policy is a deferred compensation plan subject to Section 409A); Notice 2007–34 (to same effect).

Q.184 ARE OTHER LIFE INSURANCE PLANS SUBJECT TO SECTION 409A?

Any other arrangement involving a life insurance policy may be subject to Section 409A. Also, Code Sections 101(j) and 6039I provide rules governing issuance, placement, and reporting of employer-owned life insurance to obtain tax-free treatment of death proceeds under employer-owned life insurance, independent of Section 409A.

Citation: I.R.C. §§ 101(j), 6039I; *see* Treas. Reg. §§ 1.409A-1(a)(1), (b) and (c); Notice 2007–34.

Q.185 COULD SECTION 409A APPLY IN CONNECTION WITH TERMINATION OF A SPLIT-DOLLAR LIFE INSURANCE ARRANGEMENT THAT IS GENERALLY EXEMPT FROM SECTION 409A?

On termination of an endorsement split-dollar life insurance arrangement, if the service recipient continues to own the policy and the service provider is entitled only to designate the beneficiary of any residual death benefit, the policy functions as a death-benefit-only plan, the service provider is required to recognize current income equal to the value of the coverage each year, and the benefit is not subject to Section 409A.

However, if the service recipient distributes the policy to the service provider in connection with termination of the arrangement, the arrangement might be recharacterized as an equity split dollar arrangement as to which the annual cash value increases should have been recognized as income by the service provider as they occurred or as a deferred compensation plan subject to Section 409A, under which distribution on plan termination is an impermissible acceleration. To reduce the likelihood of recharacterization in these circumstances, documentation of the split-dollar arrangement should expressly provide that the service recipient has no duty to transfer the policy to the service recipient on termination of the arrangement, and there should be no provider or practice of such policy transfers to other service providers on termination of such arrangements.

On termination of a loan regime split dollar arrangement, there is no transfer of the policy because the owner from the beginning is the service provider or someone selected by the service provider. On termination of the arrangement, the loans are either repaid from cash value or other sources or they are forgiven and the service provider recognizes income equal to the amounts forgiven. There is a chance that the arrangement would be recharacterized as a deferred compensation plan subject to Section 409A if the loans are forgiven and there is evidence that forgiveness was intended from the beginning.

Citation: Treas. Reg. §§ 1.61–22, 1.409A-3(j)(4)(ix); Notice 2007–34; Notice 2002–8.

FOREIGN PLANS

Q.186 DOES SECTION 409A APPLY TO DEFERRED COMPENSATION ATTRIBUTABLE TO SERVICES RENDERED OUTSIDE THE UNITED STATES?

Foreign deferred compensation arrangements are subject to Section 409A, with specified exceptions. In the absence of an exception, Section 409A applies to the global income of U.S. citizens and resident aliens working abroad and also to U.S. source income of non-resident aliens.

The following deferred compensation arrangements are not subject to Section 409A:

- Foreign social security arrangements.
- Non-elective deferrals of foreign earned income, plus earnings thereon, under a broad-based foreign retirement plan or a plan under which substantially all participants are bona fide residents of a U.S. possession, as long as the service provider is not eligible to participate in a U.S. tax-qualified retirement plan maintained by the employer. If the service provider is a U.S. citizen or lawful permanent resident, the exemption applies only to the extent that the non-elective deferrals would not exceed the limitations on benefits and contributions set forth in Code Sections 415(b) and (c) if the plan were a U.S. qualified plan.
- These exclusions apply even if the same plan also provides for elective deferrals and whether the plan sponsor is a U.S. or foreign employer.
- Payments pursuant to tax equalization agreements, as long as payment occurs by the end of the second full taxable year following the deadline for filing the service provider's U.S. or foreign income tax return for the year at issue (or if no foreign tax return is required, the due date of the foreign tax payment), whichever is later.

- In the alternative, these payments may be subject to the rules on tax gross-ups, audits, or litigation settlements.
- Compensation excludable from income under U.S. tax law at the time it is earned or is no longer subject to a substantial risk of forfeiture pursuant to a tax treaty or convention entered into by the United States and a foreign country, plus earnings thereon.
- Compensation excludable from income under U.S. tax law at the time it is either earned or no longer subject to a substantial risk of forfeiture, plus earnings thereon, under the following Code provisions:
  - The service provider is a non-resident alien and the compensation would be excludable as non-U.S. source income under Code Section 872.
  - The service provider is a U.S. citizen or resident living abroad and the compensation would be excludable as foreign earned income under Code Section 911, to the extent that the total amount of current and deferred compensation for a year do not exceed the limit imposed by Section 911 for the year.
  - The service provider either is not a U.S. citizen or is a dual citizen of the United States and the Republic of the Philippines and is employed by a foreign government or international organization. The compensation would be excludable under Code Section 893.
  - The service provider is a resident of Guam, American Samoa, the Northern Mariana Islands or Puerto Rico and the compensation would be excludable under Code Section 931 or 933.
- Elective deferrals of U.S. source income by a non-resident alien under a foreign plan maintained by a foreign plan sponsor up to the Section 402(g) limitation for the year, plus earnings thereon.
- Voluntary and involuntary foreign separation agreements, if payment is required by the foreign jurisdiction and payment is only from foreign-earned income sources in that jurisdiction.
- Code Section 402(b) funded foreign arrangements.

Citation: Treas. Reg. §§ 1.409A-1(a)(3), especially subparagraph (iii), and 1.409A-1(b)(8)(i)-(iv); Annotated Final Regulations, comments by Daniel L. Hogans, following Treas. Reg. § 1.409A-1(a)(3), "To determine coverage under 409A arrangements, do a transnational analysis. Look at 409A based on when and where amounts are deferred—is the person deferring income that would be subject to U.S. tax? If not, 409A would not apply. If so, if the person is a U.S. citizen or a green card holder you are talking about a deferral of U.S. taxable income subject to 409A."

Q.187 WHAT ARE THE REQUIREMENTS FOR THE TREATY EXEMPTION FROM SECTION 409A?

The treaty exemption requires that compensation be excludable from income under U.S. tax law at the time it is earned or no longer subject to a substantial risk of forfeiture pursuant to a specific income tax treaty or convention entered into by the United States and a foreign country.

A review of the specific governing treaty is required to determine whether it creates an exception for deferred compensation as defined in Section 409A. These treaties generally protect against double taxation. They do not generally cover employer-funded supplemental plans or voluntary elective deferral plans.

Citation: Treas. Reg. §§ 1.409A-1(a)(3)(i) and (b)(8)(i).

Q.188 WHAT ARE THE REQUIREMENTS FOR EXEMPTION FROM SECTION 409A FOR AMOUNTS SUBJECT TO TAX EQUALIZATION AGREEMENTS?

The tax equalization agreement exemption requires the following:

- Compensation paid to the service provider under the agreement must cover only taxes imposed by a foreign government in excess of those that would have been imposed by the service provider's home country.
- Payment must occur by the end of the second full taxable year following the deadline for filing the service provider's foreign or U.S. income tax return (including extensions) for the year at issue, whichever is later. If no foreign tax return is required, the due date of the foreign tax payment is substituted for the foreign tax return deadline for this purpose.

If the compensation is paid on a later date, the generally applicable rules on tax gross-ups or litigation settlements may apply in determining the treatment of the compensation under Section 409A (see **Q.177** and **Q.178**).

Citation: Treas. Reg. § 1.409A-1(b)(8)(iii).

Q.189 WHAT ARE THE REQUIREMENTS FOR EXEMPTION FROM SECTION 409A FOR FOREIGN SOCIAL SECURITY ARRANGEMENTS?

The amounts paid into the foreign social security system must be government-mandated or subject to a social security totalization agreement.

Citation: Treas. Reg. § 1.409A-1(a)(3)(iv).

Q.190 WHAT ARE THE REQUIREMENTS FOR EXEMPTION FROM SECTION 409A FOR BROAD-BASED FOREIGN RETIREMENT PLANS?

The foreign retirement plan must meet the following requirements:

- The plan must cover a wide range of employees, including rank and file employees, either alone or in combination with other comparable plans. Substantially all covered employees must be non-resident aliens.
- The plan must provide significant benefits to a substantial majority of covered employees.
- Plan benefits must be nondiscriminatory.
- Except for the generally applicable specified exceptions under Section 409A, the plan must prohibit in-service withdrawals for purposes other than retirement.

Citation: Treas. Reg. § 1.409A-1(a)(3)(v).

Q.191 CAN FOREIGN EARNED INCOME BE SUBJECT TO EXEMPTION FROM SECTION 409A UNDER THE GENERALLY APPLICABLE RULES?

Yes. For example, a foreign earned income arrangement might be exempt from Section 409A because it satisfies the requirements for a short-term deferral, a stock right, a Section 83 transfer, or a grandfathered plan.

Citation: Treas. Reg. § 1.409A-1(a)(3) (no provision stating that the exemptions for specific types of foreign plans are intended to be exclusive of other exemptions available under § 409A).

Q.192 HOW DOES SECTION 457A COMPARE TO SECTION 409A?

Section 457A is different from Section 409A in several ways:

- Section 457A applies only to deferred compensation of U.S. taxpayers under a nonqualified deferred compensation plan of a non-U.S. corporation or partnership that is a nonqualified entity. Section 409A applies to all types of deferred compensation of all service providers who are U.S. taxpayers, unless specifically excepted, which is a much broader class.
- For purposes of Section 457A, nonqualified entities include the following:
  - A foreign corporation whose income is 80 percent or more substantially connected to a trade or business conducted in the United States and substantially all of whose income is subject to a comprehensive foreign income tax for purposes of Section 457A.
  - An offshore hedge fund.
  - A U.S. or foreign partnership, substantially all of whose income is allocable to persons subject to U.S. taxation or comprehensive income taxation on the partnership's income.
  - A multinational company that employs U.S. expatriates in a country without a tax treaty with the United States.
  - A certain type of partnership that includes foreign entities as to its U.S. employees.

- Under Section 457A, income tax is generally incurred on the earlier of payment of the compensation or 12 months after the end of the service recipient's taxable year in which all substantial risk of forfeiture with respect to the compensation lapses or ceases to exist. Under an arrangement that is compliant with or exempt from Section 409A, the timing of income inclusion will generally be the date that the income is actually or constructively received (see **Q.102**).
- The definition of substantial risk of forfeiture includes only the requirement to perform substantial future services, making Section 457A more restrictive than the definition used under Section 409A, under which a condition related to a purpose of the compensation may also constitute a substantial risk of forfeiture (see **Q.24**).
- If the amount subject to tax under Section 457A is unknown by the deadline for payment after lapse of the substantial risk of forfeiture because of the additional risk that substantial performance goals will not be attained, then the tax is imposed at such later time when the amount of compensation based on attainment of the substantial performance goals can be determined, and the compensation is subject to an additional 20 percent income tax and an interest penalty parallel to those imposed by Section 409A. This event would not cause violation of Section 409A and would not cause imposition of any additional taxes under Section 409A.
- Section 457A applies to both cash and accrual taxpayers, and casts a wider net than Section 409A, which applies only to cash basis service providers.
- Section 457A applies to all stock appreciation rights settled in cash. It is broader in scope than Section 409A, under which stock appreciation rights measured from a value at least equal to fair market value on the date of grant may be exempt (see **Q.155**).

It is possible that both Section 409A and Section 457A would apply to the same compensation of the same service provider, and in that case, special ordering rules apply.

Citation: I.R.C. § 457A; Notice 2009–8.

Q.193 IF A PLAN IS SUBJECT TO SECTION 457A, MAY IT ALSO BE SUBJECT TO SECTION 409A?

Yes. A nonqualified deferred compensation plan subject to Section 457A may also constitute a nonqualified deferred compensation plan for purposes of Section 409A. If this is the case, the rules of Section 409A apply to such a plan separately and in addition to any requirement applicable to the plan under Section 457A.

Citation: Prop. Treas. Reg. § 1.409A-1(a)(4) (2016); Preamble to 2016 Proposed 409A Regulations § II.A.

LIMITATIONS ON LINKING PLANS

Q.194 CAN PARTICIPANT ELECTIONS UNDER A NONQUALIFIED DEFERRED COMPENSATION PLAN THAT IS AN EXCESS PLAN BE LINKED TO AND CONTROLLED BY A QUALIFIED RETIREMENT PLAN?

In the past, participant elections with respect to the time and form of distribution under an excess plan that provided benefits that would have been provided under a tax-qualified retirement plan, except for the limits on benefits, contributions, and covered compensation imposed by the Code, were linked to the underlying tax-qualified plan.

Section 409A generally prohibits linkage of participant elections under tax-qualified and nonqualified plans. The following exceptions apply:

- Legally required changes in a qualified plan that result in an increase or decrease in the amounts accrued under an excess plan subject to Section 409A will not cause a prohibited deferral or acceleration under the excess plan as long as the changes do not otherwise change the time or form of payment under the excess plan and the increase or decrease does not exceed the corresponding decrease or increase in the amount deferred under the underlying qualified plan.
- Changes in the amount accrued under the excess plan by reason of action or inaction by a participant to elect to receive a subsidized or ancillary benefit under the qualified plan.
- Changes in the amount accrued under the excess plan by reason of action or inaction by a participant with respect to making or adjusting elective deferrals and other participant pre-tax contributions

under the qualified plan, as long as the action or inaction does not increase or decrease the participant's deferrals under the nonqualified plan in excess of the combined qualified plan limits under Section 402(g)(1)(B) ($18,000 in 2017) and Section 414(v) (catch-up contributions for participants age 50 and over, $6,000 for 2017).
- A participant's action or inaction with regard to elective deferrals and other participant pre-tax and after-tax contributions under the tax-qualified plan that has an effect on the amounts credited as matching or other similar contingent amounts under the nonqualified plan, as long as the matching or contingent amounts under the nonqualified plan never exceed 100 percent of the amounts that would be provided under the qualified plan but for the qualified plan limitations on such contributions.
- An amendment to the tax-qualified plan that adds or removes a subsidized or ancillary benefit, or that freezes or limits benefit accruals.
- A mere change of form of payment from one type of annuity to another actuarially equivalent annuity that starts at the same time is not subject to the prohibition against accelerations and the requirements of the subsequent election rule (see **Q.127** and **Q.128**). This allows a participant to change an annuity form of payment under the excess plan to match the form of payment selected under the tax-qualified plan without delaying distribution for five years.

Citation: Treas. Reg. § 1.409A-2(b)(2)(ii)(A).

Q.195 CAN THE BENEFITS FROM ONE NONQUALIFIED PLAN BE OFFSET AGAINST THE BENEFITS OF ANOTHER NONQUALIFIED PLAN?

Offsetting the benefits of one nonqualified plan against the benefits of another nonqualified plan will generally result in a Section 409A violation unless the two plans have identical payment provisions. If amounts payable under one nonqualified plan affect amounts payable under another, and if the two plans provide for different times and forms of payment, increasing or decreasing benefits under one plan may result in an acceleration or deferral of nonqualified benefits under the other plan.

For example, an employer maintains one nonqualified account balance plan that provides that all benefits will be payable in a lump sum upon separation from service and another account balance plan that pays benefits in 10 equal installments upon separation from service. If the amount of the service provider's account balance under the first plan is offset by the amount of the service provider's account balance under the second plan, then an increase in the service provider's account balance under the second plan will result in a deferral of the benefits that would otherwise have been paid in a lump sum under the first plan.

Citation: Annotated Final Regulations, comments following Treas. Reg. § 1.409A-1(c)(2)(i)(C)(2): William Schmidt, "If you have two nonqualified plans that are linked together, you may have a problem"; Daniel L. Hogans, "If you have offsets between two nonqualified plans, you better make sure both those plans have identical payment provisions; otherwise you've blown yourself up."

FUNDING

Q.196 IS A PLAN SUBJECT TO SECTION 409A REQUIRED TO BE FUNDED?

Quite the opposite. To defer recognition of income by the service provider, Code Sections 61 and 451 require that nonqualified deferred compensation plans be unfunded and unsecured promises to pay amounts due under the plan in the future. In addition, nonqualified deferred compensation plans designed to be exempt from the funding, benefit accrual, and vesting rules that apply to tax-qualified plans under the Code and ERISA must be unfunded. Section 409A does not change these requirements.

In general, employers may choose to maintain reserves from which to satisfy their future obligations under deferred compensation plans subject to Section 409A without incurring a violation of Section 409A. The reserves must be completely unrestricted and remain general corporate assets that may be applied to any corporate purpose. The employer receives no current income tax deduction for amounts set aside in these reserves. The income tax deduction is not available until the year of distribution to the participant, and the amount deductible in each case is the amount of the participant's taxable distribution. Death benefits received by a service recipient under a life insurance policy that are held in a reserve for payment to the service provider's beneficiary or estate under a deferred compensation plan are treated as income in respect of a decedent of the beneficiary or estate when they are paid under federal income tax law.

Depending on the type of plan, a variety of funding media are available for these employer reserves, such as mutual funds, grantor trusts (commonly known as rabbi trusts) and business-owned life insurance policies. Because the employer retains ownership of the assets, earnings and capital gains are taxable to the employer for the year in which they are realized. To reduce the incidence of current income tax, employers sometimes choose low turnover mutual funds or business-owned life insurance policies for this purpose.

The amount of the reserve from time to time appears on the employer's balance sheet, and gains and losses on the reserved assets are reflected in the employer's income statement.

These tax and accounting consequences occur independent of Section 409A. The choice of funding method is also independent of Section 409A. Factors considered in selecting funding media include the employer's status as a for-profit or tax-exempt entity, the plan design and objectives, and the employer's overall financial approach.

Note: To address perceived abuses, use of off-shore trusts is prohibited (see **Q.198**) and use of a grantor trust to informally fund benefits for a service recipient's highest executives while it maintains a defined benefit pension plan that does not satisfy the minimum funding requirements of the Internal Revenue Code causes immediate recognition of income by the affected executives (see **Q.199**).

Citation: *See* I.R.C. § 409A(b)(2); H.R. Conf. Rep. No. 108–775 (Oct. 22, 2004) pp. 514–15, 524 (§ 409A "funding" rules); *see also* Louis R. Richey, Richard C. Baier, John Phelan, THE ADVISOR' GUIDE TO NONQUALIFIED DEFERRED COMPENSATION PLAN (2014 Ed.) (informal funding, tax, accounting, SEC, security techniques, and other nonqualified deferred compensation issues). There are still no detailed regulations interpreting the funding rules under Section 409A(b)(2) as of the date of publication of this edition.

Q.197 DOES SECTION 409A PERMIT ASSETS IN A RABBI TRUST OR OTHER TRUST TO BE APPLIED EXCLUSIVELY TO FUND A NONQUALIFIED DEFERRED COMPENSATION PLAN INCIDENT TO A CHANGE IN THE EMPLOYER'S FINANCIAL CONDITION?

No. Section 409A treats this as a taxable transfer under Section 83. This taxable transfer will occur when the assets are actually restricted to this purpose or when the plan first provides that the assets will be so restricted, whichever occurs first. Amounts treated as transferred will be subject not only to income tax, but also the additional 20 percent tax and interest penalty imposed by Section 409A.

If a plan contains a provision for funding all deferrals in connection with a change in the financial situation of the service recipient, all amounts deferred under the plan are treated as taxable transfers under Section 83. If a plan provides for funding the deferrals of specified individuals, all deferrals of those individuals are treated as taxable transfers under Section 83. Subsequent increases in value and earnings on the assets are also treated as taxable transfers of property under Section 83.

Citation: *See* I.R.C. § 409A(b)(2); H.R. Conf. Rep. No. 108–755, 70777 (Oct. 22. 2004).

Q.198 MAY AN EMPLOYER USE AN OFFSHORE TRUST TO HOLD ASSETS ACQUIRED IN CONNECTION WITH A NONQUALIFIED DEFERRED COMPENSATION PLAN COVERED BY SECTION 409A?

Generally, no. Informally funding deferred compensation with assets held in an offshore trust is a violation of Section 409A, unless the majority of the services connected with the plan are rendered offshore. The assets held in all such trusts previously in existence were required to be distributed or disassociated with the employer's deferred compensation obligation by December 31, 2007.

Citation: I.R.C. § 409A(b)(1) as amended by the Gulf Opportunity Zone Act of 2005, Pub. L. No. 109–135, 119 Stat. 2577 (GOZA).

Q.199 MAY A NONQUALIFIED DEFERRED COMPENSATION PLAN BE INFORMALLY FUNDED THROUGH A RABBI TRUST WHILE THE PLAN SPONSOR MAINTAINS AN UNDERFUNDED TAX-QUALIFIED DEFINED BENEFIT RETIREMENT PLAN?

Assets set aside in a trust or other arrangement on behalf of an "applicable covered employee" for purposes of funding nonqualified deferred compensation subject to Section 409A during any "restricted period" with respect to a tax-qualified, single-employer defined benefit plan maintained by the employer will be treated as immediately taxable under Section 83 and subject to the additional 20 percent tax and interest penalty imposed by Section 409A.

The term "applicable covered employee" means an employee described in Code Section 162(m)(3), which includes only a public company's chief executive officer, one of its four highest-paid individuals subject to reporting under the Securities Exchange Act of 1934, or persons subject to reporting under Section 16(a) of the Securities Exchange Act of 1934, which also applies only to public companies.

The term "restricted period" refers to any one of the following:

- Any period during which the defined benefit plan is in at-risk status, meaning generally that the plan is less than 80 percent funded for purposes of Code Section 412.
- Any period during which the plan sponsor is in bankruptcy proceedings under Title 11 of the United States Code.
- The 12-month period beginning on the date 18 months before the defined benefit plan is terminated if the plan is underfunded as of the termination date.

Because the requirements of Code Section 162(m)(3) and Section 16(a) of the Securities Exchange Act of 1934 apply only to individuals related to publicly held companies, it can be argued that no employees of privately held companies are "applicable covered employees" or that only the chief executive officer of a privately held company should be treated as an "applicable covered employee" for this purpose. Therefore, the restrictions on informal funding of a nonqualified deferred compensation plan through a rabbi trust while the plan sponsor maintains an underfunded defined benefit pension plan do not apply to a private company at all or or apply only to its chief executive officer. The IRS has indicated that this issue is under study.

In any event, a public company's service providers who are not within the scope of Code Section 162(m)(3) or Section 16(a) of the Securities Exchange Act of 1934 and a private company's service providers, who would not be within the scope of those provisions if the service recipient were a public company, are not subject to the restrictions on informal funding of a nonqualified deferred compensation plan through a rabbi trust while the service recipient maintains an underfunded defined benefit pension plan.

The original effective date for the rules involving bankruptcy and plan termination was January 1, 2005. The IRS subsequently extended the effective date to August 17, 2006, which was the date of adoption of Section 409A(b)(3). Because a plan's restricted period does not begin until after the end of the plan year in which the plan experiences at-risk status, the first year to which this rule could have applied was 2008.

Citation: I.R.C. §§ 162(m)(3), 409A(b)(3); Securities Exchange Act of 1934 § 16(a), 15 U.S.C. §§ 78a *et seq.* (2012); Notice 2006–33; 2009 ABA JCEB Questions, Q&A 29.

Q.200 DO THE SECTION 409A FUNDING RESTRICTIONS APPLY TO GRANDFATHERED PLANS?

Yes. The effective date of the funding provisions relating to offshore trusts and financial health triggers was January 1, 2005, including amounts set aside or restricted with respect to deferrals of compensation that were earned and vested on or before December 31, 2004. For example, amounts set aside in an offshore trust before January 1, 2005, for the purpose of paying deferred compensation and plans providing for the restriction of assets in connection with the change in the employer's financial condition before January 1, 2005 are subject to the Section 409A(b) funding rules on and after January 1, 2005. Taxpayers were granted a limited period of time to come into compliance with the new rules until December 31, 2007.

Citation: I.R.C. § 409A(b); Notice 2006–33.

PANDEMICS AND OTHER CRISES THAT DISRUPT THE ECONOMY

Q.201 WHAT ISSUES AND CONCERNS AROSE DURING THE COVID-19 PANDEMIC AS A RESULT OF RESTRICTIONS IMPOSED BY SECTION 409A?

During the Covid-19 pandemic, Section 409A created challenges in connection with urgent requests made by service providers to:

- Receive immediate distribution of nonqualified plan benefits;
- Borrow money secured by nonqualified plan benefits; and/or
- Modify or cancel deferral elections.

Service recipients had to navigate the requirements of Section 409A in connection with a number of actions taken because of financial exigencies, including the following:

- Reductions in service provider wages;
- Reductions in or cancellations of service provider bonuses;
- The modification of performance-based bonus arrangements to (i) add discretionary features, (ii) delay the timing of the establishment of performance goals, or (iii) revise previously-established performance goals; and
- Temporary or permanent reductions in or cessations of business operations.

Plan administrators were pressed into interpreting plan documents and 409A rules as applied to:

- Requests by service recipients regarding their ability to reduce matching credits or other nonqualified plan benefits;
- Requests by service recipients facing cash flow challenges regarding their ability to reduce contributions to rabbi trusts established to informally fund nonqualified plan benefits;
- Service providers on furlough or leave of absence.

Authors' Comment: We anticipate that these same issues are likely to arise during any future crisis that severely disrupts the U.S. economy.

Q.202 WHAT LEGISLATIVE OR REGULATORY RELIEF WAS ISSUED TO ADDRESS THE SECTION 409A CHALLENGES THAT AROSE DURING THE COVID-19 PANDEMIC?

A nonqualified deferred compensation plan was allowed to provide for the cancellation of a service provider's deferral election due to certain "coronavirus-related distributions" made from qualified retirement plans during 2020. Otherwise, no special relief was afforded. As a result, the issues and concerns outlined in **Q.201** must be analyzed by applying the general principles of Section 409A in the context of the particular factual scenarios arising during the pandemic.

Citation: Notice 2020-50, § 6.

Q.203 MAY A SERVICE PROVIDER ACCESS HIS OR HER NONQUALIFIED PLAN BENEFITS DUE TO A PANDEMIC?

Generally speaking, no, except in limited circumstances that are subject to stringent Section 409A requirements and the terms of the plan document. If permitted under the terms of the plan, benefits may be accessed due to:

- Unforeseeable emergency (see **Q.73**);
- Disability (see **Q.46**); or
- Plan termination (see **Q.85**).

The plan sponsor may amend a plan at any time to terminate it or to add a provision permitting payment of benefits upon an unforeseeable emergency or disability (see **Q.74 and Q.86**).

In contrast to the rules applicable to 401(k) and other qualified retirement plans, a service provider may not borrow money from a nonqualified plan (see **Q.91**).

Citation: I.R.C. § 409A(a)(2)(B)(ii); I.R.C. § 409A(a)(2)(C); Treas. Reg. §§ 1.409A-3(i)(3)(i)-(iii); Treas. Reg. §§ 1.409A-3(i)(4)(i)-(iii); Treas. Reg. § 1.409A-3(j)(2); Treas. Reg. §§ 1.409A-3(j)(4)(i) and (ix).

Q.204 UNDER WHAT CIRCUMSTANCES MAY A SERVICE PROVIDER ACCESS NONQUALIFIED PLAN BENEFITS DURING A PANDEMIC DUE TO UNFORESEEABLE EMERGENCY, AND HOW DO THESE CIRCUMSTANCES DIFFER FROM THOSE APPLICABLE TO HARDSHIP WITHDRAWALS FROM 401(K) PLANS?

The Section 409A unforeseeable emergency requirements are much more restrictive than the hardship withdrawal requirements applicable to 401(k) plans, both in scope and process. Generally speaking, the circumstances must not only cause a documented financial hardship, but also be of an extraordinary and unforeseeable nature. Hence, even a documented need to pay college or home purchase expenses (which are acceptable hardship expenses under the 401(k) rules) do not qualify as unforeseeable emergency expenses. Moreover, in contrast to a 401(k) hardship, a 409A unforeseeable emergency may not be self-certified. Before making an unforeseeable emergency distribution, the plan administrator must obtain prior documentation and make a positive determination of both the amount of the financial need and the unforeseeable nature of the financial emergency. In making the determination of financial need, the plan administrator must take into consideration the extent to which cessation of the service provider's elective nonqualified plan deferrals, plus any reimbursement available from insurance and/or the liquidation of personal assets that are reasonably available, will relieve the financial need.

In the context of an unforeseeable emergency withdrawal request as a result of the pandemic, a decline in a service recipient's investment portfolio would probably not meet the unforeseen emergency test because investment portfolios routinely increase and decrease in value and therefore are foreseeable. On the other hand, an emergency withdrawal request arising from a spouse's loss of employment (or reduction in income) because of the pandemic that results in inadequate day-to-day family income to meet current living expenses could qualify as an unforeseeable emergency.

Citation: Treas. Reg. § 1.409A-3(a)(i)(3).

Q.205 UNDER WHAT CIRCUMSTANCES MAY A SERVICE PROVIDER ACCESS NONQUALIFIED PLAN BENEFITS DURING A PANDEMIC DUE TO DISABILITY?

The service provider must suffer from a physical or mental impairment that can be expected to result in death or last for a continuous period of at least 12 months and must either qualify for Social Security disability benefits or receive income replacement benefits for at least three months under an employer's disability plan (see **Q.46**). In addition, the nonqualified plan must permit distribution on account of disability.

Authors' Comment: Since a disability determination will often require a review of medical records and the passage of time to assure the long-term nature of the disability, approval of a disability distribution will typically take longer than approval of an emergency distribution. Accordingly, an emergency distribution option, if available, may be preferable to a disability distribution.

Citation: Treas. Reg. § 1.409A-3(i)(4).

Q.206 UNDER WHAT CIRCUMSTANCES MAY A SERVICE PROVIDER BE PROVIDED ACCESS TO NONQUALIFIED PLAN BENEFITS DURING A PANDEMIC DUE TO PLAN TERMINATION?

The service recipient must initiate a voluntary plan termination (see **Q.85**) that satisfies all the following conditions:

- All plans of the same type under the special aggregation rule required under Section 409A (see **Q.107**) must also be terminated

with respect to *all* participants (not just those participants seeking a withdrawal).
- A new plan of the same type may not be established for at least three years from the date the service recipient takes all necessary action to terminate the plan.
- No payments other than those otherwise payable under the terms of the plan can be made during the 12 months following the date of plan termination.
- All payments must be made within 24 months following the date of plan termination.
- Termination cannot occur proximate to a downturn in the financial health of the service recipient.

Because of the 12-month delay provision, a plan termination will not solve any immediate financial needs of a service provider adversely impacted by the pandemic.

Citation: Treas. Reg. § 1.409A-3(j)(4)(ix)(C).

Q.207 MAY A SERVICE PROVIDER MODIFY OR CANCEL HIS OR HER NONQUALIFIED PLAN DEFERRAL ELECTION AS A RESULT OF A PANDEMIC?

If the plan so provides, a service provider may elect to cancel a nonqualified plan deferral election for the remainder of the year in the event of disability, an unforeseeable emergency distribution from the plan, or a hardship distribution from the service recipient's 401(k) plan. Cancellation or other modification of a deferral election is not otherwise permitted (see **Q.125**).

Authors' Comment 1: If a service provider desires to cancel a current nonqualified plan deferral election, a straightforward option may be available if supported by the underlying facts and circumstances and the plan documents. The service provider may make a self-certified request for a pandemic-related hardship distribution in a small amount (unless more is actually needed) under the employer's 401(k) plan and then request cancellation of his or her nonqualified plan deferral election.

Authors' Comment 2: Note that the disability standard for cancellation of a deferral election employs an "own occupation" test that is less stringent than the "any occupation" test used for disability distribution purposes (see **Q.46**).

Citation: Treas. Reg. §§ 1.409A-3(j)(4)(viii) & (xii).

Q.208 IF A SERVICE RECIPIENT REDUCES A SERVICE PROVIDER'S REGULAR COMPENSATION DURING A PANDEMIC, DOES THE SERVICE PROVIDER HAVE THE OPTION OF CANCELLING HIS OR HER NONQUALIFIED DEFERRAL ELECTION?

No, unless the reduction is significant enough to result in an unforeseeable emergency or a 401(k) plan hardship withdrawal (e.g., the service provider is unable to pay day-to-day living expenses because of the compensation reduction) (see **Q.207**).

Authors' Comment 1: Service provider elections are often made as a percentage of compensation. In this event, the service provider's deferral amount and compensation will both decline by the same percentage, mitigating to some extent the cash flow impact of the compensation reduction. If, however, the deferral amount is in the form of a fixed dollar amount, the resulting negative impact on the service provider's current income may prove more problematic.

Authors' Comment 2: Service recipients should make certain that any change in a service provider's salary deferral contribution is properly reported to those individuals who are responsible for plan administration. The failure to maintain a service provider's proper deferral election during the entire plan year, taking into account compensation changes, is one of the most common 409A errors made.

Citation: Treas. Reg. § 1.409A-3(j)(4)(viii).

Q.209 IF A SERVICE RECIPIENT REDUCES A SERVICE PROVIDER'S COMPENSATION DURING A PANDEMIC, MAY THE SERVICE RECIPIENT PROMISE TO PAY THE COMPENSATION REDUCTION TO THE SERVICE PROVIDER IN THE FUTURE?

Yes, if the service recipient does not currently maintain a nonqualified salary deferral account balance plan. The reduction in compensation, coupled with a promise to pay the compensation in a future year, will create a nonqualified salary deferral account balance plan that must fully comply with the documentary and operational requirements of Section 409A.

If the service recipient already maintains a nonqualified salary deferral account balance plan, mid-year salary deferrals for existing plan participants are not permitted even if mandated by the employer. Accordingly, with respect to existing plan participants, only a future year's reduced compensation may be deferred to subsequent years, and the terms of any such deferrals must be set forth in writing in accordance with the requirements of Section 409A before the beginning of such year. Any mid-year salary reduction amounts could be deferred for new participants in accordance with the rules set forth in Q.121.

Authors' Comment: In general, a nonqualified plan may only cover a select group of management or highly compensated employees in order to comply with ERISA. Accordingly, a service recipient's promise to pay reduced compensation in the future to a broad range of affected service providers creates potential ERISA compliance issues. This means that a nonqualified plan may not be able to cover all service providers adversely impacted by a reduction in compensation.

Citation: Treas. Reg. §§ 1.409A-2(a)&(b).

Q.210 IF A SERVICE RECIPIENT REDUCES A SERVICE PROVIDER'S BONUS OPPORTUNITY DURING A PANDEMIC, DOES THE SERVICE PROVIDER HAVE THE OPTION OF MODIFYING OR CANCELLING HIS OR HER BONUS DEFERRAL ELECTION IF THE BONUS IS NOT PERFORMANCE BASED?

No, unless the year in which the bonus is earned has not yet commenced. An election to defer bonus amounts that do not qualify as performance-based compensation (see **Q.124**) must generally be made and become irrevocable in the year prior to the year in which the bonus is earned (see **Q.121**).

Authors' Comment: Bonus amounts are often not vital to meeting a family's current living expenses and typically fluctuate from year to year. Accordingly, it might be difficult to make a case for an election change due to an unforeseen emergency merely because of a reduction in bonus opportunity.

Citation: Treas. Reg. § 1.409A-2(a)(3).

Q.211 IF A SERVICE RECIPIENT REDUCES OR OTHERWISE MODIFIES A SERVICE PROVIDER'S OPPORTUNITY TO EARN A PERFORMANCE-BASED BONUS DURING A PANDEMIC, DOES THE SERVICE PROVIDER STILL HAVE THE OPTION OF MAKING A DELAYED ELECTION IN ACCORDANCE WITH THE PERFORMANCE-BASED BONUS RULES?

It depends on when and how the service recipient takes action to modify the bonus opportunity.

If (i) the service provider communicates the new performance goals to the service provider within 90 days of the beginning of the performance period, and (ii) the new goals are based on individual or organizational criteria, and (iii) the remaining requirements set forth in **Q.124** are satisfied, the service provider may take advantage of the special rules allowing delayed deferral elections for performance-based bonuses (i.e., the election must be made by the earlier of the date the performance-based compensation has become readily ascertainable or six calendar months before the performance period ends). Otherwise, the special performance-based bonus election will not be available.

Authors' Comment: The potential for a failure to meet the requirements for a delayed performance-based election suggests the wisdom of a plan requiring a deferral election with respect to a bonus that is intended to qualify as performance-based compensation before the beginning of the year it is earned. If the requirements for a delayed performance-based election are later met, the service provider will then have an opportunity to amend his or her prior election.

Citation: Treas. Reg. § 1.409A-2(a)(8).

Q.212 IF A SERVICE RECIPIENT REDUCES OR OTHERWISE MODIFIES A SERVICE PROVIDER'S OPPORTUNITY TO EARN A PERFORMANCE-BASED BONUS MORE THAN SIX MONTHS INTO THE PERFORMANCE PERIOD DUE TO A PANDEMIC, WHAT IMPACT DOES THIS HAVE ON A SERVICE PROVIDER'S DELAYED ELECTION PURSUANT TO THE PERFORMANCE-BASED BONUS RULES?

The Final Regulations do not specifically address this question, but the only possibility for avoiding a 409A violation would be to take the position that the election is void since no qualified performance-based bonus is being paid. A 409A violation would certainly occur if the election were given effect.

Example. In March 2028, a service recipient communicates to a service provider the details of a performance-based bonus plan for the period ending December 31, 2028. The service provider elects to defer the entire bonus in June 2028. In August 2028, a pandemic begins, and the service recipient modifies the bonus arrangement to make the 2028 bonus discretionary. A bonus is declared in February 2029. The parties could take the position that no performance-based bonus has been paid, and, accordingly, the service provider's election is ineffective (i.e., the bonus should not be deferred).

Citation: Treas. Reg. § 1.409A-2(a)(8).

Q.213 WHAT IMPACT DOES A TEMPORARY SHUTDOWN OF ALL BUSINESS OPERATIONS DURING A PANDEMIC HAVE ON SERVICE PROVIDER DEFERRALS UNDER A NONQUALIFIED PLAN?

If compensation is paid during the shutdown, deferrals must continue unless the service provider meets the requirements to cancel deferrals and chooses to do so (see **Q.207**).

Q.214 MAY A SERVICE RECIPIENT REDUCE OR CANCEL MATCHING OR OTHER EMPLOYER CREDITS TO A NONQUALIFIED PLAN DURING A PANDEMIC WITHOUT VIOLATING SECTION 409A?

Yes, provided that no other compensation or benefits are substituted for the reduced or canceled credits (see **Q.90**).

Authors' Comment: Whether the service recipient has the legal ability to reduce or eliminate matching or other credits under a nonqualified plan requires an analysis of the governing plan documents, communications to service providers, and state contract law. A plan amendment may be required to accomplish this result.

Citation: Treas. Reg. § 1.409A-3(f).

Q.215 TO HELP PRESERVE CASH FLOW DURING A PANDEMIC, MAY A SERVICE RECIPIENT REDUCE OR CANCEL ASSET CONTRIBUTIONS TO A RABBI TRUST USED TO INFORMALLY TRACK THE LIABILITIES OF A PLAN WITHOUT VIOLATING SECTION 409A?

Yes. Section 409A permits a service recipient to choose to fund—or not fund—a rabbi trust (or other informal funding vehicle) that mirrors the liabilities of a plan (see **Q.196**), subject to certain limitations (see **Q.197-200**).

Authors' Comment 1: Whether the service recipient has the legal ability to reduce or eliminate contributions to a rabbi trust requires an analysis of the governing trust document, communications to service providers, and state contract law.

Authors' Comment 2: The service recipient and plan recordkeeper should discuss how the plan's liabilities will be tracked going forward before the service recipient stops setting aside assets that informally mirror the plan's liabilities. In some cases, the plan's recordkeeper records and reports the amount of a plan's liabilities based on assets in an informal funding vehicle and may not have the administrative capacity to accurately record plan liabilities absent such informal funding.

Citation: I.R.C. § 409A(b).

Q.216 IF A SERVICE RECIPIENT FURLOUGHS SERVICE PROVIDERS DURING A PANDEMIC, DOES A SEPARATION FROM SERVICE OCCUR FOR PURPOSES OF SECTION 409A?

While the Final Regulations create a rebuttable presumption that a separation from service has occurred when the level of services performed by service providers has been reduced to zero, this presumption may be rebutted based on the reasonable intent of the parties that the furlough will be temporary and the service providers will return to work once the pandemic subsides or economic conditions otherwise improve (see **Q.29**). If the furlough is intended to be temporary, the facts and circumstances supporting this intent should be documented in writing. If circumstances change and the parties determine that the suspension of services has become permanent with respect to one or more service providers, the service recipient should treat the service provider(s) as experiencing a separation from service at such time.

Authors' Comment: In contrast to the rules governing leaves of absence (see **Q.30** and **Q.217**), the Final Regulations do not set forth a maximum length of time before a furloughed service provider will be deemed to have separated from service. In most situations, as a service provider's furlough period lengthens, a return to active service becomes less likely. If a furlough period continues for six months, we recommend that the parties evaluate whether a separation from service should be deemed to have occurred.

Citation: Treas. Reg. § 1.409A-1(h)(1)(ii).

Q.217 IF A SERVICE PROVIDER TAKES A LEAVE OF ABSENCE DURING A PANDEMIC, DOES A SEPARATION FROM SERVICE OCCUR FOR PURPOSES OF SECTION 409A?

No, if a reasonable expectation exists that the service provider will return to work within six months (in limited circumstances, a longer period than six months is permitted, see **Q.30**). If the service provider does not return to active service within six months (or such longer period), then a separation of service occurs on the first day immediately following such six month (or longer) period.

Citation: Treas. Reg. § 1.409A-1(h)(1)(i).

ENFORCEMENT

Q.218 CAN AN EMPLOYER OBTAIN AN IRS LETTER RULING THAT A DEFERRED COMPENSATION PLAN SATISFIES THE REQUIREMENTS OF SECTION 409A?

In general, no. The IRS maintains a no-ruling position with respect to most Section 409A documentary and operational issues, including the following:

- The income tax consequences of establishing, operating, or participating in a plan, including withholding tax compliance.
- Whether or not a plan is subject to a totalization agreement or is a foreign-based retirement plan that might be exempt from Section 409A.
- Whether or not a plan is a bona fide vacation leave, sick pay, or compensatory time plan that might be exempt from Section 409A.
- Whether or not a plan provides for deferral of compensation within the meaning of Section 409A and therefore might be covered by Section 409A.
- Whether or not an amount might qualify as a short-term deferral that might thereby be exempt from Section 409A.
- Whether or not certain stock rights, foreign plans, and separation pay plans are subject to Section 409A.

The IRS has not suggested that any model document or language will be forthcoming with respect to plans subject to Section 409A or 457(f). Although there was no IRS-approved model nonqualified deferred compensation plan document or plan language before enactment of Section 409A, a plan sponsor could request a favorable private letter ruling from the IRS with respect to the form of a nonqualified deferred compensation plan at the outset. This is no longer possible.

Citation: Rev. Proc. 2013–3, § 3.01(46).

Q.219 ARE THERE ANY ISSUES INVOLVING DEFERRED COMPENSATION PLANS SUBJECT TO SECTION 409A ON WHICH THE IRS WILL ISSUE RULINGS?

The IRS will rule on estate and gift tax and FICA issues involving a nonqualified deferred compensation arrangement subject to Section 409A.

Citation: Rev. Proc. 2008–61, § 2.08.

Q.220 WHEN WILL THE IRS ACTIVELY AUDIT AND ENFORCE THE REQUIREMENTS OF SECTION 409A WITH RESPECT TO COVERED PLANS?

The IRS is auditing and enforcing these requirements now. During Section 409A audits, the IRS is asking the service recipient to identify and provide documentation for all of its Section 409A plans. The service recipient must also identify all of its plans that are excepted from Section 409A and the specific exception on which the service recipient is relying for each plan.

Authors' Comment: The IRS audit approach highlights the importance of documenting all employee benefit plans and indicating the exemption or exception to Section 409A for those claiming such exemption or exception.

Citation: I.R.C. §§ 409A(a)(1)(B)(i)(II), (b)(4)(A)(ii).

Q.221 DOES THE SERVICE RECIPIENT HAVE INCOME TAX REPORTING OBLIGATIONS WITH RESPECT TO AMOUNTS ACCRUED BY SERVICE PROVIDERS UNDER ITS DEFERRED COMPENSATION PLANS THAT ARE SUBJECT TO SECTION 409A?

Deferred amounts includible in the income of service providers for a taxable year on account of a violation of Section 409A must be reported by the service recipient each year.

For employees, these amounts are treated as wages reported in Box 1 and as Section 409A income reported in Box 12 of Form W-2 using Code Z. The amount includible in income is treated as supplemental wages subject to income tax withholding, but the employer has no duty to withhold based on the additional excise tax and interest imposed pursuant to Section 409A.

For independent contractors, taxable deferred compensation is reported in Box 7 and in Box 15b of Form 1099-MISC.

The statute requires a service recipient to report annually all amounts deferred for the year by all of its employees and independent contractors, but the IRS has suspended this reporting obligation indefinitely. For individual account plans, this will consist of additional amounts deferred to the service provider's account each year. For employer non-account balance plans (SERPs and excess plans), this will consist of the actuarial increase in value of the benefit, either year by year or at such later time as the amount is reasonably ascertainable within the meaning of Code Section 3121(v)(2).

Citation: I.R.C. §§ 3401(a), 6041(g)(1) and 6051(a)(13); *see* Prop. Treas. Reg. § 1.409A-4, I.R.B. 2008–51 (Dec. 22, 2008) (valuation methods); *see, e.g.,* Notice 2008–115, § III.A (interim notice on reporting and withholding requirements, including suspension of certain informational reporting requirements).

Q.222 WHAT PENALTIES MAY BE IMPOSED ON A SERVICE RECIPIENT WHEN A SECTION 409A VIOLATION OCCURS?

All adverse tax consequences imposed specifically by Section 409A fall upon the service provider unless the parties agree otherwise (see **Q.105**). Interest and penalties may be imposed on the service recipient under other Code Sections, however, if the service recipient fails to timely report income inclusion or withhold taxes associated with Section 409A violations.

Citation: I.R.C. §§ 3403 and 6672 (failure to withhold and pay over federal income tax); I.R.C. § 6601(a) (interest on underpayments); I.R.C. § 6721 (failure to file a correct W-2 or 1099-MISC); I.R.C. § 6722 (failure to furnish a correct W-2 or 1099-MISC); I.R.C. § 6651 (failure to properly file form 941 and pay tax); I.R.C. § 6662 (accuracy-related penalty on underpayments).

Q.223 IN DETERMINING COMPLIANCE WITH THE VARIOUS TIMING REQUIREMENTS IN THE SECTION 409A RULES, HOW DOES THE IRS COUNT DAYS, MONTHS, AND YEARS?

When counting days, the first day of a period is disregarded and the last day is taken into account. Months and years are computed on an anniversary basis.

Example 1. A service provider begins participation in a plan on March 1, 2021, and is entitled to make an initial deferral election within 30 days after this date (see **Q.121**). The election must be made on or before March 31, 2021.

Example 2. A plan provides for a payment to be made to a service provider on January 1, 2021. The employee makes an election on January 1, 2020 (12 months before the date of the first scheduled payment) to defer the payment until January 1, 2026 (the fifth anniversary of the date the payment would otherwise have been made). The election satisfies the subsequent election requirements (see **Q.127**).

Citation: Treas. Reg. § 1.409-2(b)(9) Examples 5 and 19; Notice 2008-113, § III(H); Notice 2010-6, § III(F).

MITIGATION— DOCUMENTARY ERRORS

Q.224 ARE THERE WAYS TO LIMIT THE NEGATIVE TAX CONSEQUENCES OF DOCUMENTARY ERRORS UNDER SECTION 409A?

Yes. Notice 2010–6, as modified by Notice 2010–80, provides rules for correcting certain documentary errors under Section 409A. Documentary failures not expressly addressed in the notices are ineligible for relief under this guidance.

Only inadvertent errors are subject to correction, and the service recipient is required to "take commercially reasonable steps" to correct all similar errors in all of its plans.

Intentional errors and listed tax shelter transactions cannot be corrected.

In some cases, correction of an operational error may also be required (see **Q.240** through **Q.255**).

Citation: See generally Notice 2010–6, as amended by Notice 2010–80 as to documentary errors.

Q.225 WHAT TYPES OF DOCUMENTARY ERRORS ARE SUBJECT TO CORRECTION UNDER NOTICE 2010-6?

Corrections pursuant to Notice 2010–6 include interpretation of ambiguous provisions without plan amendment or negative tax consequences, plan amendment without negative tax consequences, and plan amendment with service provider recognition of income under Section 409A incident to the correction.

Citation: Notice 2010–6.

Q.226 WHAT TYPES OF PLANS ARE NOT ELIGIBLE FOR CORRECTION OF DOCUMENTARY ERRORS UNDER NOTICE 2010-6?

Plans providing for payment of commissions after the service recipient's receipt of payments from a third party could have been corrected by plan amendment through December 31, 2011, but this remedy is no longer available to them.

Since January 1, 2012, documentary corrections have been available only on a restricted basis for plans providing for stock rights (see **Q.231** and **Q.232**) and plans under which the amount or time of payment is linked to other qualified or nonqualified deferred compensation plans (see **Q.233**).

Citation: Notice 2010–6, §§ III.G, XI.B-C, modified by Notice 2010–80, § III.A.

Q.227 WHAT DOCUMENTARY AMBIGUITIES IN A PLAN CAN BE ADDRESSED BY INTERPRETING THE AMBIGUOUS PROVISION CONSISTENT WITH SECTION 409A WITHOUT HAVING TO AMEND THE PLAN?

Notice 2010–6 provides for relief with respect to the following types of plan provisions without requiring a plan amendment, special reporting or negative tax consequences:

- A provision for payment as soon as practicable (or similar language) following a payment event, such as separation from service, change of control, or disability.

This type of term could be viewed as a technical breach because it contains implicit discretion as to the time of payment prohibited by Section 409A.

In such cases, the date of the payment event will be treated as the fixed date for payment required by Section 409A, and payment will be considered timely if payment occurs or begins by the end of the calendar year in which the payment event occurs or 2½ months after the payment event, whichever is later.

Correction of an operational defect under Notice 2008–113 may be required for erroneous distributions under the ambiguous provision before its correction.

Service provider plans that demonstrate a pattern or practice of non-compliant application of an ambiguous provision are not eligible for this relief.

- Use of ambiguous terms to define a payment event that could be interpreted to include an impermissible payment event or not to include a permissible payment event. Examples include use of the term "termination of employment" instead of the technically correct "separation from service" defined in accordance with Section 409A, or use of the term "acquisition" instead of the technically correct "change of control" defined in accordance with Section 409A.

An ambiguous term cannot be corrected in this way if it expressly violates Section 409A by including impermissible payment events or excluding permissible payment events.

The ambiguous term must be applied in a manner consistent with Section 409A. If the term is applied in a manner that is inconsistent with Section 409A, a documentation failure occurs. The plan must be amended to comply with Section 409A, non-compliant payments or failures to pay under the ambiguous plan provision must be corrected under Notice 2008–113 (see **Q.240** through **Q.255**), and the plan amendment must occur by the end of the service provider's taxable year of operational correction.

Plans that demonstrate a pattern or practice of non-compliant application of an ambiguous provision are not eligible for this relief. Also, if a court has interpreted an ambiguous plan provision in a manner that is inconsistent with Section 409A, neither the affected

plan nor any other plan of the service provider and its controlled group that uses the same term is eligible for this relief.
- Failed initial or subsequent deferral election provisions as applied to service providers who did not make elections under the failed provision. This relief is not available with respect to a service provider who made an election under a failed provision, even if the particular election complied with the requirements of Section 409A, nor to impermissible service provider elections to accelerate distribution, such as the old haircut provisions (see **Q.17**).

Even though plan amendment is not required in these instances, these terms invite further review of operational compliance with Section 409A if the plan becomes the subject of an IRS audit. It would be prudent to make clear in the plan's administrative procedures that the more definite terms required under Section 409A are intended. A plan provision requiring interpretation of the plan language consistent with Section 409A is useful in this context (see **Q.19**).

Citation: Notice 2010–6, § IV.

Q.228 WHAT TYPES OF ERRORS IN PLAN DOCUMENTATION CAN BE CORRECTED BY PLAN AMENDMENT WITHOUT RECOGNITION OF INCOME BY A SERVICE PROVIDER?

If correction occurs before occurrence of an impermissible payment event with respect to the service provider, the following types of documentary errors are subject to correction by plan amendment without recognition of income by a service provider:

- *Impermissible definition of disability*. Correction requires adoption of a definition of disability that complies with Section 409A or a plan amendment removing disability as a payment event. It is possible to correct the definition after payment pursuant to an impermissible definition. The affected payments must be treated as an operational defect and corrected pursuant to Notice 2008–113.

- *Impermissible provision for payment after the service provider provides a required release, non-compete agreement, etc.* Correction requires a plan amendment that either makes the payment date independent of the date the service provider provides the release, provides a fixed date that gives ample time for the service provider to return the release, or provides for payment at any time during a specified period up to 90 days following the permissible payment event, subject to the requirement that payment occur in the later year if the specified period spans two taxable years.
- *Impermissible service recipient discretion to accelerate payment.* Correction requires elimination of the discretion to accelerate payment before the earlier of the date the service recipient irrevocably exercises its discretion under the plan or the date of payment pursuant to exercise of the service recipient's discretion. Impermissible service provider discretion to accelerate payment, such as in the old haircut provisions, cannot be corrected.

Correction by plan amendment is not available if either the service recipient or the service provider is under IRS audit at the time of correction. For an individual service recipient or service provider, this includes any IRS audit. For other taxpayers, it includes only an IRS request for documents or audit relating to its nonqualified deferred compensation plans.

Citation: Notice 2010–6, §§ III.C, V.A-C, VI.B, modified by Notice 2010–80, § III.B.

Q.229 WHAT TYPES OF DOCUMENTARY ERRORS CAN BE CORRECTED BY PLAN AMENDMENT WITH LIMITED RECOGNITION OF INCOME FOR SERVICE PROVIDERS WHO WERE SUBJECT TO THE DOCUMENTARY ERROR BEFORE THE CORRECTIVE AMENDMENT?

Certain types of documentary error can be corrected by plan amendment, subject to recognition of current income under Section 409A by a service provider who experiences a defective payment event within one year after the date of correction. The service provider must treat 50 percent of his or her vested deferred compensation under the corrected provision (25 percent for a defective definition of change of control) as current income taxable under Section 409A for the year of occurrence of the defective payment event, whether or not the service provider receives a distribution under the plan pursuant to the defective plan provision. Documentary errors correctable by plan amendment include:

- *Impermissible definition of separation from service.* Examples include a change in status from full-time to part-time employment or from employee to independent contractor, transfer from employment with one member of a controlled group of service recipients to another, or failure to include separation from service as a payment event. Correction requires adoption of a definition of separation from service that complies with Section 409A.
- *Impermissible definition of change of control.* Correction requires adoption of a definition that complies with Section 409A. This correction is not available for a definition of change of control that treats a change of control as a payment event for employees of a parent company that sells a subsidiary who remain employed by the parent after the sale.
- *Different payment schedules for voluntary and involuntary separation.* Correction requires a plan amendment before the service provider's separation from service that makes the form of payment for voluntary separation the same as the existing form for involuntary separation (subject to the six-month rule if the service provider is a specified employee).
- *Impermissible additional payment schedules under the anti-toggle rule* (see **Q.58**). Correction requires a plan amendment eliminating the extra forms of payment. In determining which of two forms to eliminate and which to retain, the surviving form must be the one with the latest or potentially latest final payment date. If there is a tie, the one commencing or potentially commencing on the latest possible date survives. If there is a second, the one generally anticipated to result in the amount deferred being paid later than

the other one survives. This process of elimination continues until the proper number of forms is retained in the plan.

If a plan contains too many forms of payment but a service provider is not eligible for more than the proper number of forms of payment, this requirement does not apply to that service provider.

- *Impermissible reimbursement and in-kind benefit provisions.* Correction requires a plan amendment that complies with Section 409A before a payment event that makes the service provider eligible for reimbursement or in-kind benefits. The amount eligible for in-kind benefits must be prorated over the period of eligibility. If the eligibility period is the service provider's lifetime, the actuarially determined life expectancy must be used. If the eligibility period is based on an event, the time of the event must be reasonably determined and cannot be less than three years.
- *Failure to include the rule that distribution to a specified employee on account of separation from service cannot begin until six months after the separation from service.* The deadline for including this provision is the first day a specified employee is covered by the plan, which is the first specified employee effective date. Corrective amendment must provide that payment cannot begin until expiration of 18 months after the plan amendment making the correction or six months after the specified employee's separation from service, whichever is later.
- *Any other impermissible payment event in a plan that contains both permissible and impermissible payment events.* Correction requires a plan amendment removing the impermissible payment events. This relief is not available for impermissible payment events that include discretion on the part of either party.
- *Impermissible service provider or service recipient discretion to change a payment schedule, including subsequent deferral elections.* Correction requires elimination of the impermissible discretion and replacing it with the default time and form of payment provided for in the plan, or the form with the latest payment date if the plan does not contain a default. If there is a tie in that case, use the form with the latest commencement date. If there is a tie in that case, use the form reasonably expected to end at the latest time. If any

participant has made an election under the impermissible provision, even if the actual election complies with the requirements of Section 409A, the corrective plan amendment must be adopted by the end of the second taxable year following the year of the tainted election and any resulting operational failures must be corrected under Notice 2008–113.

- *Impermissible initial deferral elections.* Correction requires deleting the provision. If any participant has made an election under the impermissible provision, even if the actual election complies with the requirements of Section 409A, the corrective plan amendment must be adopted by the end of the second taxable year following the year of the tainted election and the resulting operational failures must be corrected under Notice 2008–113. Any defective elections that occurred before the first taxable year to which the amendment applies cannot be corrected by this method and are in breach of Section 409A.

One type of documentary error can be corrected by plan amendment, subject to recognition of current income under Section 409A by a service provider who experiences a defective payment event before correction, as long as the correction is made within a reasonable time. The service provider must treat 50 percent of his or her vested deferred compensation under the corrected provision as current income taxable under Section 409A for the year of occurrence of the permissible payment event, whether or not the service provider receives a distribution under the plan pursuant to the defective plan provision. This type of error is described as follows:

- *Impermissible provision for payment or commencement period longer than 90 days following a payment event.* Correction requires a plan amendment that either limits the payment period to 90 days or less or removes the period for payment after the event, and also forecloses the service provider from selecting the taxable year of payment. This correction is not available if the defective payment or commencement period exceeds 365 days.

Correction by plan amendment is not available if either the service recipient or the service provider is under IRS audit at the time of correction. For an individual service recipient or service provider, this includes any IRS audit. For other taxpayers, it includes only an IRS request for documents or audit relating to its nonqualified deferred compensation plans.

Citation: Notice 2010–6, §§ III.C, VI.A, VII.C, VII. F, VIII, IX.

Q.230 WHAT TYPE OF DOCUMENTARY ERRORS CAN BE CORRECTED BY PLAN AMENDMENT WITH RECOGNITION OF SECTION 409A INCOME BY AFFECTED SERVICE PROVIDERS WITHOUT EXCEPTION?

The following type of documentary error can be corrected by plan amendment subject to recognition of 50 percent of the amount deferred as Section 409A income by affected service providers in the year of correction without exception:

- *Impermissible payment events in a plan that contains only impermissible payment events.* Correction requires replacement of any impermissible payment event with a provision for payment on the later of separation from service or the sixth anniversary of the correction. This correction is not available after the impermissible payment event occurs.

Correction by plan amendment is not available if either the service recipient or the service provider is under IRS audit at the time of correction. For an individual service recipient or service provider, this includes any IRS audit. For other taxpayers, it includes only an IRS request for documents or audit relating to its nonqualified deferred compensation plans.

Citation: Notice 2010–6, §§ III.C, VII. B.

Q.231 WHAT SPECIAL RULES APPLY TO STOCK PLANS?

Until December 31, 2011, a plan providing for grants of stock or stock rights could be amended as appropriate to cause the plan either to satisfy the exception to the application of Section 409A for plans providing for stock options or stock appreciation rights or to satisfy the requirements of Section 409A. After December 31, 2011, corrective amendments pursuant to Notice 2010–6 are available only to stock or stock appreciation rights plans intended to comply with Section 409A either at the time of grant or as corrected by December 31, 2011.

Citation: Notice 2010–6, § III.G; Notice 2010–80, § III.A; Notice 2008–113, §§ V.D and E.

Q.232 IN WHAT CIRCUMSTANCES CAN A DOCUMENTARY ERROR RELATING TO A STOCK RIGHT INTENDED TO BE EXEMPT FROM SECTION 409A BE CORRECTED?

If a stock right that was exempt from Section 409A is changed such that the stock right becomes subject to Section 409A, the change can be rescinded before the earlier of the date the stock right is exercised or by the last day of the calendar year during which the change occurred to avoid the consequences of a Section 409A violation. There are no reporting requirements associated with this type of correction.

Example. An employee is granted a stock right that is exempt from Section 409A on January 3, 2013. On March 1, 2018, while the stock right is in the money, the exercise period is extended for an additional five years. This extension would generally cause the stock right to become subject to Section 409A and cause an immediate violation of Section 409A (see **Q.154** and **Q.155**). If the extension is rescinded on or before December 31, 2018, and before exercise, then the extension is disregarded and the stock right remains exempt from Section 409A.

Citation: Treas. Reg. § 1.409A-1(b)(5)(v)(I).

Q.233 WHAT SPECIAL RULES APPLY TO LINKED PLANS?

A linked plan is a plan under which the amount or time of payment is linked to another qualified or nonqualified deferred compensation plan. Until December 31, 2011, a linked plan could be amended as appropriate to cause the plan to satisfy the requirements of Section 409A. After December 31, 2011, corrective amendments pursuant to Notice 2010–6 are available only if the linkage to another plan does not affect the time and form of payment under either plan.

Citation: Notice 2010–6, §§ III.C, XI.B.

Q.234 WHEN IS CORRECTION DEEMED TO OCCUR FOR PURPOSES OF NOTICE 2010-6?

The date of correction for purposes of Notice 2010–6, including any one-year period measured from the date of correction for purposes of determining whether a prohibited payment event has occurred with respect to a participant, is the latest of the date of adoption of the change, the effective date of the change, or the date that the change is reduced to writing.

Citation: Notice 2010–6, § III.F.

Q.235 WHAT ARE THE RULES FOR RECOGNITION OF SERVICE PROVIDER INCOME INCIDENT TO A DOCUMENTARY CORRECTION PURSUANT TO NOTICE 2010-6?

If a service provider is required to recognize current income under Section 409A incident to a documentary correction, the amount subject to recognition pursuant to Notice 2010–6 is limited to 50 percent, or 25 percent in the case of a defective change of control provision, of the amount to which the previously defective provision being corrected would have applied, rather than the value of the entire vested benefit that would have to be recognized under the general rules on breach of Section 409A. The amount recognized is determined as of the end of the taxable year of correction, and is based on the defective plan provision in effect immediately before the correction.

If correction of more than one error requires recognition of current income in the same taxable year, only the amount required to be recognized under the most burdensome correction is recognized.

The amount required to be recognized as current income incident to a documentary correction is subject to income tax at the ordinary rates, plus the additional 20 percent tax imposed by Section 409A. It is not subject to the premium interest tax otherwise due under Section 409A.

Any income recognized incident to a correction of this kind is treated as an amount previously included in income in determining amounts includable in income in later taxable years under Section 409A. If two or more documentary errors apply to the same plan in a single taxable year, only the correction that requires the highest percentage of income to be taken into account will apply. If correction is required with respect to the same documentary error in two or more taxable years, the amount treated in a subsequent year as corrected in a prior year is two times the amount actually recognized as income in the prior year.

These consequences are less burdensome to the taxpayer than would be required by statute on breach of Section 409A.

Citation: Notice 2010–6, §§ III.E, F.

Q.236 WHAT ADDITIONAL REPORTING AND DISCLOSURE REQUIREMENTS ARE IMPOSED IN CONNECTION WITH CORRECTION OF A DOCUMENTARY ERROR THAT REQUIRES A PLAN AMENDMENT?

With the exception of correction of a brand new plan (see **Q.237**), the following rules apply if a correction requires a plan amendment:

- The service recipient must furnish each affected service provider a detailed statement for the year of correction describing the documentary failure and the correction, the name and Social Security number or taxpayer identification number of the service provider and the amount, if any, of the taxable income the service provider must recognize on account of the failure pursuant to Section 409A. If the service provider is required to recognize income in any

subsequent year in connection with the correction, the service recipient must provide the same information for the subsequent year.
- The service recipient must attach the same statements to its federal income tax return for each affected year.
- The service recipient must report income tax due pursuant to Section 409A on the Form W-2, Box 1 and Box 12, Code Z, of each affected employee and on the Form 1099 of each affected independent contractor for each affected year.
- Any service provider required to pay federal income tax on account of the failure must report the tax due on Form 1040. The service provider must also pay the tax and file the detailed statement from the service recipient with the service provider's federal income tax return for the year of correction and any subsequent year in which the service provider is required to pay federal income tax pursuant to Section 409A in connection with the correction.

Note that neither the service recipient nor the service provider can be under audit at the time of correction. For an individual service recipient or service provider, this includes any audit. For other taxpayers, it includes only an IRS request for documents or audit relating to its nonqualified deferred compensation plans (see **Q.256, Q.257** and **Q.261**).

See **Exhibit 6** for sample statements for attachment to the service recipient and service provider's federal income tax returns for correction of a documentary failure to comply with Section 409A pursuant to Notice 2010–6.

Citation: Notice 2010–6, § XII, modified by Notice 2010–80, § III.E.

Q.237 CAN A DOCUMENTARY ERROR IN A NEW PLAN BE CORRECTED BY PLAN AMENDMENT WITHOUT BEING SUBJECT TO THE TAX AND REPORTING REQUIREMENTS GENERALLY REQUIRED?

Yes. If a Section 409A plan documentation error is discovered and corrected, either by the end of the calendar year during which the first legally binding right to deferred compensation arose under the new plan or within 2½ months following the date on which such first legally binding right arose, whichever is later, it need not comply with the rest of the generally applicable correction, reporting and disclosure requirements. Operational correction may also be required (see **Q.240** through **Q.255**).

For this purpose, a plan is treated as a new plan only if it is the first plan of the same type adopted by the service recipient and its controlled group members.

Citation: Notice 2010–6, § X.

Q.238 WHAT CORRECTION IS AVAILABLE IN THE EVENT OF A SCRIVENER'S ERROR?

Notice 2010–6 does not address scriveners' errors. If a scrivener's error does not affect the time or amount of deferral or distribution, it should be corrected as soon as possible after discovery.

Q.239 ARE THERE ANY CIRCUMSTANCES IN WHICH A DOCUMENTARY ERROR IN A PLAN SUBJECT TO SECTION 409A CAN BE CORRECTED WITHOUT COMPLYING WITH NOTICE 2010-6?

Yes.

If any of a service provider's deferred compensation under a plan subject to Section 409A is nonvested on the last day of a calendar year, the nonvested deferred compensation is not includible in the service provider's income under Section 409A for the year in the absence of abusive practices (see **Q.103** and **Q.104**). This is true whether or not the form of the plan complies with Section 409A.

Accordingly, if a documentary violation of Section 409A is corrected before the beginning of the first calendar year in which any deferred compensation payable under the plan becomes vested, the documentary violation has no adverse tax consequences for any service provider under Section 409A and no reporting or disclosure requirements apply to the correction.

Citation: Prop. Treas. Reg. § 1.409A-4, I.R.B. 2008–51 (Dec. 22, 2008); CCA 20158013; Annotated Notice 2010–6, comments by Stephen Tackney, following § III.I, "To the extent the failure involves a nonvested amount that wouldn't be included in income, the way to change that is under the income inclusion regulations, which are not affected by [Notice 2010–6]."

MITIGATION OF CONSEQUENCES— OPERATIONAL ERRORS

Q.240 HAS THE IRS PUBLISHED GUIDANCE ON CORRECTION OF INADVERTENT ERRORS IN THE ADMINISTRATION OF DEFERRED COMPENSATION PLANS SUBJECT TO SECTION 409A?

Yes, in Notice 2008–113, as modified by Notice 2010–6 and Notice 2010–80.

The requirements for correction are detailed and specific. There are six categories of error. The correction for each category of error varies with the year of correction. No correction is available after the second calendar year following the calendar year in which the error occurs.

If an error is corrected as specified in the year of occurrence, or in some cases in the year following the year of occurrence, no additional income tax or premium interest tax otherwise required by Section 409A must be paid. Other correction methods require only payment of the 20 percent additional income tax on the amount involved in the error. The rest of the service provider's vested account or other deferred compensation is not subject to the 20 percent additional income tax, and no premium interest tax is due.

The IRS has taken the position that these correction methods are the only ones available with respect to plans subject to Section 409A. This includes not only plans intended to be subject to Section 409A, but also plans intended to beyond the scope of Section 409A that by their terms or operational defects fall within its scope. Service providers who use other correction techniques do so at their peril.

Citation: Notice 2010–80; Notice 2010–6; Notice 2008–113; *see also* Rosina B. Barker and Kevin P. O'Brien, *409A Failures: Correcting With and Without Notice 2008-113*, Tax Notes (Aug. 10, 2009) at 557 (arguing that correction of operational errors should be possible, especially in the year of failure, even if the requirements of Notice 2008–113 cannot be satisfied); Brian W. Berglund, Lisa A. Van Fleet and Carolyn G. Wolff, *Section 409A in Action,* Exec. Comp. Library on the Web (BNA) (Oct. 16, 2009).

Q.241 IS THERE A MINIMAL LEVEL OF ADMINISTRATIVE ERROR UNDER SECTION 409A FOR WHICH THE IRS DOES NOT REQUIRE FORMAL CORRECTION AND REPORTING?

Technically, no. Even the least burdensome corrections authorized in Notice 2008–113 that involve amounts less than the limitation on elective deferrals require documentation and reporting of the corrective action and the amount involved (see **Q.244** through **Q.249**). There is no stated exception even for very small errors in the amount of a distribution due to actuarial or accounting calculations involving only a few dollars in Notice 2008–113 or other official IRS guidance. The IRS rarely pursues errors of this magnitude when it audits a taxpayer for other requirements of the Internal Revenue Code. For example, an overpayment up to $100 and an underpayment up to $75 in connection with a distribution from a tax-qualified retirement plan need not be corrected if the reasonable direct cost of correction exceeds the amount of the distribution. In addition, IRS representatives have informally suggested that *de minimis* Section 409A operational errors of $25 or less may be insufficient to warrant IRS enforcement action. Therefore, it appears that the risk of a problem is remote under these circumstances. However, to obtain absolute certainty, the procedures in Notice 2008–113 must be followed.

Citation: Rev. Proc. 2008–50, §§ 6.02(5)(b), (c).

Q.242 ARE THERE ANY PLANS FOR WHICH THE CORRECTION OF OPERATIONAL DEFECTS PURSUANT TO NOTICE 2008-113 DOES NOT APPLY?

Yes. Grandfathered plans remain covered by the rules governing contract correction and tax accounting that applied before enactment of Section 409A.

Citation: Treas. Reg. § 1.409A-6(a); Notice 2010–6; Notice 2008–113.

Q.243 WHAT ANALYSIS SHOULD BE DONE TO DETERMINE WHETHER CORRECTION OF AN OPERATIONAL ERROR PURSUANT TO NOTICE 2008-113 IS NECESSARY?

It is possible that an operational failure requiring correction has not occurred, even though the specific provisions of the plan have not been followed to the letter. For example, a distribution that occurs after the designated payment date may be saved from noncompliance by the rule on refusal to pay (see **Q.71**), the rule on when a payment is considered to have been made on the designated payment date (see **Q.48**), or the rule on late payment due to administrative impracticability (see **Q.61**). A distribution that occurs before the designated payment date may be saved from noncompliance by one of rules permitting acceleration, such as the rule on discretionary cash-outs of small amounts (see **Q.72** and **Q.78**). A recordkeeping error regarding the amount of the benefit due may be corrected provided no benefit payments have already been made at the time the error is discovered.

It is also possible that part or all of the compensation deferred under the plan is grandfathered from the application of Section 409A.

Example 1. A plan provides for a distribution of nonqualified deferred compensation to a service provider on November 1, 2015. The service recipient unilaterally delays the payment to the service provider until January 10, 2016. No operational failure has occurred because the distribution was made within 2½ months after the scheduled distribution date and the service provider was not allowed to elect the taxable year of payment (see **Q.48**).

Example 2. A plan provides for distribution of nonqualified deferred compensation in connection with a service provider's separation from service. A service provider who is not a specified employee retires on October 1, 2015. On her last day of work, the service provider meets with representatives of the service recipient and completes withholding forms relating to her nonqualified plan distribution. On December 20, 2015, the service provider has not received the distribution, and she sends an email to the service recipient's senior vice president of human resources stating that she has not received the distribution and asking when the distribution will occur. Through the service recipient's inadvertence, the distribution is not paid by December 31, 2015. The service provider asks about the distribution again on January 20, 2016, and the service recipient makes the payment three days later. The rule on refusal or failure to pay (see **Q.71**) protects this distribution from treatment as a violation of Section 409A.

Example 3. A service provider defers $10,000 under a plan subject to Section 409A in 2015. The service recipient maintains no other plans of the same type. The plan provides that distribution will occur incident to separation from service. In October 2016, the service provider states that he will terminate employment at the end of the month, and the service recipient's benefits specialist in charge of plan administration is advised accordingly. The service provider later reverses the decision to terminate and continues to work for the service recipient, but the service recipient distributes the service provider's entire balance of $11,000, including deferrals and income, in December 2016. Even though the service provider is still employed by the service recipient and even if the plan does not provide for cash-outs, the distribution can be characterized as a discretionary cash-out of small benefits by the service recipient that is not in violation of Section 409A (see **Q.72** and **Q.78**).

Example 4. A nonqualified defined contribution plan includes an account that is based upon a stock value, including any declared dividend. The recordkeeper overlooks a dividend and, as a result, the reported account balances for all participants are inaccurate. As long as no distributions are made based on the inaccurate account balance values, no operational error has occurred for purposes of Section 409A which requires correction under the IRS correction procedures. The recordkeeper need only record the correct account balances to reflect the missed dividend credits.

Citation: Treas. Reg. §§ 1.409A-3(c), (d), (g) and (j)(4)(v).

Q.244 WHAT CORRECTION IS AVAILABLE FOR FAILURE TO DEFER COMPENSATION PURSUANT TO THE PLAN, THE SERVICE PROVIDER'S DEFERRAL ELECTION, AND SECTION 409A?

NOTE: This **Q.244** does not address correction of early payment to a specified employee that should have been delayed for six months after separation from service. See **Q.246** for available corrections.

i. Correction may be made in the calendar year of error. The correction may be made as follows:
- This correction is available to both insiders and non-insiders. Special rules apply to insiders (see **Q.252** for definition of insider.)
- In general, the service provider must repay the amount distributed in error by the end of the calendar year of error. For this purpose, the amount distributed in error generally includes not only the net amount received by the service provider but also any amounts withheld by the service recipient, including any payroll and income taxes. Federal taxes withheld need not be repaid if the service recipient makes an adjustment on Form 941X based on the amounts withheld from the early distribution. The same is true if the service recipient makes a corresponding adjustment for state tax.
- Repayment may occur in installments by future salary reduction completed in the same taxable year. In this event, interest is applied to the declining balance due in the case of an insider.
- If the service provider is not an insider at any time during the calendar year and repayment within the same calendar year would cause an immediate and heavy financial need for purposes of Code Section 401(k), repayment can be spread by agreement over up to 24 months from the due date (without extensions) of the

service provider's federal income tax return for the year of error, plus interest on the declining balance due.
- If the amount distributed in error exceeds the limitation on elective deferrals provided for in Section 402(g)(1)(B) for the year of error and the service provider is an insider at any time during the calendar year, the service provider is required to pay interest on the amount distributed in error from the date of error to the date of repayment. Interest is calculated by applying the annually compounded interest rate described in the next paragraph, dividing the number of days in the period between error and correction by the number of days in the calendar year.
- The interest rate applied in any case cannot be less than the annually compounded short-term applicable federal rate (AFR) for the month of error. Interest on installments is applied to the declining balance due from time to time.
- Upon repayment or agreement to repay, the service provider must have the same right to deferred compensation under the plan as if the error had not occurred, including the time and form of distribution.
- Adjustment of the service provider's account balance or other deferred compensation for earnings or losses retroactive to the date of error is optional. Any adjustment must occur by the end of the year of error.
- The service recipient must take commercially reasonable steps to avoid recurrence of a similar operational failure, in this case by making sure that service providers' deferral elections are properly designed and implemented on time.
- This correction is not available if during the calendar year of error the service recipient is experiencing a substantial financial downturn or other issues which indicate a significant risk of nonpayment when due (see **Q.62**).
- For additional reporting and disclosure requirements, see **Q.255**.

FEDERAL INCOME TAX CONSEQUENCES: The amount paid in error is not includible in the service provider's income for federal tax purposes. Any interest paid by the service provider to the service recipient in connection with repayment is income to the service recipient. If repayment is accomplished by means of future salary reductions, the salary reduction amount (including any interest component) is treated as income to the service provider and must be reported as wages on Form W-2 for the year of the salary reduction installments and included in the service provider's income on Form 1040 for the same year.

Citation: Notice 2008–113, § IV.A, modified by Notice 2010–6, § XIII.A with respect to adjustment of the repayment amount for withheld taxes.

ii. Correction may be made in the calendar year following the calendar year of error. The correction may be made as follows:
- This correction is available only if the service provider is not an insider at any time in either calendar year (see **Q.252** for definition of insider).
- In general, the service provider must repay the amount distributed in error by the end of the calendar year following the calendar year of error, plus interest from the date of error to the date of repayment. For this purpose, the amount distributed in error generally includes not only the net amount received by the service provider but also any amounts withheld by the service recipient, including any payroll and income taxes.
- There is a partial exception if the amount paid in error would have been paid in the calendar year following the year of error if there had been no error. In that case, repayment of the amount distributed in error is not required, but interest must be paid for the period from the date of error to the first day payment could have been made in compliance with the plan terms.
- Repayment may occur in installments completed in the calendar year following the error, such as by future salary reductions, plus interest on the declining balance due.
- In addition, if repayment by the end of the calendar year following the error would cause an immediate and heavy financial

need for purposes of Code Section 401(k), repayment can be spread by agreement over up to 24 months from the due date (without extensions) of the service provider's federal income tax return for the year of error, plus interest on the declining balance due.
- The interest rate applied in any case cannot be less than the annually compounded short-term applicable federal rate (AFR) for the month of error. If repayment occurs in installments, interest is applied to the declining balance due from time to time.
- Upon repayment or agreement to repay, the service provider must have the same right to deferred compensation under the plan as if the error had not occurred, including the time and form of distribution.
- Adjustment of the service provider's account balance or other deferred compensation for earnings or losses retroactive to the date of the error is optional. Any adjustment must occur by the end of the year of repayment.
- The service recipient must take commercially reasonable steps to avoid recurrence of a similar operational failure, in this case by making sure that service providers' deferral elections are properly designed and implemented on time.
- The service provider's federal income tax return for the year of error cannot be under IRS examination at the time of correction.
- This correction is not available if during the calendar year of error the service recipient is experiencing a substantial financial downturn or other issues which indicate a significant risk of nonpayment when due (see **Q.62**).
- For additional reporting and disclosure requirements, see **Q.255**.

FEDERAL INCOME TAX CONSEQUENCES: The amount paid in error is includible in the service provider's income for the year of error. The service provider is permitted a deduction for the amount paid in error for the year of repayment, but not for the interest paid. If repayment is accomplished by means of future salary reductions, both the amount repaid in correction of the error and the interest component of the salary reduction amount are treated as income to the service provider. They must be reported as wages on Form W-2 for the year of the salary reduction installments, and they must be included in the service provider's income on Form 1040 for the same year.

Citation: Notice 2008–113, § V.B.

iii. Correction may be made by the end of the second calendar year following the calendar year of error, if the amount involved does not exceed the limitation on elective deferrals under Code Section 402(g)(1)(B) (see **Q.251**) for the year of error.
- This correction method can be used in the alternative to the correction methods described in Parts ii and iv, subject to the limitation on the amount involved.
- This correction method is available to both insiders and non-insiders (see **Q.252** for definition of insider).
- All improperly distributed amounts paid to the service provider in a calendar year under all plans of the same type are aggregated in determining whether the amount involved satisfies the limitation on deferrals under Section 402(g)(1)(B). For this purpose, improperly distributed amounts include not only amounts that should have been deferred but were not deferred, but also previously deferred compensation paid before the year in which it was scheduled for payment.
- The service provider's federal income tax return for the year of error cannot be under IRS examination at the time of correction.
- The service recipient must report the amount distributed as Section 409A compensation subject to income tax and payroll tax on an original or corrected Form 1099 or W-2 for the year of error, using Code Z in Box 12 of Form W-2.
- The service provider must include the amount distributed as Section 409A income on an original or amended Form 1040 for the year of error. Such return must be filed no later than December 31 of the second year following the year of the error.
- The service recipient must take commercially reasonable steps to avoid recurrence of a similar operational failure by making sure that service providers' deferral elections are properly designed and implemented on time.
- For additional reporting and disclosure requirements, see **Q.255**.

FEDERAL INCOME TAX CONSEQUENCES: The amount paid in error is includible in the service provider's income for the year of error. The service provider is subject to the 20 percent additional tax on the amount involved, but not the premium interest tax.

Citation: Notice 2008–113, § VI.B.

iv. Correction may be made by the end of the second calendar year following the calendar year of error, notwithstanding the amount involved. The correction may be made as follows:
- This correction method can be used in the alternative to the correction methods described in Parts ii and iii.
- This correction is available to both insiders and non-insiders (see **Q.252** for definition of insider).
- The service provider must repay the amount distributed in error by the end of the second calendar year following the calendar year of error. For this purpose, the amount distributed in error generally includes not only the net amount received by the service provider but also any amounts withheld by the service recipient, including any payroll and income taxes.
- If the service provider is an insider, the service provider is required to pay interest on the amount distributed in error from the date of error to the date of repayment.
- If repayment by the insider occurs in installments, interest is required on the declining balance due.
- The interest rate applied in any case cannot be less than the annually compounded short-term applicable federal rate (AFR) for the month of error. Interest on installments is applied to the declining balance due from time to time. If payments span two calendar years, interest is compounded at the beginning of the second calendar year.
- Adjustment of the service provider's account balance or other deferred compensation for earnings or losses retroactive to the date of the error is optional. Any adjustment must occur by the deadline for repayment.
- This correction is not available if during the calendar year of error the service recipient is experiencing a substantial financial

downturn or other issues which indicate a significant risk of nonpayment when due (see **Q.62**).
- The service recipient must take commercially reasonable steps to avoid recurrence of a similar operational failure, in this case by making sure that service providers' deferral elections are properly designed and implemented on time.
- The service provider's federal income tax return for the year of error cannot be under IRS examination at the time of correction.
- The service recipient must report the amount involved as Section 409A compensation on an original or corrected Form 1099 or W-2 for the year of error, using Code Z in Box 12 of Form W-2.
- The service provider must include the amount involved as Section 409A income on an original or amended Form 1040 for the year of error. The return must be filed no later than December 31 of the second year following the year of the error.
- For additional reporting and disclosure requirements, see **Q.255**.

FEDERAL INCOME TAX CONSEQUENCES: The amount paid in error is includible in the service provider's income for the year of error. The service provider is subject to the 20 percent additional tax on the amount involved, but not the premium interest tax. The service provider is not entitled to a deduction for the amount repaid or any interest paid, but may apply that amount as basis against future deferred compensation under the plan. The service recipient is not subject to penalties for failure to withhold federal income taxes for the year of error.

Citation: Notice 2008–113, § VII.B.

Q.245 WHAT CORRECTION IS AVAILABLE FOR LATE DISTRIBUTION OF PREVIOUSLY DEFERRED COMPENSATION?

i. If the deferred compensation is distributed in the calendar year of error, correction is not available or necessary. Treasury Regulation § 1.409A-3(d) treats a payment as made on the date specified under the plan if the payment is made later in the same calendar year, or if later, by the 15th day of the third calendar month following the due date specified under the plan, provided that the service provider is not permitted to designate the calendar year of payment.

Citation: Notice 2008–113, § IV.C.

ii. Correction may be made in the calendar year following the calendar year of error as follows:
- This correction is available only if the service provider is not an insider at any time during either calendar year (see **Q.252** for definition of insider).
- The amount improperly deferred must be paid to the service provider, and the service provider's individual account or other deferred compensation under the plan must be adjusted to reflect this payment.
- The service recipient cannot pay interest to or otherwise compensate the service provider to reflect the time value of money with respect to the late payment.
- The service provider's account balance or other deferred compensation under the plan must be adjusted for any earnings accrued on the amount improperly deferred between the date of error and the date of correction. Adjustment for losses is optional.
- All payments and adjustments to the service provider's account under the plan, including the corrective distribution, corresponding reduction of the service provider's account balance or other deferred compensation and all adjustments due to earnings or losses, must occur by the end of the calendar year following the calendar year of error.
- The service provider's federal income tax return for the year of error cannot be under IRS examination at the time of correction.
- The service recipient must take commercially reasonable steps to avoid recurrence of a similar operational failure. In this case, the service recipient must establish practices and procedures designed to assure that distribution of service providers' deferred compensation occurs promptly and accurately.
- For additional reporting and disclosure requirements, see **Q.255**.

FEDERAL INCOME TAX CONSEQUENCES: The service recipient reports the distribution on Form 1099 or W-2 for the year of correction and the service provider includes the amount in income on Form 1040 for the same year. No additional income tax is due under Section 409A.

Citation: Notice 2008–113, § V.D, modified by Notice 2010–6, § XIII.B.

iii. Correction may be made by the end of the second calendar year following the calendar year of error if the amount involved does not exceed the limitation on elective deferrals under Code Section 402(g)(1)(B) (see **Q.251**) for the year of error. The correction may be made as follows:
  - This correction method can be used in the alternative to the correction methods described in Parts ii and iv, subject to the limitation on the amount involved.
  - This correction method is available to both insiders and non-insiders (see **Q.252** for definition of insider).
  - All amounts improperly deferred with respect to the service provider in a calendar year under all plans of the same type must be aggregated in determining whether the amount improperly deferred satisfies the limitation under Code Section 402(g)(1)(B). For this purpose, the amount improperly deferred includes not only amounts deferred in prior years that should have been distributed in the year of error but also amounts erroneously deferred during the year of error.
  - The amount improperly deferred must be paid to the service provider by the end of the second calendar year following the calendar year of error.
  - Any earnings allocable to the amount improperly deferred from the date of error through the date of correction must either be forfeited or paid to the service provider, and any losses during that period must either be permanently disregarded or reduce the amount paid to the service provider.
  - The service provider's federal income tax return for the year of error cannot be under IRS examination at the time of correction.

- The service recipient must report the amount involved as Section 409A compensation on Form 1099 or W-2 for the year of correction, using Code Z in Box 12 of Form W-2.
- The service provider must include the amount involved as Section 409A income on Form 1040 for the year of correction.
- The service recipient must take commercially reasonable steps to avoid recurrence of a similar operational failure. In this case, the service recipient must establish practices and procedures designed to assure that distribution of service providers' deferred compensation occurs promptly and accurately.
- For additional reporting and disclosure requirements, see **Q.255**.

FEDERAL INCOME TAX CONSEQUENCES: The amount improperly deferred is includible in the service provider's income for the year of correction. The service provider is subject to the 20 percent additional tax on the amount involved, but not the premium interest tax. The service recipient is not subject to penalties for failure to withhold federal income taxes for the year of error.

Citation: Notice 2008–113, § VI.C.

iv. Correction may be made by the end of the second calendar year following the calendar year of error, notwithstanding the amount involved. The correction may be made as follows:
   - This correction method can be used in the alternative to the correction methods described in Parts ii and iii.
   - This correction method is available to both insiders and non-insiders (see **Q.252** for definition of insider).
   - The amount improperly deferred must be paid to the service provider, and the service provider's individual account or other deferred compensation under the plan must be adjusted to reflect this payment.
   - The service recipient cannot pay interest to or otherwise compensate the service provider to reflect the time value of money with respect to the late payment.

- The service provider's account balance or other deferred compensation under the plan must be adjusted for any earnings accrued on the amount improperly deferred between the date of error and the date of correction. Adjustment for losses is optional.
- All payments and adjustments to the service provider's account under the plan, including the corrective distribution, corresponding reduction of the service provider's account balance or other deferred compensation and all adjustments due to earnings or losses, must occur by the end of the calendar year of correction.
- The service provider's federal income tax return for the year of error cannot be under IRS examination at the time of correction.
- The service recipient must report the amount involved as Section 409A compensation on an original or corrected Form 1099 or W-2 for the year of error, using Code Z in Box 12 of Form W-2.
- The service provider must include the amount involved as Section 409A income on an original or amended Form 1040 for the year of error. Such return must be filed no later than December 31 of the second year following the year of the error.
- The service recipient must take commercially reasonable steps to avoid recurrence of a similar operational failure. In this case, the service recipient must establish practices and procedures designed to assure that distribution of service providers' deferred compensation occurs promptly and accurately.
- For additional reporting and disclosure requirements, see **Q.255**.

FEDERAL INCOME TAX CONSEQUENCES: The amount improperly deferred is includible in the service provider's income for the year of error. The service provider is subject to the 20 percent additional tax on the amount involved, but not the premium interest tax. The service recipient is not subject to penalties for failure to withhold federal income tax for the year of error. The service provider may treat the amount improperly deferred as basis with respect to subsequent distributions under the plan.

Citation: Notice 2008–113, § VII.D.

Q.246 WHAT CORRECTION IS AVAILABLE IN THE CASE OF OTHERWISE PROPER PAYMENT OF AMOUNTS DUE A SPECIFIED EMPLOYEE UPON SEPARATION FROM SERVICE DURING THE SIX MONTHS FOLLOWING THE SEPARATION?

i. Correction may occur in the calendar year of error as follows:
- This correction method is available to both insiders and non-insiders (see **Q.252** for definition of insider).
- The service provider must repay the amount distributed in error by the end of the calendar year of error. For this purpose, the amount distributed in error generally includes not only the net amount received by the service provider but also any amounts withheld by the service recipient, including any payroll and income taxes. Federal taxes withheld need not be repaid if the service recipient makes an adjustment on Form 941X based on the amounts withheld from the early distribution. The same is true if the service recipient makes a corresponding adjustment for state tax.
- The service provider is not responsible for payment of interest for the period between the date of error and the date of correction.
- The plan must redistribute the amount paid in error at a later time.
- If correction occurs on or before expiration of six months after separation from service, the date the plan is required to redistribute the amount paid in error is determined by counting the number of days between the date of error and the date of the service provider's corrective repayment and adding that number of days to the date which is six months after the separation from service.
- If the service provider repays the early distribution after expiration of six months after separation from service, the date the plan is required to redistribute the amount paid in error is determined by counting the number of days between the date of error and the expiration of six months after the separation from service

and adding that number of days to the date of the service provider's corrective repayment.
- Adjustment of the service provider's account balance or other deferred compensation for losses retroactive to the date of error is optional. The service provider's account balance or other deferred compensation cannot be adjusted for earnings during that period. All adjustments must occur by the deadline for redistribution.
- The service recipient must take commercially reasonable steps to avoid recurrence of a similar operational failure, in this case by properly identifying specified employees in connection with their separation and delaying any payments otherwise due within six months after separation until six months after separation.
- This correction is not available if during the calendar year of error the service recipient is experiencing a substantial financial downturn or other issues which indicate a significant risk of nonpayment when due (see **Q.62**).
- For additional reporting and disclosure requirements, see **Q.255**.

FEDERAL INCOME TAX CONSEQUENCES: The amount distributed in error is not includible in the service provider's income for federal tax purposes. The plan's subsequent distribution is treated as compensation to the service provider on Forms W-2 or 1099 and 1040 and is subject to employment taxes. The year the service recipient deducts the distribution depends on the service recipient's method of accounting.

Citation: Notice 2008–113, § IV.B, modified by Notice 2010–6, § XIII.A with respect to adjustment of the repayment amount for withheld taxes.

ii. Correction may be made in the calendar year following the calendar year of error as follows:
- The service provider cannot be an insider at any time during either calendar year (see **Q.252** for definition of insider).
- The service provider must repay the amount distributed in error by the end of the calendar year following the calendar year of error. For this purpose, the amount distributed in error generally

includes not only the net amount received by the service provider but also any amounts withheld by the service recipient, including any payroll and income taxes.
- The service provider will not be responsible for payment of interest for the period between the date of error and the date of correction.
- The plan must redistribute the amount involved at a later time. The redistribution date is determined by counting the number of days between the date of error and the date of expiration of six months after the service provider's separation and adding that number of days to the date of the service provider's corrective repayment.
- Adjustment of the service provider's account balance or other deferred compensation under the plan for losses on the amount of the error from the date of error to the date of the service provider's corrective repayment is optional. The service provider's account balance or other deferred compensation cannot be adjusted for earnings during that period. All adjustments must occur by the deadline for redistribution.
- The service recipient must take commercially reasonable steps to avoid recurrence of a similar operational failure, in this case by properly identifying specified employees in connection with their separation and delaying any payments otherwise due within six months after separation until expiration of six months after separation.
- The service provider's federal income tax return for the year of error cannot be under IRS examination at the time of correction.
- This correction is not available if during the calendar year of error the service recipient is experiencing a substantial financial downturn or other issues which indicate a significant risk of non-payment when due (see **Q.62**).
- For additional reporting and disclosure requirements, see **Q.255**.

FEDERAL INCOME TAX CONSEQUENCES: The amount distributed in error is includible in the service provider's income for the calendar year of error. If both the service provider's corrective repayment and the plan's subsequent redistribution occur within the calendar year following the year of error, the service recipient does not report the plan's subsequent redistribution as compensation to the service provider, the service provider does not include the subsequent redistribution in income, and the service provider cannot deduct the corrective repayment. If the service provider's corrective repayment occurs in the calendar year after the calendar year of error but the plan's subsequent redistribution does not occur until the second calendar year following the year of error, the service recipient must report the plan's subsequent redistribution as compensation to the service provider, the service provider can deduct the corrective repayment, and the service provider recognizes the plan's subsequent redistribution as income under federal income tax law. Alternatively, if the service provider's compensation is reduced in lieu of corrective repayment, the compensation foregone is treated as compensation to the service provider and the service provider can deduct such repayment amount.

Citation: Notice 2008–113, § V.C.

iii. Correction may be made by the end of the second calendar year following the calendar year of error if the amount involved does not exceed the limitation on elective deferrals under Code Section 402(g)(1)(B) (see **Q.251**) for the year of error. The correction may be made as follows:
- This correction method can be used in the alternative to the correction methods described in Parts ii and iv, subject to the limitation on the amount involved.
- This correction method is available to both insiders and non-insiders (see **Q.252** for definition of insider).
- All amounts improperly distributed to the service provider in a calendar year under all plans of the same type are aggregated in determining whether the improperly distributed amount satisfies the limitation under Section 402(g)(1)(B). For this purpose, amounts improperly distributed include not only amounts erroneously distributed to a specified employee before expiration of six months after separation from service, but also other

amounts deferred in prior years and distributed more than 30 days before schedule during the year of error and amounts that should have been deferred but were not deferred during the year of error.
- The service provider's federal income tax return for the year of error cannot be under IRS examination at the time of correction.
- The service recipient must report the amount distributed as Section 409A compensation subject to income tax and payroll tax on an original or corrected Form 1099 or W-2 for the year of error, using Code Z in Box 12 of Form W-2.
- The service provider must include the amount distributed as Section 409A income on an original or amended Form 1040 for the year of error. Such return must be filed by December 31 of the second calendar year following the year of the error.
- This correction is not available if during the calendar year of error the service recipient is experiencing a substantial financial downturn or other issues which indicate a significant risk of non-payment when due (see **Q.62**).
- The service recipient must take commercially reasonable steps to avoid recurrence of a similar operational failure, in this case by properly identifying specified employees in connection with their separation and delaying any payments otherwise due within six months after separation until expiration of six months after separation.
- For additional reporting and disclosure requirements, see **Q.255**.

FEDERAL INCOME TAX CONSEQUENCES: The amount distributed in error is includible in the service provider's income for the year of error. The service provider is subject to the 20 percent additional tax on the amount involved, but not the premium interest tax.

Citation: Notice 2008–113, § VI.B.

iv. Correction may be made by the end of the second calendar year following the calendar year of error, notwithstanding the amount involved. The correction may be made as follows:

- This correction method can be used in the alternative to the correction methods described in Parts ii and iii.
- This correction method is available to both insiders and non-insiders (see **Q.252** for definition of insider).
- The service provider must repay the amount distributed in error by the end of the second calendar year following the calendar year of error. For this purpose, the amount distributed in error generally includes not only the net amount received by the service provider but also any amounts withheld by the service recipient, including any payroll and income taxes.
- The service provider will not be responsible for payment of earnings, but may adjust for losses for the period between the date of error and the date of the service provider's corrective repayment, provided any adjustment for losses is made by the deadline for repayment.
- The plan must redistribute the amount involved at a later time. The redistribution date is determined by counting the number of days between the date of error and the expiration of six months after the service provider's separation from service, and adding that number of days to the date of the service provider's corrective repayment.
- This correction is not available if during the calendar year of error the service recipient is experiencing a substantial financial downturn or other issues which indicate a significant risk of nonpayment when due (see **Q.62**).
- The service recipient must take commercially reasonable steps to avoid recurrence of a similar operational failure, in this case by properly identifying specified employees in connection with their separation and delaying any payments otherwise due within six months after separation until expiration of six months after separation.
- The service provider's federal income tax return for the year of error cannot be under IRS examination at the time of correction.
- The service recipient must report the amount involved as Section 409A compensation on an original or corrected Form W-2 for the year of error, using Code Z in Box 12 of Form W-2.

- The service provider must include the amount involved as Section 409A income on an original or amended Form 1040 for the year of error. Such return must be filed no later than December 31 of the second year following the year of the error.
- For additional reporting and disclosure requirements, see **Q.255**.

FEDERAL INCOME TAX CONSEQUENCES: The amount distributed in error is includible in the service provider's income for the year of error. The service provider is subject to the 20 percent additional tax on the amount involved, but not the premium interest tax. The service recipient is not subject to penalties for failure to withhold federal income taxes for the year of error. The amount repaid by the service provider is not deductible for the year of repayment but may be treated as basis with respect to subsequent distributions under the plan.

Citation: Notice 2008–113, § VII.C.

Q.247 WHAT CORRECTION IS AVAILABLE IF THE AMOUNT DEFERRED ON BEHALF OF A SERVICE PROVIDER UNDER THE PLAN IS GREATER THAN PROVIDED FOR IN THE PLAN OR THE SERVICE PROVIDER'S DEFERRAL ELECTION?

i. Correction may be made in the calendar year of error as follows:
- This correction is available to both insiders and non-insiders (see **Q.252** for definition of insider).
- The amount deferred in error must be paid to the service provider, and the service provider's individual account or other deferred compensation under the plan must be adjusted to reflect this payment during the calendar year of error.
- The service recipient may pay reasonable interest or other reasonable compensation for the use of the amount improperly deferred from the date of error to the date of correction.
- If the service provider is an insider at any time during the year of error, the service provider's account balance or other deferred

compensation under the plan must be adjusted for earnings accrued on the amount improperly deferred between the date of error and the date of correction. Adjustment for losses is optional.
- If the service provider is not an insider at any time during the year of error, adjustments for both income and losses are optional.
- All payments and adjustments to the service provider's account under the plan, including the corrective distribution, corresponding reduction of the service provider's account balance or other deferred compensation, all adjustments due to earnings or losses, and any payments to the service provider reflecting the time value of the money, must occur by the end of the calendar year of error.
- The service recipient must take commercially reasonable steps to avoid recurrence of a similar operational failure. In this case, the service recipient must establish practices and procedures designed to assure that deferrals are implemented promptly and accurately.
- For additional reporting and disclosure requirements, see **Q.255**.

FEDERAL INCOME TAX CONSEQUENCES: The service recipient reports the distribution on Form 1099 or W-2 for the year of correction and the service provider includes the amount in income on Form 1040 for the same year.

Citation: Notice 2008–113, § IV.C.

ii. Correction may be made in the calendar year following the calendar year of error as follows:
- This correction is available only if the service provider is not an insider at any time during either calendar year. (See **Q.252** for definition of insider.)
- The amount improperly deferred must be paid to the service provider and the service provider's individual account or other deferred compensation under the plan must be adjusted to reflect this payment.
- The service recipient cannot pay interest to or otherwise compensate the service provider to reflect the time value of money with respect to the late payment.

- The service provider's account balance or other deferred compensation under the plan must be adjusted for any earnings accrued on the amount improperly deferred between the date of error and the date of correction. Adjustment for losses is optional.
- All payments and adjustments to the service provider's account under the plan, including the corrective distribution, corresponding reduction of the service provider's account balance or other deferred compensation, and all adjustments due to earnings or losses, must occur by the end of the calendar year following the calendar year of error.
- The service provider's federal income tax return for the year of error cannot be under IRS examination at the time of correction.
- The service recipient must take commercially reasonable steps to avoid recurrence of a similar operational failure. In this case, the service recipient must establish practices and procedures designed to assure that employees' deferral elections are implemented promptly and accurately.
- For additional reporting and disclosure requirements, see **Q.255**.

FEDERAL INCOME TAX CONSEQUENCES: The service recipient reports the distribution on Form 1099 or W-2 for the year of correction and the service provider includes the amount in income on Form 1040 for the same year. No additional income tax is due under Section 409A.

Citation: Notice 2008–113, § V.D.

iii. Correction may be made by the end of the second calendar year following the calendar year of error if the amount involved does not exceed the limitation on elective deferrals under Code Section 402(g)(1)(B) (see **Q.251**) for the year of error. The correction may be made as follows:
- This correction method can be used in the alternative to the correction methods described in Parts ii and iv, subject to the limitation on the amount involved.

- This correction method is available to both insiders and non-insiders (see **Q.252** for definition of insider).
- All amounts improperly deferred with respect to the service provider in a calendar year under all plans of the same type must be aggregated in determining whether the amount improperly deferred satisfies the limitation under Section 402(g)(1)(B). For this purpose, the amount improperly deferred includes not only amounts erroneously deferred during the year of error, but also amounts deferred in prior years that should have been distributed during the year of error.
- The amount improperly deferred must be paid to the service provider by the end of the second calendar year following the calendar year of error.
- Any earnings allocable to the amount improperly deferred from the date of error through the date of correction must be forfeited or paid to the service provider, and any losses during that period must be permanently disregarded or reduce the amount paid to the service provider.
- The service provider's federal income tax return for the year of error cannot be under IRS examination at the time of correction.
- The service recipient must report the amount involved as Section 409A compensation on Form 1099 or W-2 for the year of correction, using Code Z in Box 12 of Form W-2.
- The service provider must include the amount involved as Section 409A income on Form 1040 for the year of correction.
- The service recipient must take commercially reasonable steps to avoid recurrence of a similar operational failure. In this case, the service recipient must establish practices and procedures designed to assure that employees' deferral elections are implemented promptly and accurately.
- For additional reporting and disclosure requirements, see **Q.255**.

FEDERAL INCOME TAX CONSEQUENCES: The amount improperly deferred is includible in the service provider's income for the year of correction. The service provider is subject to the 20 percent additional tax on the amount involved, but not the premium interest tax. The service recipient is not subject to penalties for failure to withhold federal income taxes for the year of error.

Citation: Notice 2008–113, § VI.C.

iv. Correction may be made by the end of the second calendar year following the calendar year of error as follows, notwithstanding the amount involved.
   - This correction method can be used in the alternative to the correction methods described in Parts ii and iii.
   - This correction method is available to both insiders and non-insiders (see **Q.252** for definition of insider).
   - The amount improperly deferred must be paid to the service provider and the service provider's individual account or other deferred compensation under the plan must be adjusted to reflect this payment.
   - The service recipient cannot pay interest to or otherwise compensate the service provider to reflect the time value of money with respect to the late payment.
   - The service provider's account balance or other deferred compensation under the plan must be adjusted for any earnings accrued on the amount improperly deferred between the date of error and the date of correction. Adjustment for losses is optional.
   - All payments and adjustments to the service provider's account under the plan, including the corrective distribution, corresponding reduction of the service provider's account balance or other deferred compensation, and all adjustments due to earnings or losses, must occur by the end of the calendar year of correction.
   - The service provider's federal income tax return for the year of error cannot be under IRS examination at the time of correction.
   - The service recipient must report the amount involved as Section 409A compensation on an original or corrected Form 1099 or W-2 for the year of error, using Code Z in Box 12 of Form W-2.
   - The service provider must include the amount involved as Section 409A income on an original or amended Form 1040 for the

year of error. Such return must be filed no later than December 31 of the second year following the year of the error.
- The service recipient must take commercially reasonable steps to avoid recurrence of a similar operational failure. In this case, the service recipient must establish practices and procedures designed to assure that employees' deferral elections are implemented promptly and accurately.
- For additional reporting and disclosure requirements, see **Q.255**.

FEDERAL INCOME TAX CONSEQUENCES: The amount improperly deferred is includible in the service provider's income for the year of error. The service provider is subject to the 20 percent additional tax on the amount involved, but not the premium interest tax. The service recipient is not subject to penalties for failure to withhold federal income tax for the year of error. The service provider may treat the amount improperly deferred as basis with respect to subsequent distributions under the plan.

Citation: Notice 2008–113, § VII.D.

Q.248 WHAT CORRECTION IS AVAILABLE FOR PAYMENT OF DEFERRED COMPENSATION BEFORE THE CALENDAR YEAR IT IS SCHEDULED TO BE PAID?

NOTE: This **Q.248** does not address correction of early payment to a specified employee that should have been delayed for six months after separation from service. See **Q.246** for available corrections.

i. Correction may be made in the calendar year of error as follows:
- This correction is available to both insiders and non-insiders (see **Q.252** for definition of insider).
- In general, the service provider must repay the amount distributed in error by the end of the calendar year of error. For this purpose, the amount distributed in error generally includes not only the net amount received by the service provider but also any amounts withheld by the service recipient, including any payroll

and income taxes. Federal taxes withheld need not be repaid if the service recipient makes an adjustment on Form 941X based on the amounts withheld from the early distribution. The same is true if the service recipient makes a corresponding adjustment for state tax.
- Repayment may occur in installments completed in the same calendar year, such as by future salary reduction. In that case, interest is applied to the declining balance due.
- In addition, if the service provider is not an insider at any time during the calendar year and repayment within the same calendar year would cause an immediate and heavy financial need for purposes of Code Section 401(k), repayment can be spread by agreement over up to 24 months from the due date (without extensions) of the service provider's federal income tax return for the year of error, plus interest on the installments.
- If the amount distributed in error exceeds the limitation on elective deferrals provided for in Section 402(g)(1)(B) for the year of error and the service provider is an insider at any time during the calendar year, the service provider is required to pay interest on the amount distributed in error from the date of error to the date of repayment.
- The interest rate applied in any case cannot be less than the annually compounded short-term applicable federal rate (AFR) for the month of error. Interest on installments is applied to the declining balance due from time to time.
- Upon repayment or agreement to repay, the service provider must have the same right to deferred compensation under the plan as if the error had not occurred, including the time and form of distribution.
- Adjustment of the service provider's account balance or other deferred compensation for earnings or losses retroactive to the date of error is optional. Any adjustment must occur by the end of the year of error.
- The service recipient must take commercially reasonable steps to avoid recurrence of a similar operational failure, in this case

by making sure that service providers' distribution elections are properly designed and implemented.
- This correction is not available if during the calendar year of error the service recipient is experiencing a substantial financial downturn or other issues which indicate a significant risk of nonpayment when due (see **Q.62**).
- For additional reporting and disclosure requirements, see **Q.255**.
- Under the general rule (see **Q.93**), reimbursement cannot be made by offset against amounts owed to the service provider under the plan.

FEDERAL INCOME TAX CONSEQUENCES: The amount paid in error is not includible in the service provider's income for federal tax purposes. Any interest paid by the service provider to the service recipient in connection with repayment is income to the service recipient. If repayment is accomplished by means of future salary reductions, the interest component of the salary reduction amount is treated as income to the service provider and must be reported as wages on Form W-2 for the year of the salary reduction installments and included in the service provider's income on Form 1040 for the same year.

Citation: Notice 2008–113, § IV.A, modified by Notice 2010–6, § XIII.A with respect to adjustment of the repayment amount for withheld taxes.

ii. Correction may be made in the calendar year following the calendar year of error as follows:
- This correction is available only if the service provider is not an insider at any time in either calendar year (see **Q.252** for definition of insider).
- In general, the service provider must repay the amount distributed in error by the end of the calendar year following the calendar year of error, plus interest from the date of error to the date of repayment. For this purpose, the amount distributed in error generally includes not only the net amount received by the

service provider but also any amounts withheld by the service recipient, including any payroll and income taxes.
- There is a partial exception if the amount paid in error would have been paid in the calendar year following the error had there been no error. In that case, repayment of the amount distributed in error is not required, but interest must be paid for the period from the date of error to the first day of the following calendar year.
- Repayment may occur in installments completed in the calendar year following the calendar year of error, such as by future salary reductions, plus interest on the declining balance due.
- In addition, if repayment by the end of the calendar year following the error would cause an immediate and heavy financial need for purposes of Code Section 401(k), repayment can be spread by agreement over up to 24 months from the due date (without extensions) of the service provider's federal income tax return for the year of error, plus interest on the declining balance due.
- The interest rate applied in any case cannot be less than the annually compounded short-term applicable federal rate (AFR) for the month of error. If repayment occurs in installments, interest is applied to the declining balance due from time to time.
- Upon repayment or agreement to repay, the service provider must have the same right to deferred compensation under the plan as if the error had not occurred, including the time and form of distribution.
- Adjustment of the service provider's account balance or other deferred compensation for earnings or losses retroactive to the date of error is optional. Any adjustment must occur by the end of the year of repayment.
- The service recipient must take commercially reasonable steps to avoid recurrence of a similar operational failure, in this case by making sure that service providers' distribution elections are properly designed and implemented.
- The service provider's federal income tax return for the year of error cannot be under IRS examination at the time of correction.

- This correction is not available if during the calendar year of error the service recipient is experiencing a substantial financial downturn or other issues which indicate a significant risk of non-payment when due (see **Q.62**).
- For additional reporting and disclosure requirements, see **Q.255**.
- Under the general rule (see **Q.93**) reimbursement cannot be made by offset against amounts owed to the service provider under the plan.

FEDERAL INCOME TAX CONSEQUENCES: The amount paid in error is includible in the service provider's income for the year of error. The service provider is permitted a deduction for the amount paid in error for the year of repayment, but not for the interest. If repayment is accomplished by means of future salary reductions, both the amount repaid in correction of the error and the interest component of the salary reduction amount are treated as income to the service provider. They must be reported as wages on Form W-2 for the year of the salary reduction installments, and they must be included in the service provider's income on Form 1040 for the same year.

Citation: Notice 2008–113, § V.B.

iii. Correction may be made by the end of the second calendar year following the calendar year of error if the amount involved does not exceed the limitation on elective deferrals under Code Section 402(g)(1)(B) (see **Q.251**) for the year of error. The correction may be made as follows:
- This correction method can be used in the alternative to the correction methods described in Parts ii and iv, subject to the limitation on the amount involved.
- This correction method is available to both insiders and non-insiders (see **Q.252** for definition of insider).
- All amounts improperly distributed to the service provider in a calendar year under all plans of the same type are aggregated in determining whether the amount involved satisfies the limitation on deferrals under Section 402(g)(1)(B). For this purpose,

amounts improperly distributed include not only previously deferred compensation paid before the year in which it was scheduled for payment, but also amounts distributed that should have been deferred to a later year pursuant to the service provider's deferral election.
- The service provider's federal income tax return for the year of error cannot be under IRS examination at the time of correction.
- The service recipient must report the amount distributed as Section 409A compensation subject to income tax and payroll tax on an original or corrected Form 1099 or W-2 for the year of error, using Code Z in Box 12 of Form W-2.
- The service provider must include the amount distributed as Section 409A income on an original or amended Form 1040 for the year of error. The return must be filed by December 31 of the second calendar year following the year of the error.
- The service recipient must take commercially reasonable steps to avoid recurrence of a similar operational failure, in this case by making sure that service providers' distribution elections are properly implemented.
- For additional reporting and disclosure requirements, see **Q.255**.
- Under the general rule (see **Q.93**), reimbursement cannot be made by offset against amounts owed to the service provider under the plan.

FEDERAL INCOME TAX CONSEQUENCES: The amount paid in error is includible in the service provider's income for the year of error. The service provider is subject to the 20 percent additional tax on the amount involved, but not the premium interest tax.

Citation: Notice 2008–113, § VI.B.

iv. Correction may be made by the end of the second calendar year following the calendar year of error, notwithstanding the amount involved. The correction may be made as follows:
- This correction method can be used in the alternative to the correction methods described in Parts ii and iii.

- This correction method is available to both insiders and non-insiders (see **Q.252** for definition of insider).
- The service provider must repay the amount distributed in error by the end of the second calendar year following the calendar year of error. For this purpose, the amount distributed in error generally includes not only the net amount received by the service provider, but also any amounts withheld by the service recipient, including any payroll and income taxes.
- If the service provider is an insider, the service provider is required to pay interest on the amount distributed in error from the date of error to the date of repayment.
- If repayment occurs in installments, interest is required on the declining balance due.
- The interest rate applied in any case cannot be less than the annually compounded short-term applicable federal rate (AFR) for the month of error. Interest on installments is applied to the declining balance due from time to time. If payments span two calendar years, interest is compounded at the beginning of the second calendar year.
- Adjustment of the service provider's account balance or other deferred compensation for earnings or losses retroactive to the date of error is optional. Any adjustment must occur by the deadline for repayment.
- This correction is not available if during the calendar year of error the service recipient is experiencing a substantial financial downturn or other issues which indicate a significant risk of non-payment when due (see **Q.62**).
- The service recipient must take commercially reasonable steps to avoid recurrence of a similar operational failure, in this case by making sure that service providers' distribution elections are properly designed and implemented.
- The service provider's federal income tax return for the year of error cannot be under IRS examination at the time of correction.
- The service recipient must report the amount involved as Section 409A compensation on an original or corrected Form 1099 or W-2 for the year of error, using Code Z in Box 12 of Form W-2.

- The service provider must include the amount involved as Section 409A income on an original or amended Form 1040 for the year of error. Such return must be filed by December 31 of the second calendar year following the year of the error.
- For additional reporting and disclosure requirements, see **Q.255**.
- Under the general rule (see **Q.93**), reimbursement cannot be made by offset against amounts owed to the service provider under the plan.

FEDERAL INCOME TAX CONSEQUENCES: The amount paid in error is includible in the service provider's income for the year of error. The service provider is subject to the 20 percent additional tax on the amount involved, but not the premium interest tax. The service provider is not entitled to a deduction for the amount repaid or any interest paid, but may apply that amount as basis against future deferred compensation under the plan. The service recipient is not subject to penalties for failure to withhold federal income taxes for the year of error.

Citation: Notice 2008–113, § VII.C.

Q.249 WHAT CORRECTION IS AVAILABLE IF DISTRIBUTION OCCURS IN THE CORRECT CALENDAR YEAR BUT EARLIER THAN THE SCHEDULED DISTRIBUTION DATE?

i. No correction is required if the actual date of distribution is within 30 days of the date scheduled for distribution.

Treasury Regulation § 1.409A-3(d) gives a pass for this discrepancy, as long as the service provider does not have discretion to choose the taxable year of distribution.

Citation: Treas. Reg. § 1.409A-3(d).

ii. Correction may be made in the calendar year of error if the actual date of distribution is more than 30 days before the date scheduled for distribution. The correction may be made as follows:
- This correction method is available to both insiders and non-insiders (see **Q.252** for definition of insider).
- The service provider must repay the amount distributed in error by the end of the calendar year of error. For this purpose, the amount distributed in error generally includes not only the net amount received by the service provider but also any amounts withheld by the service recipient, including any payroll and income taxes. Federal taxes withheld need not be repaid if the service recipient makes an adjustment on Form 941X based on the amounts withheld from the early distribution. The same is true if the service recipient makes a corresponding adjustment for state tax.
- The service provider is not responsible for payment of interest for the period between the date of error and date of correction.
- The plan must redistribute the amount paid in error at a later time.
- If the service provider repays the amount on or before the scheduled distribution date, the date for redistribution is determined by counting the number of days between the date of error and the date of the service provider's corrective repayment and adding that number of days to the scheduled distribution date.
- If the service provider repays the amount after the scheduled distribution date, the date for redistribution is determined by counting the number of days between the date of error and the scheduled distribution date and adding that number of days to the date of the service provider's corrective repayment.
- Adjustment of the service provider's account balance or other deferred compensation for losses retroactive to the date of error is optional. The service provider's account balance or other deferred compensation cannot be adjusted for earnings during that period. All adjustments must occur by the deadline for redistribution.

- The service recipient must take commercially reasonable steps to avoid recurrence of a similar operational failure, in this case by making sure that distributions do not occur before schedule.
- This correction is not available if during the calendar year of error the service recipient is experiencing a substantial financial downturn or other issues which indicate a significant risk of nonpayment when due (see **Q.62**).
- For additional reporting and disclosure requirements, see **Q.255**.
- Under the general rule (see **Q.93**), reimbursement cannot be made by offset against amounts owed to the service provider under the plan.

FEDERAL INCOME TAX CONSEQUENCES: The amount distributed in error is not includible in the service provider's income for federal tax purposes. The plan's subsequent distribution is treated as compensation to the service provider on Forms W-2 or 1099 and 1040 and is subject to employment taxes. The year the service recipient deducts the distribution depends on the service recipient's method of accounting.

Citation: Notice 2008–113, § IV.B, modified by Notice 2010–6, § XIII.A with respect to adjustment of the repayment amount for withheld taxes.

iii. Correction may be made in the calendar year following the calendar year of error as follows:
- The service provider cannot be an insider at any time during either calendar year. (See **Q.252** for definition of insider.)
- The service provider must repay the amount distributed in error by the end of the calendar year following the calendar year of error. For this purpose, the amount distributed in error generally includes not only the net amount received by the service provider but also any amounts withheld by the service recipient, including any payroll and income taxes. Federal taxes withheld need not be repaid if the service recipient makes an adjustment on Form 941X based on the amounts withheld from the early distribution. The

same is true if the service recipient makes a corresponding adjustment for state tax.
- The service provider will not be responsible for payment of interest for the period between the date of error and date of correction.
- The plan must redistribute the amount involved at a later time. The redistribution date is determined by counting the number of days between the date of error and the scheduled distribution date and adding that number of days to the date of the service provider's corrective repayment.
- Adjustment of the service provider's account balance or other deferred compensation under the plan for losses on the amount of the error from the date of error to the date of the service provider's corrective repayment is optional. The service provider's account balance or other deferred compensation cannot be adjusted for earnings during that period. All adjustments must occur by the deadline for redistribution.
- The service recipient must take commercially reasonable steps to avoid recurrence of a similar operational failure, in this case by making sure that distributions do not occur before schedule.
- The service provider's federal income tax return for the year of error cannot be under IRS examination at the time of correction.
- This correction is not available if during the calendar year of error the service recipient is experiencing a substantial financial downturn or other issues which indicate a significant risk of nonpayment when due (see **Q.62**).
- For additional reporting and disclosure requirements, see **Q.255**.
- In no event may reimbursement be made by offset against amounts owed to the service provider under the plan.

FEDERAL INCOME TAX CONSEQUENCES: The amount distributed in error is includible in the service provider's income for the calendar year of error. If both the service provider's corrective repayment and the plan's subsequent redistribution occur within the calendar year following the year of error, the service recipient does not report the plan's subsequent redistribution as compensation to the service provider, the service provider does not include the subsequent redistribution in income, and the service provider cannot deduct the corrective repayment. If the service provider's corrective repayment occurs in the first calendar year following the calendar year of error, but the plan's subsequent redistribution does not occur until the second calendar year following the year of error, the service recipient must report the plan's subsequent redistribution as compensation to the service provider, the service provider can deduct the corrective repayment, and the service provider recognizes the plan's subsequent redistribution as income under federal income tax law. Alternatively, if the service provider's compensation is reduced in lieu of repayment, the compensation foregone is treated as compensation to the service provider and the service provider can deduct the repayment amount.

Citation: Notice 2008–113, § V.C, modified by Notice 2010–6, § XIII.A with respect to adjustment of the repayment amount for withheld taxes.

> iv. Correction may be made by the end of the second calendar year following the calendar year if the amount involved does not exceed the limitation on elective deferrals under Code Section 402(g)(1)(B) (see **Q.251**) for the year of error. The correction may be made as follows:
> - This correction method can be used in the alternative to the correction methods described in Parts iii and v, subject to the limitation on the amount involved.
> - This correction method is available to both insiders and non-insiders (see **Q.252** for definition of insider).
> - All amounts improperly distributed to the service provider in a calendar year under all plans of the same type are aggregated in determining whether the amount improperly distributed satisfies the limitation under Section 402(g)(1)(B). For this purpose, amounts improperly distributed include not only amounts distributed more than 30 days before schedule in the correct calendar year, but also erroneous distribution of previously deferred amounts, erroneous distribution of current compensation that the service provider elected to defer, and erroneous distributions

to specified employees before expiration of six months after separation from service during the same calendar year.
- The service provider's federal income tax return for the year of error cannot be under IRS examination at the time of correction.
- The service recipient must report the amount distributed as Section 409A compensation subject to income tax and payroll tax on an original or corrected Form 1099 or W-2 for the year of error, using Code Z in Box 12 of Form W-2.
- The service provider must include the amount distributed as Section 409A income on an original or amended Form 1040 for the year of error. The return must be filed by December 31 of the second calendar year following the year of the error.
- The service recipient must take commercially reasonable steps to avoid recurrence of a similar operational failure, in this case by making sure that distributions do not occur before schedule.
- This correction is not available if during the calendar year of error the service recipient is experiencing a substantial financial downturn or other issues which indicate a significant risk of nonpayment when due (see **Q.62**).
- For additional reporting and disclosure requirements, see **Q.255**.

FEDERAL INCOME TAX CONSEQUENCES: The amount distributed in error is includible in the service provider's income for the year of error. The service provider is subject to the 20 percent additional tax on the amount involved, but not the premium interest tax.

Citation: Notice 2008–113, § VI.B.

v. Correction may be made by the end of the second calendar year following the calendar year of error, notwithstanding the amount involved. Correction may be made as follows:
- This correction method can be used in the alternative to the correction methods described in Parts iii and iv.
- This correction method is available to both insiders and non-insiders (see **Q.252** for definition of insider).

- The service provider must repay the amount distributed in error by the end of the second calendar year following the calendar year of error. For this purpose, the amount distributed in error generally includes not only the net amount received by the service provider but also any amounts withheld by the service recipient, including any payroll and income taxes. Federal taxes withheld need not be repaid if the service recipient makes an adjustment on Form 941X based on the amounts withheld from the early distribution. The same is true if the service recipient makes a corresponding adjustment for state tax.
- The service provider will not be responsible for payment of earnings, but may adjust for losses, for the period between the date of error and the date of the service provider's corrective repayment, provided any adjustment for losses is made by the deadline for repayment.
- The plan must redistribute the amount involved at a later time. The redistribution date is determined by counting the number of days between the date of error and the scheduled distribution date and adding that number of days to the date of the service provider's corrective repayment.
- This correction is not available if during the calendar year of error the service recipient is experiencing a substantial financial downturn or other issues which indicate a significant risk of nonpayment when due (see **Q.62**).
- The service recipient must take commercially reasonable steps to avoid recurrence of a similar operational failure, in this case by making sure that distributions do not occur before schedule.
- The service provider's federal income tax return for the year of error cannot be under IRS examination at the time of correction.
- The service recipient must report the amount involved as Section 409A compensation on an original or corrected Form 1099 or W-2 for the year of error, using Code Z in Box 12 of Form W-2.
- The service provider must include the amount involved as Section 409A income on an original or amended Form 1040 for the year of error. Such return must be filed by December 31 of the second calendar year following the year of the error.

- For additional reporting and disclosure requirements, see **Q.255**.
- Under the general rule (see **Q.93**), reimbursement cannot be made by offset against amounts owed to the service provider under the plan.

FEDERAL INCOME TAX CONSEQUENCES: The amount paid in error is includible in the service provider's income for the year of error. The service provider is subject to the 20 percent additional tax on the amount involved, but not the premium interest tax. The service recipient is not subject to penalties for failure to withhold federal income taxes for the year of error. The amount repaid by the service provider is not deductible for the year of repayment but may be treated as basis with respect to subsequent distributions under the plan.

Citation: Notice 2008–113, § VII.C, modified by Notice 2010–6, § XIII.A with respect to adjustment of the repayment amount for withheld taxes.

Q.250 WHAT CORRECTION IS AVAILABLE FOR ERRONEOUSLY ESTABLISHING THE EXERCISE PRICE OF A STOCK RIGHT BELOW FAIR MARKET VALUE OF THE UNDERLYING STOCK ON THE DATE OF GRANT?

i. Correction may be made in the calendar year of error as follows:
   - This correction is available to both insiders and non-insiders (see **Q.252** for definition of insider).
   - The exercise price of the stock right must be reset to an amount not less than the fair market value of the underlying stock on the date of grant no later than the last day of the calendar year in which the stock right was granted or the date of exercise if earlier.
   - The service recipient must take commercially reasonable steps to avoid recurrence of a similar operational failure, in this case by making sure that future stock right grants have an exercise price

no less than the fair market value of the underlying stock on the date of grant.
- No additional reporting and disclosure requirements are required with respect to this correction (see **Q. 255**).

FEDERAL INCOME TAX CONSEQUENCES: The stock right will be treated as not providing for a deferral of compensation, and therefore will not be subject to Section 409A, assuming that all other requirements for exemption from Section 409A are satisfied (see **Q.154** and **Q.155**).

Citation: Notice 2008–113, §§ IV.D, IX.A.

ii. Correction may be made in the calendar year following the calendar year of error as follows:
- This correction is available only to non-insiders (see **Q.252** for definition of insider).
- The exercise price of the stock right must be reset to an amount not less than the fair market value of the underlying stock on the date of grant no later than the last day of the calendar year following the calendar year in which the stock right was granted or the date of exercise if earlier.
- The service recipient must take commercially reasonable steps to avoid recurrence of a similar operational failure, in this case by making sure that future stock right grants have an exercise price no less than the fair market value of the underlying stock on the date of grant.
- For additional reporting and disclosure requirements, see **Q.255**.

FEDERAL INCOME TAX CONSEQUENCES: The stock right will be treated as not providing for a deferral of compensation and will not be subject to Section 409A, assuming that all other requirements for exemption from Section 409A are satisfied (see **Q.154** and **Q.155**).

Citation: Notice 2008–113, §§ V.E, IX.A.

- Except as provided above, no correction is available for a stock right with an exercise price below fair market value on the date of grant.

Perhaps because of the negative public perception surrounding the backdating of options issued by certain public companies, the IRS provided only limited relief for stock rights priced below fair market value on the date of grant.

Q.251 WHAT IS THE LIMITATION ON ELECTIVE DEFERRALS UNDER SECTION 402(g)(1)(B) OF THE CODE?

The Section 402(g)(1)(B) dollar amount is equal to the maximum salary deferral amount which an individual who has not reached age 50 may contribute to a 401(k) or 403(b) plan for a calendar year. For 2017, this maximum amount is $18,000. This amount will be adjusted in future years in $500 increments to reflect cost-of-living adjustments.

Citation: I.R.C. §§ 402(g)(1)(B), (4); IR-2012–77.

Q.252 WHO IS AN INSIDER UNDER NOTICE 2008-113?

For this purpose, an insider is an employee or other service provider who is a director or officer of the service recipient or is a direct or indirect beneficial owner of more than 10 percent of any class of any equity security of the service recipient.

The threshold for 10 percent beneficial ownership is determined under Section 16 of the Securities Exchange Act of 1934. For this purpose, Section 16 applies to all types of service recipients, whether they are public or private, corporate or non-corporate.

For non-corporate entities without formal directors or officers, the beneficial ownership rules are applied by analogy. Logically, the terms director and officer should also be determined by analogy, but this is not directly addressed in the Notice.

If an individual is an insider with respect to a service recipient at any time in a calendar year, the individual is treated as an insider for the entire calendar year.

Citation: 17 C.F.R. §§ 240.13d-3 and 16a-1(f) (2012); Notice 2008–113, § III.G.

Q.253 IF THE TERM "OFFICER" IS DETERMINED BY REFERENCE TO THE SECTION 16 RULES WHEN IDENTIFYING WHO IS AN "INSIDER" FOR 409A CORRECTION PURPOSES, WHICH INDIVIDUALS WOULD BE CONSIDERED OFFICERS?

Regulations issued under Section 16 of the Securities Exchange Act of 1934 provide that the term "officer" means the following individuals associated with a business entity subject to the Act:

- The president;
- The principal financial officer;
- The principal accounting officer (or, if there is no such accounting officer, the controller);
- Any vice-president in charge of a principal business unit, division, or function (such as sales, administration, or finance); and
- Any other officer or person who performs a policy-making function for the employer. When the issuer is a limited partnership, officers or employees of the general partner(s) who perform policy-making functions for the limited partnership are deemed officers of the limited partnership. When the issuer is a trust, officers or employees of the trustee(s) who perform policy-making functions for the trust are deemed officers of the trust.

Citation: 17 C.F.R. § 240.16a-1(f).

Q.254 IF EARNINGS OR LOSSES ARE TO BE CREDITED IN CONNECTION WITH AN APPLICABLE CORRECTION, BUT IT IS ADMINISTRATIVELY IMPRACTICABLE TO MAKE THE ADJUSTMENT FOR EARNINGS OR LOSSES BY THE DEADLINE FOR CORRECTIONS SET FORTH IN NOTICE 2008-113, IS ANY RELIEF AVAILABLE?

If it is impractical to make the adjustment for earnings or losses by the applicable deadline set forth in Notice 2008–113, the adjustment will be treated as timely made if the service provider and service recipient have entered into a legally binding agreement to have such adjustment made.

Citation: Notice 2008–113, § III.I.

Q.255 WHAT ARE THE ADDITIONAL REPORTING AND DISCLOSURE REQUIREMENTS REGARDING CORRECTIONS PURSUANT TO NOTICE 2008-113?

The service recipient is required to attach the information contained in the sample statement below to its timely filed (including extensions) original federal income tax return for the year of correction.

For corrections that occur after the year of error, the service recipient is required to disclose substantially the same information to affected service providers by the due date of their Forms 1099 or W-2 for the year of correction (or January 31 of the following year, if no Form 1099 or W-2 is required). Affected service providers are required to attach substantially the same information to their timely filed (including extensions) original federal individual income tax returns for the year of correction.

The service recipient may report to the IRS with respect to all service providers affected by the same error under the same plan in a single statement as shown in the sample statement, but information provided to a service provider and a service provider's filing with the IRS should include only information pertaining to the particular service provider.

See **Appendix G** for sample statements for attachment to the service recipient and service provider's federal income tax returns for correction of an operational failure to comply with Section 409A pursuant to Notice 2008–113.

Citation: Notice 2008–113, § IX, modified by Notice 2010–80, § III.H.

MITIGATION—DISQUALIFICATION BY IRS EXAMINATION

Q.256 WHEN IS A SERVICE RECIPIENT CONSIDERED TO BE UNDER IRS EXAMINATION FOR PURPOSES OF THE DOCUMENTARY AND OPERATIONAL CORRECTION PROGRAMS?

Neither the documentary nor the operational correction program is available if either the service recipient or the service provider is under IRS examination at the time of correction.

A service recipient other than an individual is considered to be under examination for a year when the service recipient has received written notice from the IRS specifically identifying deferred compensation as an audit target. Otherwise, the correction programs would not be available to large businesses whose returns are perpetually under audit. If deferred compensation becomes a routine IRS audit focus for large businesses in the future, then the correction programs may be available to this group of service recipients only in limited circumstances.

An individual service recipient is considered to be under examination when the service recipient has received written notice from the IRS that his or her individual tax return is under examination. Unlike a service recipient other than an individual, any audit notice, whether or not deferred compensation is identified as an audit target, is sufficient to disqualify an individual service recipient from the documentary and operational correction programs.

Although this guidance is informal and was provided in a discussion of the documentary corrections program, it is appropriate to assume that it applies both to documentary and operational corrections because the purpose of the rule is the same in both cases.

Citation: Annotated Notice 2010–6, comments by Stephen Tackney, following § III.C.

Q.257 WHEN IS A SERVICE PROVIDER CONSIDERED TO BE UNDER IRS EXAMINATION FOR PURPOSES OF THE DOCUMENTARY AND OPERATIONAL CORRECTIONS PROGRAMS?

Neither the documentary nor the operational correction program is available if either the service recipient or the service provider is under IRS examination at the time of correction.

A service provider is considered to be under examination when the service provider has received written notice from the IRS that his or her individual tax return is under examination. Any audit notice, whether or not deferred compensation is identified as an audit target, is sufficient to disqualify a service provider from the documentary and operational correction programs.

Although this guidance is informal and was provided in a discussion of the documentary corrections program, it is appropriate to assume that it applies both to documentary and operational corrections because the purpose of the rule is the same in both cases.

Citation: Annotated Notice 2010–6, comments by Stephen Tackney and Keith Ranta, following § III.C.

Q.258 HOW SHOULD A SERVICE RECIPIENT THAT USES A CORRECTION PROCEDURE ADDRESS THE AUDIT STATUS OF ITS AFFECTED SERVICE PROVIDERS?

Neither the documentary nor the operational correction program is available if either the service recipient or the service provider is under IRS examination at the time of correction.

The service recipient generally does not know this kind of information about its service providers and the IRS does not intend to require that knowledge. Instead of asking all of its service providers to provide this information, the service recipient can simply notify all affected service providers that they are not eligible for relief if they are under audit. An affected service provider who is under audit at the time of correction will have to address the Section 409A issue with the IRS examiner.

Although this guidance is informal and was provided in a discussion of the documentary corrections program, it is appropriate to assume that it applies both to documentary and operational corrections because the purpose of the rule is the same in both cases.

Citation: Annotated Notice 2010–6, comments by Stephen Tackney, following § III.C.

Q.259 WHEN WILL A CORRECTION BE CONSIDERED COMPLETE FOR PURPOSES OF DETERMINING WHETHER THE SERVICE PROVIDER OR SERVICE RECIPIENT IS UNDER IRS EXAMINATION AT THE TIME OF CORRECTION?

Both the documentary and operational correction programs are available only if neither the service recipient nor the service provider is under examination at the time of correction.

Correction is considered complete when all legal steps have been taken to carry out the correction, except that a correction is not considered incomplete if the taxpayer receives an audit letter at a time when the only task remaining to be done is to file the required notices with income tax returns that are not yet due.

Although the authority for this rule is informal and was provided in a discussion of the documentary corrections program, it is appropriate to assume that it applies both to documentary and operational corrections.

Citation: Annotated Notice 2010–6, comments by Stephen Tackney, following § III.C.

Q.260 WHAT SHOULD A TAXPAYER DO IF THE IRS AUDITS THE TAXPAYER'S RETURN FOR A YEAR IN WHICH A CORRECTION AFTER THE YEAR OF ERROR OCCURRED?

If the IRS audits a taxpayer's federal income tax return for a year in which a correction after the year of error occurred, the taxpayer must make reasonable efforts to place the examining agent on notice when the audit begins that the taxpayer is relying on Notice 2008–113 for the years covered by the audit.

Citation: Notice 2008–113, § IX.B.

Q.261 WILL PARTICIPATION IN A CORRECTION PROGRAM INCREASE A TAXPAYER'S AUDIT RISK?

IRS representatives have stated that the Section 409A correction programs were not intended as an audit flag and are not used for that purpose. This makes sense as a practical matter, since an increase in audit risk would deter the compliance which is the goal of the correction programs. Nonetheless, taxpayers must weigh the protections of the corrections programs against the risk that accompanies the filing of any return attachment that raises compliance issues.

Although this guidance is informal and was provided in a discussion of the documentary corrections program, it is appropriate to assume that it applies both to documentary and operational corrections, since the purpose of the rule is the same in both cases.

Citation: Annotated Notice 2010–6, comments by John Richards, following § XII.A.

Q.262 IF AN OPERATIONAL FAILURE IS CORRECTED UNDER THE PRINCIPLES DESCRIBED IN NOTICE 2008-113 AND A SUBSTANTIALLY SIMILAR OPERATIONAL FAILURE SUBSEQUENTLY OCCURS, CAN THE SUBSEQUENT FAILURE BE CORRECTED BY APPLYING THESE PRINCIPLES AGAIN?

Correctional relief is not available for a subsequent operational failure substantially similar to one that was previously corrected unless incident to the earlier correction the employer established practices and procedures reasonably designed to ensure that the same type of operational failure would not recur and took commercially reasonable steps to avoid a recurrence, but the subsequent failure occurred despite the employer's diligent efforts.

Citation: Notice 2008–113, § III.B.

Q.263 WHY DOESN'T THE IRS OFFER A SECTION 409A CORRECTION PROGRAM LIKE THE EMPLOYEE PLANS COMPLIANCE RESOLUTION SYSTEM (EPCRS) FOR TAX-QUALIFIED RETIREMENT PLANS?

The EPCRS permits the employer to pay a sanction in return for relief from all negative tax consequences related to a particular violation of the Internal Revenue Code that would otherwise apply to a tax-qualified retirement plan, its associated trust or other funding medium, the employer maintaining the plan, and all of the individual active and former plan participants who are owed benefits under the plan.

Unlike a tax-qualified plan, a plan subject to Section 409A is not a separate taxable entity, and only the individual service providers affected by a violation of Section 409A realize adverse income tax consequences on account of the violation. Therefore, according to informal statements of IRS representatives, the IRS has not developed a broad program for relief in connection with violations of Section 409A.

Citation: Annotated Notice 2010–6, comments by Stephen Tackney, at the beginning of § I.

Q.264 WHAT OPTIONS ARE AVAILABLE IF A 409A FAILURE IS DISCOVERED WHEN CORRECTION IS NO LONGER AVAILABLE UNDER THE IRS CORRECTION GUIDANCE?

No good can arise from the discovery of a 409A failure after the last year when correction may be made under the published IRS guidance. It may be possible to avoid the harsh adverse consequences associated with a 409A violation if the limitations period for assessing tax with respect to the 409A violation has lapsed (see **Q.265** to **Q.268**).

Q.265 WHAT IS THE STATUTE OF LIMITATIONS FOR BREACH OF SECTION 409A?

The general statutes of limitations under the Internal Revenue Code with respect to income tax apply to liability for violation of Section 409A. The statute of limitations generally runs three years after the due date of the tax return for the taxable year in which the violation occurred or the actual filing date, whichever is later.

If the unreported income exceeds 25 percent of gross income, the statute of limitations runs six years after the due date of the tax return for the taxable year in which the violation occurred or the actual filing date, whichever is later.

The statute of limitations is unlimited in cases of fraud and failure to file a return.

Citation: I.R.C. §§ 6501(a), (c)(2) and (e); Prop. Treas. Reg. §§ 1.409A-4(a)(1)(ii) and (a)(3) and Preamble, Part III.E.2, I.R.B. 2008–51 (Dec. 22, 2008).

Q.266 HOW DO STATUTE OF LIMITATIONS PRINCIPLES APPLY IN THE CONTEXT OF 409A VIOLATIONS?

No continuing or permanent failure occurs with respect to a plan that violates 409A during an earlier year (see **Q.113**). Accordingly, each taxable year is analyzed independently to determine if a 409A failure has occurred. As a result, assessment of tax liabilities due to a plan's failure to comply with the requirements of 409A in a closed year (see **Q.265**) are time-barred if the plan complies with Section 409A in form and operation in subsequent years.

Example. A service provider wishes to elect to defer $100,000 of 2012 compensation until January 1, 2030. Under the plan's terms, her election must be made no later than December 31, 2011. However, she mistakenly fills out, dates, and files her election form on January 2, 2012. The plan administrator does not notice that her election is untimely, and $100,000 of the service provider's compensation is withheld and deferred in 2012. This operational failure is first discovered in 2025. The plan has been administered in full compliance with 409A in all years after 2012. Assessment of tax liabilities due to the plan's failure to comply with the requirements of 409A in 2012 are time-barred.

Citation: Preamble to 2008 Proposed 409A Regulations § II; Prop. Treas. Reg. § 1.409A-4(a)(1)(ii)(A).

Q.267 MAY A SERVICE RECIPIENT TAKE THE POSITION THAT THE ASSESSMENT OF 409A TAX LIABILITIES IS TIME-BARRED WHEN SUCH LIABILITIES ARISE FROM A FAILURE TO TIMELY DISTRIBUTE NONQUALIFIED DEFERRED COMPENSATION IN A CLOSED TAX YEAR?

Although the answer to this question is not free from doubt, a reasonable position exists that the assessment of taxes is time-barred in this situation based on the principles discussed in **Q.266**. This position is based on the assumption that no 409A violation with respect to the service provider occurs in any year after the year of the failure to distribute the deferred compensation. The IRS could make the argument, however, that the failure to distribute the deferred compensation creates a continuing documentary failure since the plan document does not explicitly provide for a time of payment with respect to the undistributed amounts. To minimize the force of this potential argument, the deferred compensation should be distributed as soon as possible after the failure to distribute is discovered.

Example. A service provider is due $100,000 in deferred compensation upon her separation from service in 2012, but the payment is not made. The parties discover the error in 2025, and distribution of all deferred amounts, plus earnings, is promptly made to the service provider. The service recipient reports the distribution as taxable income for 2025 but does not report a 409A violation based on the position that the assessment of 409A taxes is time-barred. Although the matter is not entirely free from doubt, the service recipient's position is reasonable given the absence of guidance on this issue.

Citation: Preamble to 2008 Proposed 409A Regulations § II; Prop. Treas. Reg. § 1.409A-4(a)(1)(ii)(A); for an excellent discussion of this issue, see Jeffrey W. Kroh and William P. Fogelman, *View from Groom: An Open (or Closed) Section 409A Case*, Pension and Benefits Daily (June 6, 2017).

Q.268 IF A SERVICE PROVIDER FAILS TO PROPERLY INCLUDE AMOUNTS IN INCOME ARISING FROM A SECTION 409A FAILURE, AND ASSESSMENT OF TAXES BECOMES BARRED BY THE STATUTE OF LIMITATIONS, CAN THE TAXPAYER CLAIM THAT SUCH AMOUNTS CAN NEVER BE TAXED?

No. The taxpayer's duty of consistency would prevent the service provider from claiming a tax benefit in a later year with respect to such amounts (such as, for example, by claiming any type of "basis" or "investment in the contract" in the year the service recipient paid such amount to the service provider pursuant to the plan's terms). In other words, a taxpayer who benefits from the statute of limitations with respect to a failure to recognize income under 409A in a closed year cannot take the position upon subsequent distribution that the income that should have been recognized in the prior closed year should not be treated as income for the subsequent year or that the amount that should have been treated as income in the prior closed year should be treated as basis in determining the amount that must be recognized as income in the subsequent year.

Example. On January 1, 2030, the service provider in the example in **Q.266** receives a distribution of $100,000 in deferred 2012 compensation, plus earnings, in accordance with her untimely election. She must include the entire amount in income in 2030. She cannot claim that part of the distribution is nontaxable merely because a portion of the distribution should have been taxed in 2012 as a result of the 409A operational failure.

Citation: Preamble to 2008 Proposed 409A Regulations § II.

EFFECTIVE DATES

Q.269 WHAT WAS THE STATUTORY EFFECTIVE DATE OF SECTION 409A?

By its terms, Section 409A applies generally on and after January 1, 2005. However, deferred amounts to which the service provider had a legally binding right and that were both earned and vested as of December 31, 2004, and earnings on such amounts under plans in existence on October 3, 2004, are not subject to Section 409A unless there is a material modification of the plan provisions governing those amounts after October 3, 2004. Amounts that were not both earned and vested as of December 31, 2004 are not grandfathered and therefore are subject to Section 409A, even if they were accrued under a plan which also includes amounts that are grandfathered.

Citation: Treas. Reg. § 1.409A-6(a)(1)(i).

Q.270 WHEN IS A GRANDFATHERED PLAN CONSIDERED TO HAVE BEEN MATERIALLY MODIFIED?

Deferred amounts that were both earned and vested as of December 31, 2004, and subsequent earnings on those amounts are eligible for grandfathering, as long as the plan under which they are subject is not materially modified after October 3, 2004 (see **Q.269**). For this purpose, material modification means the addition of a material benefit or right or the material enhancement of a benefit or right but not the exercise or reduction of an existing benefit, right or feature. The following are examples of actions will cause loss of grandfathered status:

- Accelerated vesting of amounts accrued but not vested as of October 3, 2004, even if the acceleration occurred before January 1, 2005.
- Addition of a haircut provision.
- Addition of a provision permitting the exercise of discretion.
- A plan amendment providing for distribution in the case of an unforeseeable emergency or for subsequent elections to change the time or form of payment.

Other actions affecting grandfathered plans would not constitute material modifications and would not cause loss of grandfathered status. These actions include:

- Removal of a haircut provision from a grandfathered plan.
- Exercise of discretion permitted under a provision included in a grandfathered plan on October 3, 2004.
- Establishment of or contributions to a rabbi trust to set aside a reserve to satisfy future obligations under a grandfathered plan.
- Amendment of a grandfathered plan to require compliance with a domestic relations order with respect to payments to an individual other than the service provider.
- Amendment of a grandfathered plan providing payment in the form of a life annuity to permit an election between the existing life annuity form and other actuarially equivalent forms of annuity payments.
- Amendment of a grandfathered plan to add a limited cash-out feature consistent with the limited cash-out feature allowed under a Section 409A-compliant plan.
- Termination of a grandfathered plan pursuant to the provisions of the plan.
- Addition of new notional investment options under an account balance plan to the extent that the new investment options are based on a predetermined actual investment, as defined in Treasury Regulation § 31.3121(b)(2)-1(d)(2) or a reasonable interest crediting rate.

If a plan is inadvertently materially modified in a way that causes loss of grandfathered treatment, grandfathered status may be preserved if the material modification is rescinded before the last day of the calendar year in which the change is made or before any new discretionary right is exercised, whichever occurs first.

Example. An employer modifies the terms of a grandfathered plan on March 1 to allow an employee to elect a new change in the time or form of payment without realizing that the change constitutes a material modification but rescinds the modification on the following November 1. The plan will not lose grandfathered treatment as long as no participant has elected to change the time or form of payment is made before November 1.

At a practical level, grandfathered amounts must be identifiable to claim the protection of grandfathering (see **Q.269**). If a single plan document governs grandfathered amounts and amounts subject to Section 409A, care must be taken not to cause an inadvertent material modification of the plan provisions governing the grandfathered amounts by plan amendment or restatement. Care must also be taken that the grandfathered assets remain subject to the prior plan rules in operation as well as form, being sure that any more favorable current rules are not inadvertently applied to the grandfathered amounts. To avoid such issues, some plan sponsors froze the plan governing the grandfathered amounts and created a separate new plan designed to comply with the requirements of Section 409A for amounts accrued but not vested as of December 31, 2004, and subsequent deferrals.

Citation: I.R.C. § 409A(D)(2)(B); Treas. Reg. § 1.409A-6(a)(1)-(4); *see also* American Jobs Creation Act of 2004, § 885(d); H.R. Conf. Rep. No. 108–755, 737 (Oct. 22, 2004).

Q.271 CAN A GRANDFATHERED PLAN BE AMENDED TO PERMIT ADDITION OF A LIFE INSURANCE CONTRACT FOR NOTIONAL INVESTMENT CREDITING PURPOSES WITHOUT CAUSING THE PLAN TO LOSE GRANDFATHERED STATUS?

Yes and no. The plan can be amended to add a notional investment measure, so addition of cash value increases under a life insurance contract as a measure of periodic investment return on a service provider's account is permitted.

Because it relates to mortality risk and not investment return, addition of the death benefit under a life insurance policy to increase the value of a service provider's account incident to death is unlikely to be treated as a notional investment measure.

In any event, the plan amendment should state that the plan remains unfunded for purposes of the Code and ERISA and has no ownership interest in any insurance policy.

Citation: Treas. Reg. § 1.409A-6(a)(4)(iv).

Q.272 IF A GRANDFATHERED PLAN IS AMENDED TO CHANGE THE FORM AND TIME OF PAYMENTS UNDER THE PLAN, WILL SUCH A MATERIAL MODIFICATION RESULT IN A VIOLATION OF SECTION 409A?

Exercise of discretion over the time and manner of payment of a benefit provided for under the terms of a grandfathered plan is permitted. To the extent that the grandfathered plan does not provide for discretion to alter the form or time of payments, an amendment to the plan altering the form or time of payment constitutes a new material benefit or right that causes the loss of grandfathered status (see **Q.269**).

It appears that if a materially modified grandfathered plan loses its grandfathered status but the plan complies in form and operation with the requirements of Section 409A as modified, Section 409A will not be applied retroactively to January 1, 2005 and no Section 409A violation results.

Example. An employer maintains a grandfathered plan not subject to Section 409A that provides that benefits will be paid in a lump sum upon separation from service. The employer amends the plan to provide prospectively that benefits will be paid in 20 annual installments rather than a lump sum. When amending the plan, the employer includes all documentary provisions required to comply with Section 409A. The plan complies with Section 409A on the effective date of the plan amendment. Consequently, Section 409A is not applied retroactively to January 1, 2005, and no breach of Section 409A occurs on account of the plan amendment.

Citation: Treas. Reg. § 1.409A-6(a)(1)(i), second sentence.

Q.273 HOW ARE AMOUNTS ELIGIBLE FOR GRANDFATHERING DETERMINED?

Account Balance Plans

The amount of compensation that is considered grandfathered under a grandfathered account balance plan is the portion of the service provider's account balance that was both earned and vested as of December 31, 2004, plus subsequent earnings on that portion of the account balance. For this purpose, a right to earnings that is subject either to a substantial risk of forfeiture or a requirement of performance of further services is not treated as earnings on the grandfathered amount, but a separate right to deferred compensation which is subject to Section 409A.

Example. On December 31, 2004, an executive has a fully vested right to a nonqualified deferred compensation account balance of $100,000. Interest on the account balance is credited based on the five-year Treasury rate. If the executive remains in employment with the employer to age 55, interest is retroactively recalculated based on the five-year Treasury rate plus one percent. As of December 31, 2004, the executive is age 45. The amount of the executive's grandfathered compensation is $100,000 plus interest at the five-year Treasury rate. If the executive works until age 55 and thereby earns the right to the additional one percent annual interest, the additional interest is not part of the grandfathered account balance because the right to the additional interest was subject to a substantial risk of forfeiture as of December 31, 2004 due to the risk that the executive would not remain in employment with the employer until age 55. Therefore, the additional interest is deferred compensation subject to the requirements of Section 409A.

Non-account Balance Plans

The amount of grandfathered compensation under a nonqualified deferred compensation plan that is a non-account balance plan equals the present value of the amount to which the service provider would have been entitled under the plan if the service provider voluntarily terminated employment without cause on December 31, 2004, and received payment of the benefits available from the plan on the earliest possible date allowed under the plan in the form of benefit with the greatest value. The grandfathered amount may increase after December 31, 2004, applying the interest rate used to determine the present value of the benefit as of December 31, 2004. The present value of the benefit may also increase as a result of the service provider's survival each year, applying the mortality assumptions used to calculate the present value of the grandfathered benefit as of December 31, 2004. The grandfathered amount cannot be increased after December 31, 2004, on account of either an increase in compensation under a final average pay plan or qualification for an early retirement subsidy after December 31, 2004. Any increase due to these factors after December 31, 2004 is subject to Section 409A.

Split-Dollar Life Insurance Programs

The grandfathered portion of a split-dollar life insurance program can be calculated by use of any reasonable method that allocates increases in cash value attributable to premiums earned and vested on or before December 31, 2004.

Citation: Treas. Reg. § 1.409A-6(a)(3).

Q.274 ARE GRANDFATHERED AMOUNTS SUBJECT TO ANY RESTRICTIONS ON DISTRIBUTION?

Yes. Although grandfathered plans need not satisfy the requirements of Section 409A, they must continue to satisfy governing plan provisions and the constructive receipt and other income tax rules in effect prior to the January 1, 2005 effective date of Section 409A (see **Q.114**).

Citation: I.R.C. § 409A(c).

Q.275 WHAT WAS THE EFFECTIVE DATE FOR ACTUAL COMPLIANCE WITH SECTION 409A?

Because of the complexity of the subject matter, it took a long time to develop the regulatory framework for enforcement of Section 409A. Final regulations were published in April 2007 and, after a series of extensions, became generally applicable for service providers' taxable years beginning on or after January 1, 2009, with respect to both documentary and operational compliance. However, Notice 2010–6 permitted retroactive correction of documentary errors through December 31, 2010, effective retroactive to January 1, 2009 (see **Q.224**).

Citation: Notice 2007–86, extending Treas. Reg. § 1.409A-6(b) (original effective date January 1, 2008).

Q.276 WHAT WERE THE STANDARDS FOR COMPLIANCE WITH SECTION 409A FOR THE TRANSITION PERIOD BETWEEN THE STATUTORY EFFECTIVE DATE, JANUARY 1, 2005, AND DECEMBER 31, 2008?

Section 409A became applicable by its terms as of January 1, 2005. Final regulations were not issued until 2007 and the operational effective date was extended on a year-to-year basis to January 1, 2009. In the intervening transition period, taxpayers were required to operate in good faith compliance with Section 409A and IRS guidance issued during the transition period, including proposed and final regulations and IRS notices. A plan's good faith compliance during the transition period need not be documented in the plan, but good faith compliance must be demonstrable on audit, which requires at the least adequate documentation of the way the plan was administered.

Citation: *See, e.g.*, Notice 2005–1, Q&A 19.

Q.277 HAS CONGRESS EVER INTRODUCED LEGISLATION TO REPEAL SECTION 409A?

Yes. Early versions of the 2017 Tax Cuts and Jobs Creation Act in both the House and Senate would have repealed Section 409A and replaced it with a regime under which nonqualified deferred compensation would have been taxed in the first taxable year in which there was no substantial risk of forfeiture with respect to such deferred compensation. This "repeal and replace" arrangement would have become effective for services performed on and after January 1, 2018, creating a construct similar to that applicable to tax-exempt employers under I.R.C. §457(f) (see **Q.279**). The Joint Tax Committee estimated that the proposed legislative change would increase revenues by $16.2 billion between 2018 and 2027.

The Tax Reform Act of 2014, which was never enacted, included a substantially similar "repeal and replace" arrangement.

While legislation to repeal and replace Section 409A has thus far not been enacted, it is entirely possible that Congress will revisit this concept in the future because it raises revenue.

PLANS OF TAX-EXEMPT ENTITIES

Q.278 WHAT REGULATORY GUIDANCE HAS BEEN ISSUED WITH RESPECT TO DEFERRED COMPENSATION PLANS OF TAX-EXEMPT AND GOVERNMENTAL ENTITIES, AND WHEN IS THE REGULATORY GUIDANCE EFFECTIVE?

Treasury issued proposed Section 457 regulations governing deferred compensation plans of tax-exempt and governmental entities on June 22, 2016. Treasury expects that the regulations will apply to deferred compensation for calendar years beginning after the date of publication of the final regulations, and to deferred amounts to which the legally binding right arose during previous calendar years to the extent such amounts were not previously included in income. While taxpayers may rely on the proposed regulations until they become final, no implication is intended regarding application of the law before the regulations become final. With respect to the rules regarding recurring part-year compensation (see **Q.292**) for periods before the final regulations become effective, taxpayers may rely either on the rules set forth in the proposed regulations or the rules set forth in Notice 2008-62. It is anticipated that, once the regulations become final, there will be special effective date rules for collectively bargained plans and governmental plans.

Citation: Preamble to 2016 Proposed 457 Regulations § V.

Q.279 WHAT ARE THE GENERAL TAX RULES GOVERNING NONQUALIFIED DEFERRED COMPENSATION ARRANGEMENTS OF TAX-EXEMPT ENTITIES?

Nonqualified deferred compensation payable to employees of tax-exempt entities is generally subject to tax on the later of the date there is a legally binding right to the compensation or the date there is no substantial risk of forfeiture with respect to the compensation.

Citation: I.R.C. § 457(f); Prop. Treas. Reg. § 1.457-12(a)(2) (2016).

Q.280 WHY ARE THE RULES ASSOCIATED WITH THE TAXATION OF DEFERRED COMPENSATION FOR TAX-EXEMPT ENTITIES DIFFERENT FROM THE RULES APPLICABLE TO TAXABLE EMPLOYERS?

In the case of an employer which is subject to federal income tax, the employer does not receive a deduction for compensation due to an employee until the employee recognizes income. Accordingly, in situations in which the employer's marginal tax rate is roughly equivalent to that of its employees, there is often little or no deferment of income payable to the Treasury when an employee defers compensation. In the case of a tax-exempt employer, however, this is not the case. If the employee is allowed to defer compensation and not pay taxes until receipt of such compensation, the loss of the deduction to the tax-exempt entity will not result in a corresponding increase of income to Treasury since the tax-exempt entity pays no taxes. In essence, allowing a highly paid employee of a tax-exempt entity unlimited opportunities to defer compensation to a future date would afford all the advantages of a qualified retirement plan (deferral of current income, tax-free buildup of earnings, and no tax until the compensation is distributed) with none of the nondiscrimination or other rules applicable to qualified retirement plans.

Q.281 WHAT IS THE DEFINITION OF DEFERRED COMPENSATION IN THE TAX-EXEMPT EMPLOYER CONTEXT?

The basic definition is the same definition used in the Section 409A context (see **Q.3**). A deferral of compensation occurs when, under the terms of the agreement and the relevant facts and circumstances, the plan participant acquires a legally binding right in one year to receive compensation that is or may be due and payable in a later year. A deferral of compensation does not occur with respect to an amount which constitutes a short-term deferral (see **Q.20** and **Q.21**).

Citation: Prop. Treas. Reg. § 457-12(d) (2016).

Q.282 IF A PLAN IS SUBJECT TO SECTION 457, MAY IT ALSO BE SUBJECT TO SECTION 409A?

Yes. A nonqualified deferred compensation plan subject to Section 457 may also constitute a nonqualified deferred compensation plan for purposes of Section 409A. If this is the case, the rules of Section 409A apply to such plan separately and in addition to any requirement applicable to the plan under Section 457.

Citation: Treas. Reg. § 1.409A-1(a)(4).

Q.283 WHAT PLANS ARE TREATED AS NOT PROVIDING FOR A DEFERRAL OF COMPENSATION FOR PURPOSES OF SECTION 457?

The following plans of tax-exempt entities are not subject to Section 457:

- Bona fide vacation and sick leave plans (see **Q.289**);
- Bona fide severance pay plans (see **Q.285**);
- Bona fide death benefit plans (see **Q.287**);
- Bona fide disability pay plans (see **Q.288**);
- A plan paying solely length of service awards to bona fide volunteers on account of qualified services performed by such volunteers;

- Plans providing for payment of recurring part-year compensation (see **Q.292**);
- Non-elective deferred compensation plans for non-employees (all individuals other than those who have not satisfied any applicable initial service requirements who have the same relationship to the service recipient must be covered under the same plan with no individual variations or options); and
- Section 457(b) plans (such plans provide for limited deferral opportunities; the limit for 2017 for nongovernmental employees is $18,000).

Citation: I.R.C. §§ 457(e)(11) & (12); Prop. Treas. Reg. § 1.457-11 (2016).

Q.284 WHEN IS A PLAN LEGALLY BINDING FOR PURPOSES OF SECTION 457?

A service provider has a legally binding right to compensation under a plan of a service recipient unless the service recipient can unilaterally reduce or eliminate the duty to pay the compensation. Even in that case, if the facts and circumstances suggest that the right to reduce or eliminate compensation lacks substantial significance or can only be exercised upon a condition, the right to deferred compensation is treated as legally binding for purposes of Section 457. The determination of whether a legally binding right to compensation exists is basically the same as under Section 409A (see **Q.5**).

Citation: Prop. Treas. Reg. § 1.457-12(d)(1)(i) (2016).

Q.285 WHAT IS A BONA FIDE SEVERANCE PAY PLAN FOR PURPOSES OF SECTION 457?

Severance payments are exempt from Section 457 if they satisfy all of the following requirements:

- The severance payments must occur only on involuntary severance from service, voluntary severance for good reason (see **Q.147**), or pursuant to a window program (see **Q.152**).

- The severance payments cannot exceed two times the participant's annualized compensation for the year before the separation.
- Payment must be complete by the end of the second calendar year following the year the participant separates from service.

Citation: Preamble to 2016 Proposed 457 Regulations § III.B.1; Prop. Treas. Reg. § 1.457-11(d) (2016).

Q.286 HOW DOES THE DEFINITION OF "BONA FIDE SEVERANCE PAY PLAN" DIFFER FOR PURPOSES OF SECTIONS 409A AND 457?

The two definitions are very similar, including the definitions of window program (see **Q.152**), involuntary severance from employment and severance from employment for good reason (see **Q.147**). The main difference is that the Section 409A regulations provide an additional requirement in order for a plan to qualify as a bona fide severance pay plan: the total amount of severance benefits payable to a participant cannot exceed two times the Section 401(a)(17) compensation limit ($270,000 for 2017). See **Q.142**.

Example. A tax-exempt hospital and its Chief Executive Officer ("CEO") enter into an employment arrangement which provides that the CEO will receive 24 months of salary continuation following the CEO's involuntary separation from service without cause. Payments are to be made on the first day of each month commencing with the month following an involuntary separation from service. The CEO's salary is $100,000 per month. The plan does not designate the separation payments as separate payments. This plan constitutes a separation pay plan for purposes of Section 457 but not for purposes of Section 409A. While the salary continuation arrangement is subject to Section 409A, it is structured to meet the Section 409A rules. As a result, each payment is taxed when paid. If, however, the payments were accelerated into a lump sum following the CEO's separation from service, a violation of Section 409A would occur, resulting in a 20 percent additional tax under the Section 409A rules.

Citation: Treas. Reg. §§ 1.409A-1(b)(4) and 1.409A-1(b)(9); Prop. Treas. Reg. § 1.457-11(b) (2016).

Q.287 WHAT CONSTITUTES A BONA FIDE DEATH BENEFIT PLAN EXEMPT FROM SECTION 457?

A plan will be considered a bona fide death benefit plan to the extent that the total benefits payable under the plan exceed the lifetime benefits payable under the plan. The definition is the same as under Section 409A (see **Q.12**).

Example. A tax-exempt entity provides that $50,000 per year will be credited to a bookkeeping account on behalf of its Chief Executive Officer, with investment earnings or losses credited or debited to the account based on investment indices selected by the executive. Upon the executive's death, the executive's hypothetical account balance will be paid to the executive's designated beneficiary. No benefits are payable during the executive's lifetime, however. This plan qualifies as a bona fide death benefit plan and, as a result, the benefits due are not taxable until paid to the executive's designated beneficiary.

Citation: Preamble to 2016 Proposed 457 Regulations § III.C; Prop. Treas. Reg. § 1.457-11(e)(1) (2016).

Q.288 WHAT IS A BONA FIDE DISABILITY PAY PLAN FOR PURPOSES OF SECTION 457?

A bona fide disability pay plan is a plan that pays benefits (whether or not insured) only in the event that a participant is disabled. A participant is considered disabled only if the participant meets one of the following conditions:

- The participant is unable to engage in any substantial gainful activity by reason of any medically determinable physical or mental impairment that can be expected to result in death or last for a continuous period of not less than 12 months; or
- The participant is, by reason of any medically determinable physical or mental impairment that can be expected to result in death or last for a continuous period of not less than 12 months, receiving income replacement benefits for a period of not less than three

months under an accident and health plan covering employees of the service recipient; or
- The participant is determined to be totally disabled by the Social Security Administration or Railroad Retirement Board.

Citation: Preamble to 2016 Proposed 457 Regulations § III.D; Prop. Treas. Reg. § 1.457-11(e)(2) (2016).

Q.289 WHAT IS A BONA FIDE SICK AND VACATION LEAVE PLAN?

A sick or vacation leave plan is generally treated as bona fide (and therefore not as a plan providing for the deferral of compensation) if the facts and circumstances demonstrate that the primary purpose of the plan is to provide employees with paid time off from work because of sickness, vacation, or other personal reasons. The relevant facts and circumstances are the following:

- Whether the amount of leave provided could reasonably be expected to be used by the employee in the normal course before severance from employment;
- Limits, if any, on the ability to exchange unused accumulated leave for cash or other benefits and any restrictions on accruing leave (for example, the use of leave forfeiture provisions, sometimes referred to as "use it or lose it rules");
- The amount and frequency of any in-service distributions of cash or other benefits offered in exchange for accumulated and unused leave;
- Whether the payment of unused sick or vacation leave is made promptly upon severance from employment rather than over a period of time after severance from employment; and
- Whether the leave is broadly available or is available only to a select group of employees.

Citation: Preamble to 2016 Proposed 457 Regulations § III.E; Prop. Treas. Reg. § 1.457-11(f) (2016).

Q.290 WHAT IS THE SHORT-TERM DEFERRAL RULE IN THE CONTEXT OF SECTION 457?

Section 457 does not apply to any payment that is not a "deferred payment" as long as the service provider actually or constructively receives the payment within 2½ months after the close of either the service provider's or service recipient's taxable year in which the payment is no longer subject to a substantial risk of forfeiture. The rule is basically the same as the short-term deferral rule under Section 409A (see **Q.21**), except that the definition of substantial risk of forfeiture under Section 457 is broader than under Section 409A.

Citation: Preamble to 2016 Proposed 457 Regulations § IV.C.2; Prop. Treas. Reg. § 1.457-12(d)(2) (2016).

Q.291 HOW DOES THE DEFINITION OF "SUBSTANTIAL RISK OF FORFEITURE" DIFFER FOR PURPOSES OF SECTIONS 409A AND 457?

The basic definitions are very similar. Compensation is subject to a substantial risk of forfeiture for purposes of both Sections 409A and 457 if the compensation is conditioned on the performance of substantial future services or the occurrence of a condition related to a purpose of the compensation, and the possibility of forfeiture is substantial. For purposes of Section 457, a condition is considered related to the purpose of the compensation only if it relates to either (i) the service provider's performance or (ii) the service recipient's governmental or tax-exempt activities or organizational goals (compare with **Q.24**). However, under Section 457, but not Section 409A, an agreement not to compete can be a substantial risk of forfeiture if the following conditions are satisfied:

- The right to the compensation must be expressly conditioned on the employee refraining from the performance of future services pursuant to a written agreement that is enforceable under applicable law;

- The employer must consistently make reasonable efforts to verify compliance with all of the non-competition agreements to which it is a party; and
- At the time the non-competition agreement becomes binding, the facts and circumstances must show that (i) the employer has a substantial and bona fide interest in preventing the employee from performing the prohibited services and (ii) the employee has a bona fide interest in engaging in the prohibited competition. Factors taken into account for this purpose include the employer's ability to show significant adverse economic consequences that would likely result from the prohibited services; the marketability of the employee based on specialized skills, reputation, or other factors; and the employee's interest, financial need, and ability to engage in the prohibited services.

Example 1. A tax-exempt university enters into an employment agreement with its basketball coach. The agreement provides for the payment of salary continuation over a period of two years following the coach's separation from service for any reason provided that the coach agrees not to coach basketball at another Division 1 university during the salary continuation period. The agreement specifies that the separation payments will be made monthly beginning on the first day of the month following separation. Assume that the university has a substantial and bona fide interest in preventing the coach from coaching basketball and that the coach has a bona fide interest in, and ability to, coach basketball following her separation from service with the university. This arrangement is subject to a substantial risk of forfeiture for Section 457(f) purposes, but not for Section 409A purposes. However, the separation payments are structured to comply with Section 409A. Accordingly, upon the coach's separation from service with the university, payments will be taxed when made provided they are paid in accordance with the written monthly schedule.

Example 2. Assume the same facts as in Example 1, except that after the coach separates from service and receives three monthly payments, the university agrees to waive the non-competition agreement with the coach and allow her to coach basketball at another Division 1 university. If the payments continue as scheduled, then the present value of the future payments are immediately taxed under the Section 457(f) rules. Under the 2008 final regulations, no 409A violation has occurred because the actual "payment" of monthly amounts has not been accelerated. However, under the 2016 proposed regulations, the acceleration of vesting under Section 457(f) would accelerate "payment" for purposes of Section 409A and thereby trigger a 409A violation (see **Q.49**). Until and unless the 2016 proposed regulations are finalized, the employer and coach should be able to take the position that the 2008 final regulations govern when a payment is considered made such that no 409A violation occurs.

Citation: Treas. Reg. § 1.409A-1(a)(4); Prop. Treas. Reg. § 1.409A-1(q)(2016); Preamble to Final 409A Regulations § II.B (2007); Preamble to 2016 Proposed 409A Regulations §§ IV.C.2 and E.

Q.292 WHAT IS RECURRING PART-YEAR COMPENSATION?

This is compensation paid for services rendered in a position that the employer and employee reasonably anticipate will continue under similar terms and conditions in future years, and under which the employee will be required to provide services during successive periods comprising less than 12 months each. For example, a faculty member who provides services during a school year from September through May might be paid over a period of 12 months even though he or she does not teach during the summer. A deferral of compensation for purposes of Section 457 does not occur with respect to such recurring part-year compensation if (i) the arrangement does not defer payment of any of the recurring part-year compensation to a date beyond the last day of the 13th month following the first day of the service period for which the recurring part-year compensation is paid, and (ii) the amount of the recurring part-year compensation does not exceed the annual compensation limit under Section 401(a)(17) for the calendar year in which the service period commences. The rules are basically the same as the recurring part-year compensation rules under Section 409A (see **Q.126**).

Citation: Prop. Treas. Reg. § 1.457-12(d)(3) (2016); Preamble to 2016 Proposed 457 Regulations § IV.C.3.

Q.293 MAY AN EMPLOYEE OF A TAX-EXEMPT ORGANIZATION ELECT TO DEFER SALARY OR OTHER VESTED COMPENSATION SUBJECT TO A SUBSTANTIAL RISK OF FORFEITURE AND THEREBY ACHIEVE DEFERRAL OF INCOME TAXATION UNDER SECTION 457?

Deferrals of current compensation subject to a substantial risk of forfeiture will result in a deferral of income tax if all of the following requirements are met:

- The present value of the amount to be paid upon the lapse of the substantial risk of forfeiture must be materially greater than the amount the employee otherwise would be paid in the absence of a substantial risk of forfeiture. An amount is materially greater for this purpose only if the present value of the amount to be paid upon the lapse of a substantial risk of forfeiture, determined as of a date the amount would have otherwise been paid, is more than 125 percent of the amount the participant otherwise would have received on that date in the absence of the substantial risk of forfeiture.
- The substantial risk of forfeiture must be based upon the future performance of substantial services or adherence to an agreement not to compete. It may not be based solely on the occurrence of a condition related to the purpose of the transfer (although such a condition may be combined with a sufficient service condition).
- The period for which substantial future services must be performed may not be less than two years absent an intervening event such as death, disability, or involuntary severance from employment.

- The agreement subjecting the amount to a substantial risk of forfeiture must be made in writing before the beginning of the calendar year in which any services giving rise to the compensation are performed.

Example. On December 31, 2017, an employee enters into an agreement to defer $15,000 of the employee's current compensation that would otherwise be paid during 2018, with payment of the deferred amount to be made on December 31, 2024, but only if the employee continues to provide substantial services until December 31, 2024. Under the terms of the agreement, the participant's periodic payments of 2018 salary are reduced and credited (with a 30 percent employer match) to an account earning a reasonable rate of interest. Because the present value of the amount payable on December 31, 2024 is 130 percent of the present value of the amount deferred, such deferred amount is not taxable until December 31, 2024.

Citation: Prop. Treas. Reg. § 1.457-12(e)(2) (2016); Preamble to 2016 Proposed 457 Regulations § IV.E.

Q.294 MAY AN EMPLOYEE OF A TAX-EXEMPT EMPLOYER ACHIEVE A DEFERRAL OF INCOME TAXATION OF AN AMOUNT SUBJECT TO A SUBSTANTIAL RISK OF FORFEITURE BY EXTENDING THE SUBSTANTIAL RISK OF FORFEITURE TO A FUTURE DATE?

Yes. Proposed regulations issued under Section 457 would permit deferral of taxation through what is commonly referred to as a "rolling risk of forfeiture" provided the following conditions are satisfied:

- The present value of the amount to be paid upon the lapse of the extended substantial risk of forfeiture must be materially greater than the amount the employee would otherwise be paid in the absence of the extended substantial risk of forfeiture. An amount is materially greater for this purpose only if the present value of the

amount to be paid upon the extended lapse of the substantial risk of forfeiture, measured as of the date the substantial risk of forfeiture would have lapsed without regard to the extension, is more than 125 percent of the amount the participant otherwise would have received on such date in the absence of the extension.
- The extended substantial risk of forfeiture must be based upon the future performance of substantial services or adherence to an agreement not to compete. It may not be based solely on the occurrence of a condition related to the purpose of a transfer, although that type of condition may be combined with a sufficient service condition.
- The period for which substantial future services must be performed may not be less than two years (absent an intervening event such as death, disability, or involuntary severance from employment).
- The agreement subjecting the amount to an extended substantial risk of forfeiture must be made in writing at least 90 days before the date on which the existing substantial risk of forfeiture would have lapsed absent the extension.

Citation: Prop. Treas. Reg. § 1.457-12(e)(2) (2016); Preamble to 2016 Proposed 457 Regulations § IV.E.

Q.295 HOW DO THE RULES UNDER SECTION 457 RELATING TO ROLLING RISKS OF FORFEITURE DIFFER FROM THE SECTION 409A RULES?

Rolling risks of forfeiture are expressly disregarded under Section 409A unless the present value of the amount subject to the extended substantial risk of forfeiture is "materially greater" than the amount which would have otherwise been paid upon lapse of the original substantial risk of forfeiture. The term "materially greater" is not defined under Section 409A, but the Section 457 definition might be applied by analogy (see **Q.294**). In addition, a non-competition agreement may constitute a substantial risk of forfeiture for purposes of Section 457, but may never constitute a substantial risk of forfeiture for purposes of Section 409A.

Example. On January 1, 2017, a tax-exempt entity agrees to pay an executive $100,000 on December 31, 2020 if the executive continues employment until that date. On September 1, 2020, the parties agree to extend the payment date to December 31, 2022 provided the executive agrees to abide by a non-competition agreement. Assume, for purposes of this example, that the non-competition agreement constitutes a substantial risk of forfeiture under all the facts and circumstances for purposes of Section 457. The parties also agree that the amount payable on December 31, 2022 will be increased from $100,000 to $150,000. While this arrangement would constitute a rolling risk of forfeiture which would be sufficient to defer income taxes for purposes of Section 457, the arrangement violates Section 409A because the non-competition agreement is not recognized as a substantial risk of forfeiture and the deferral of the compensation does not meet the Section 409A rules. In order to comply with Section 409A in this situation, the deferral of compensation would need to meet the subsequent deferral rules described in **Q.127**, which would require (i) that the redeferral election be made at least one year before December 31, 2020 and (ii) a minimum redeferral period of an additional five years.

Q.296 IF AN AMOUNT IS INCLUDABLE IN INCOME UNDER SECTION 457(f) BEFORE PAYMENT OF THE DEFERRED AMOUNT IS MADE, HOW IS THE TAXABLE AMOUNT OF COMPENSATION DETERMINED?

The amount of the compensation deferred that is includable in gross income on the date a substantial risk of forfeiture lapses is the present value, as of that date, of the amount of compensation deferred. The rules for determining present value under Section 457 are similar to the rules for determining present value under Section 409A, except that the present value calculation under Section 457 is determined as of the later of the date there is a legally binding right to compensation or the date the substantial risk of forfeiture lapses, whereas income inclusion under Section 409A is determined as of the end of the service provider's taxable year.

Citation: Preamble to 2016 Proposed 457 Regulations § IV.B.2; Prop. Treas. Reg. § 1.457-12(c)(1)(i) (2016).

Q.297 HOW IS THE PRESENT VALUE OF COMPENSATION DEFERRED UNDER AN ACCOUNT BALANCE PLAN DETERMINED FOR PURPOSES OF SECTION 457?

If the account balance is determined using a predetermined actual investment or a reasonable rate of interest, the present value of an amount payable under an account balance plan is the amount credited to the account, i.e., the principle and any earnings or losses through the applicable date. If the account balance is not determined using a predetermined actual investment or a reasonable rate of interest, the present value of the deferred compensation is equal to the amount credited to the participant's account as of that date, plus the present value of the excess, if any, of the earnings to be credited under the plan after the applicable date and through the projected payment date over the earnings that would be credited during that period using a reasonable rate of interest.

Citation: Preamble to 2016 Proposed 457 Regulations § IV.B.2; Prop. Treas. Reg. § 1.457-12(c)(1)(iv) (2016).

Q.298 HOW IS THE PRESENT VALUE OF DEFERRED COMPENSATION UNDER A PLAN THAT IS NOT AN ACCOUNT BALANCE PLAN DETERMINED?

The calculation must be based on reasonable actuarial assumptions determined based on all of the relevant facts and circumstances.

Citation: Preamble to 2016 Proposed 457 Regulations § IV.B.3; Prop. Treas. Reg. § 1.457-12(c)(1) (2016).

Q.299 IF AN AMOUNT IS INCLUDABLE IN INCOME UNDER SECTION 457 BEFORE PAYMENT IS MADE, HOW ARE EARNINGS ACCRUING AFTER THE DATE OF INCOME INCLUSION TREATED?

The additional earnings will constitute a deferred compensation plan subject to Section 409A and, if the Section 409A rules are satisfied, will be taxed upon payment.

Example. A tax-exempt entity provides for payment of a specified dollar amount plus earnings credited at a reasonable rate of interest upon separation from service, with vesting to occur when the service provider has completed three years of service. The service provider completes three years of service, and, as a result, the specified dollar amount plus earnings accruing to the date of the lapse of the substantial risk of forfeiture are included in the service provider's income even though the service provider will not receive actual payment of her deferred compensation until her separation from service. Five years later, the service provider separates from service and receives payment of the specified dollar amount plus all earnings from the date of establishment of the arrangement. The arrangement satisfies Section 409A, and the additional earnings accruing after the vesting date are taxable upon distribution to the service provider.

Citation: Preamble to 2016 Proposed 409A Regulations § IV, footnote 2.

Q.300 IF AN AMOUNT IS INCLUDABLE IN INCOME UNDER SECTION 457(f) BEFORE PAYMENT IS MADE, MAY BENEFITS UNDER THE PLAN BE REDUCED TO PAY REQUIRED TAX WITHHOLDINGS?

Yes. A plan subject to section 457(f) may provide for an acceleration of benefits to pay federal, state, local, and foreign income taxes due upon a vesting event. The amount of such payment must not be more than the tax withholding that would have been due had there been a payment of wages equal to the income includible by the service provider under section 457(f) at the time of the vesting event.

Citation: Treas. Reg. §§ 1.409A-3(j)(4)(iv).

APPENDIX A
CHECKLIST FOR STRUCTURING NONQUALIFIED DEFERRED COMPENSATION AND BENEFITS

1. Assume that the arrangement is subject to Section 409A until proven otherwise. The scope of Section 409A is very broad and the tax penalty for breach is very costly (see **Q.101–Q.103**). This includes all commitments to pay deferred compensation, including those contained in individual employment agreements.
2. For a plan in existence before October 3, 2004, determine whether part or all of the plan is grandfathered. Certain changes to a grandfathered plan can cause loss of grandfathering (see **Q.270–Q.272**).
3. See whether the arrangement can be structured to fall outside the scope of Section 409A under the short-term deferral rule by providing that payment will occur within 2½ months after the end of the taxable year in which the service provider becomes vested in the right to receive the promised compensation (see **Q.21**).
4. See whether the arrangement can be structured to fall outside the scope of Section 409A under another statutory or regulatory exemption (see **Q.2**), such as:
   a. an arrangement between two accrual basis taxpayers.
   b. a group life insurance plan.

c. an exempt Section 457(b) plan rather than a covered Section 457(f) plan.
   d. a life insurance arrangement between an employer and a service provider that uses an exempt loan or an endorsement split-dollar arrangement (see **Q.186**).
5. If the plan cannot be structured to avoid Section 409A, make certain that the arrangement conforms to the detailed requirements of Section 409A in both form and operation.

Copyright 2005–2021 Infosys McCamish Systems, LLC. Used by permission (Question references added). All rights reserved. For more information or reprint permission contact Richard_Magner @Infosys.com.

APPENDIX B
CHECKLIST FOR DRAFTING PLANS SUBJECT TO SECTION 409A

There is no particular format for documentation of a plan subject to Section 409A, except that it must be documented. A single document is permitted, but two or more documents may also constitute a single plan. Even e-mails or other electronic communications may be sufficient to satisfy the documentation requirements, particularly with respect to participant elections.

At a minimum, the plan must state all of the following:

- Either the amount of deferred compensation or the method or formula for determining the amount.
- The time and form of payment.
- Initial employee election procedures if applicable.
- Definitions of key terms that comply with the requirements of Section 409A.

It is also appropriate to consider including the following provisions:

For All Plans:

- Definitions with respect to distribution events, such as separation from service, leave of absence, disability, unforeseeable emergency and change of control (see **Q.29–35, 46, 73,** and **82**).
- A provision for designated payment dates or payment dates measured from the separation date, such as 90 days after separation (see **Q.48**).

- A provision for grandfathering any amounts that were earned and vested on December 31, 2004 (see **Q.269**).
- An optional provision for cash-outs of small distributions.
- An optional provision for the limited available offset of the service provider's obligations to the service recipient against the amounts due the service provider under the plan (see **Q.93**).
- Optional provisions stating other desired exceptions to the prohibition against benefit accelerations. Examples include permitting distribution (i) pursuant to a domestic relations order incident to a divorce or legal separation, (ii) to pay FICA taxes due on compensation deferred under the plan and any associated income taxes, or (iii) to pay taxes due on account of breach of Section 409A.
- A provision for voluntary plan termination by the service recipient (see **Q.85**).
- A provision for interpretation of all terms and provisions consistent with Section 409A, especially as to all undefined, ambiguous, or incomplete definitions and provisions (see **Q.227**).
- A provision under which the employer either disclaims or accepts responsibility for any adverse tax consequences arising under Section 409A (see **Q.106**).
- A spendthrift or nonassignability provision.
- A provision that the plan constitutes an unsecured and unfunded contractual promise to pay benefits rather than a funded plan.
- Provisions designed to comply with state law employment requirements and choice of law.
- If the plan is informally funded through a rabbi trust, a provision prohibiting transfer of assets used to fund the plan to an irrevocable trust in connection with deterioration of the employer's financial health or to an offshore trust (see **Q.198**).
- If the plan is informally funded through a rabbi trust, a provision prohibiting setting aside assets in the rabbi trust during any "restricted period" with respect to a tax-qualified defined benefit pension plan of the employer that does not satisfy statutory minimum funding levels (see **Q.199**).

For Any Plan of a Publicly Held Employer:

- A provision for a six-month delay of payments due upon separation from service of a specified employee (see **Q.36**). A plan need not include a six-month delay provision with respect to a service provider who is not a specified employee, but if a non-specified employee becomes a specified employee, the six-month delay provision must be added with respect to the service provider no later than the date the service provider first becomes a specified employee.
- A provision stating whether all payments suspended during the six-month waiting period will be paid in a single sum on expiration of the waiting period or whether instead all individual payments due the specified employee will be delayed for six months (see **Q.36**).
- A provision stating the date for valuation of the amount due the service provider.

For Any Plan That Gives Participants the Right to Select the Time and Form of Payment (see **Q.120**):

- An optional provision allowing for subsequent elections changing the previously designated form and time of payment, including a provision for treating a prior election to receive payment in installments as a unitary single election or a series of individual elections for this purpose (see **Q.127**).

For an Account Balance Plan:

- A provision for a reasonable rate of return or an objective measure for the rate of return, such as a stock or bond index.

For an Elective Deferral Plan:

- A provision stating the date by which elections to defer base pay, bonuses, and performance-based pay must be made, both for

existing participants and those who become eligible after the beginning of a year (see **Q.121**).
- If applicable, special provisions for elections to defer performance-based compensation (see **Q.121** and **Q.124**).
- A provision for treatment of a participant whose eligibility terminates and then resumes at a later time (see **Q.121**).
- A provision for automatic cancellation of a participant's deferrals on the participant's receipt of a hardship distribution from a 401(k) or 403(b) plan (see **Q.135**).

For an Employer Non-account Balance Plan:

- A provision prohibiting suspension of payment on reemployment after periodic retirement distributions have begun (see **Q.70**).

Provisions That Are Not Permitted or Not Advisable:

- Previously used haircut provisions under which the participant could elect early distribution subject to a penalty, other conditional event-based distributions and accelerations (such as the employee's child being admitted to college), and offset provisions that do not satisfy the requirements of Section 409A must be removed from the plan (see **Q.17**).
- Blanket Section 409A savings clauses that purport to reform the document to disregard terms that violate Section 409A or to incorporate by general reference any provisions required to cause the plan to comply with Section 409A. A savings clause will not automatically disqualify a plan from meeting the requirements of Section 409A, but it will not bring a plan into compliance if the plan document includes provisions that contravene or omit requirements of Section 409A. However, a provision for application of all terms and provisions consistent with Section 409A, especially as to all undefined, ambiguous, or incomplete definitions and provisions, is permissible and useful. The distinction is between

reformation of a provision that is inconsistent with Section 409A and interpretation of an ambiguous provision as consistent with Section 409A (see **Q.277**).

Note: *Notices 2010–6 and 2010–80, which address correction of documentation errors under Section 409A, also provide useful guidelines and checklists for documentary compliance to avoid such errors.*

APPENDIX C
UNFORESEEABLE EMERGENCY DISTRIBUTION REQUEST FORM

Designed for Use Under a Nonqualified Deferred Compensation Plan Subject to Section 409A

Specimen for Review of Counsel Only

Introduction: Your balance in this plan is not generally available before retirement, other separation of service, or a fixed future date, except in the instance of an "unforeseeable emergency" that is an unanticipated severe financial hardship. The determination of whether you qualify for an "unforeseeable emergency" distribution is made by the Plan Administrator following guidelines under Internal Revenue Code Section 409A that govern and limit such distributions.

In general, you may only receive such a distribution if your financial hardship situation was unforeseeable. Please note that the IRS does not consider college expenses or expenses in connection with the purchase of a home as unforeseeable. Such a distribution must be limited to the amount necessary to relieve the hardship, not to exceed your account balance. The distribution from your account, if authorized, will be made lump sum. In the alternative or in addition, you may request your deferral election be terminated for the balance of the plan year to address the financial emergency, if your emergency would be solved by the additional cash flow provided by the termination of your deferral for the year. However, the company reserves the right to determine which approach(es) will meet the requirements and limitations of Code Section 409A. By law, the amount cannot exceed your need as the company in its sole discretion and judgment may best determine under any circumstances.

To request an "unforeseen emergency" distribution, complete the following form, sign and fax to the Plan Administrator c/o: _____. Questions concerning this distribution may be directed to this fax number, or by email at _____.

REQUEST (check either or both):

I wish to request an "unforeseeable emergency":

[ ] distribution of my account under the Plan in the amount shown below or my total account, if less.

[ ] distribution of the salary deferrals under my current deferral election form in the amount shown below by the termination of the deferral of these amounts from my salary payroll for the balance of the current Plan Year.

I request distribution based upon the following information provided. I understand that I am only entitled to this emergency distribution subject to certain requirements, conditions and limitations as outlined by Internal Revenue Code Section 409A and the guidance thereto. I affirm that the information here provided is true and correct to the best of my knowledge as of the date hereafter noted. I agree to provide any other or additional information or documentation as may be requested to establish the nature and extent of my financial hardship for purposes of this hardship distribution.

 VI. Participant Information
   1. Name: _____
   2. Address: _____, _____, ____, _____
     (Street Address) (City) (State) (ZIP)
   3. Employee Identification Code: _____
   4. Phone: ( )____-_____ Email: _____
    Fax: ( )____-_____

VII. **W-4 Card Information**

This distribution is subject to federal withholding tax. The amount of tax withheld will depend on the W-4 you have currently filed with the company. It is suggested that 20 percent to 40 percent be withheld to cover additional taxes caused by this distribution. If you wish the withholding to be larger than that based upon your current W-4 (by filing a special W-4) for this distribution, please indicate below:

Larger withholding desired? Yes__ No __

VIII. **Hardship Information (check and complete as appropriate)**

1. The nature of my financial hardship was unforeseeable and not under my control.

    Yes___ No ___

2. The nature of my current financial situation constitutes a real financial emergency that threatens to cause me great financial hardship or detriment if not relieved by an immediate distribution from my account and/or complete termination of my deferrals.

    Yes ___ No ___

3. The nature of my financial hardship is as follows:

    a. a sudden or unexpected illness or accident (me/spouse/dependent) causing loss of income (by loss of employment, disability) and/or unexpected medical expenses related to the illness or accident _____; **or**

    b. a loss of my property (for example, home, auto) due to an unforeseen casualty loss (for example, fire, earthquake, flood) _____; **or**

    c. another extraordinary and financial loss or emergency beyond my control as follows (Detail the nature of the situation. For example, death, loss of employment of spouse, reduction of living income by divorce, etc.):

    _____
    _____
    _____

4. The magnitude of my financial emergency in a lump sum is: $_____.
   Income from all other readily available sources to apply to debt: $_____.
   (From regular income, insurance, liquid assets)
5. Total amount of distribution needed to relieve financial hardship: (#4 minus #5) $_____.
6. The total amount in my Plan account as of __/__/____ was: $_____.
7. Total amount available from cessation of remaining salary deferral this calendar year beginning as of __/__/____: $_____.

Submission Date: ___/___/_____
Participant Name: _____
Participant Signature: _____

Due to the time necessary to evaluate an "unforeseeable emergency" distribution and to process a surrender of an account under the Plan, payment should not be expected for two to four weeks from receipt of completed paperwork by the Plan Administrator. (Rev. 1–06)

Administrator's Review Checklist (for use by the Company to determine action):
1. Event is a qualified unforeseeable emergency under 409A?
   ( ) YES
   ( ) NO (If "NO," no distribution may be made by reason of Code Section 409A limitations that includes penalties).
2. Other financial resources are ( ) wholly unavailable; ( ) or are inadequate to the extent of $_____ lump sum.
3. The financial emergency can be resolved by:
   ( ) distribution from the participant's account the lump sum of $_____, plus taxes in the amount of $_____.
   ( ) distribution by cessation of the participant's salary deferrals for the balance of the calendar year
   ( ) both

4. The Company will notify the participant that:
( ) the request for distribution is denied because the event is NOT a qualified "unforeseeable emergency" under 409A.
( ) the event is a qualified "unforeseeable emergency," but no distribution can be made because the participant has other resources that can be used to meet the emergency.
( ) the event qualifies as an "unforeseeable emergency," other resources are inadequate to meet the financial emergency to the extent of $_____, and a distribution will be made:
    ( ) from the participant's account of $_____, plus taxes on that distribution of $_____.
    ( ) by cessation of the participant's salary deferral for the balance of the calendar year beginning __/__/____ amounting to $_____ total.

Approved for the following total plan distribution:
$_____
Company Official: _____
Date: _____, 20__
Company Official's Signature: _____
Disapproved for any plan distribution. _____
Company Official:
Date: _____, 20__
Company Official's Signature: _____

DISCLAIMER

THIS FORM IS A SPECIMEN OF THE TYPE OF FORM TO BE USED IN CONNECTION WITH A PARTICIPANT'S REQUEST FOR DISTRIBUTION OF BENEFITS FROM A NONQUALIFIED DEFERRED COMPENSATION PLAN BY REASON OF AN "UNFORESEEABLE EMERGENCY" UNDER CODE Section 409A, AND THE GUIDANCE TO IT.

Copyright 2007–2021 Infosys McCamish Systems. Used by permission. All rights reserved. For more Information or reprint/use permission, contact Richard_Magner@Infosys.com

APPENDIX D
DOMESTIC RELATIONS ORDER

Designed for Use Under a Nonqualified Deferred Compensation Plan Subject to Section 409A

Specimen for Review of Counsel Only

_____ is a participant in the_____ _____ (Plan), which is a nonqualified defined contribution deferred compensation plan, and is not subject to a Qualified Domestic Relations Order under 414(p) because it is not a qualified plan under 414(p), but is an ERISA exempt unfunded plan for a select group of executives and highly compensated individuals under ERISA, and thereby has no plan assets. However, the Plan is subject to Treas. Reg. Section 1.409A-3(i)(3), allowing for splitting and distribution of a nonqualified plan account. On_____, this matter was before the Court, and the Court having heard evidence and the Findings of Fact, Conclusions of Law and Judgment of Divorce having been filed, and certain provisions therein having awarded _____ _____an interest in _____'s vested accrued benefit promise in the Plan, and this Order being necessary to carry forth such provisions:

IT IS ORDERED that the following disposition be made:

Upon receipt of a certified copy of this judgment and if the above-referenced nonqualified deferred compensation plan so allows, the administrator(s) of the Plan, which is_____, the nonqualified Plan's sponsor who is the Participant's employer, shall direct its recordkeeper of the Plan's hypothetical accounts, _____ (hereafter "Recordkeeper"), to divide the hypothetical account(s) of _____, into two (2) parts: one for _____, consisting of [one-half] of each specific account as of _____ [date] after adjustments for earnings, appreciation, and contributions; the remaining balance in each specific account shall be retained for _____. No credit shall be made to the [Respondent's] account with respect to contributions made by the [Petitioner] or by the employer or with respect to any other crediting to each specific account in the Plan after _____ [date].

And, if the Plan so allows, the plan administrator(s) shall direct distribute to [Respondent] in a single total lump-sum, from any sources that the plan administrator shall determine appropriate for this unsecured promise-to-pay plan, an amount of cash in the currency of the United States of America equal to the value of his/her portion of the hypothetical account(s) maintained by Recordkeeper, as outlined above. Receipt of a certified copy of this judgment by the plan administrator(s) shall fulfill any and all requirements of the Plan as to necessary notice and request by [Respondent] for a distribution from the Plan in consequence of a separation of marital property between the [Petitioner] and [Respondent], and protect the Plan Sponsor, the Plan and the other Plan participants from any adverse federal or State (local) income tax consequences, especially under Section 409A, based upon compliance with this Order.

Distribution to [Respondent] shall be made as soon as administratively possible, as permitted by IRC Reg. § 1.409A-3(j)(4)(ii), but in compliance with IRC § 409A generally, and IRC Reg. § 1.409A-2 specifically, and this distribution shall occur not later than would a distribution to the participant in the Plan under a specified future date election, except that this distribution shall not be subject to any application of the "6-month delay rule" under IRC § 409A and the regulations thereto as provided for domestic relations orders on 409A nonqualified deferred compensation plans. This provision is designed to meet the definition of a Qualified Domestic Relations Order under IRC § 414(p) *only to the extent* necessary to satisfy the requirements for a domestic relations order under IRC § 409A and the regulations thereto, and nothing in this order is intended to suggest that the Plan is either a funded plan for ERISA (one with plan assets) or income tax purposes (a secured plan). The parallel requisites for this Order are fulfilled in the following provisions of this instrument.

The name, address, and Social Security number of the participant [the Petitioner] are as follows: _____
_____
_____
_____

The name, address, and Social Security number of the alternate payee [the Respondent] are as follows: _____
_____
_____
_____

The [Respondent's] interest shall be determined by taking [one-half] of the value of each hypothetical Plan account as of _____ [date]. The benefit for the [Petitioner] shall be the balance of each hypothetical Plan account. The [Respondent's] interest also shall include any interest, dividends, or other proceeds attributable to [Respondent's] share up to the date the specific account(s) is/are actually divided. In addition, the [Respondent] shall be treated as a surviving spouse for the full value of his/her share until the hypothetical account(s) actually is/are divided.

The number of payments required is [one (1)] from the Plan.

The name of the Nonqualified Deferred Compensation Plan (Plan) for which this order applies is:
_____.

The terms and provisions of this Order are not to be construed to:

Require a plan to provide any type or form of benefit or any option (with the exception of the payment to the [Respondent] as provided above) not otherwise provided under the plan; Require a plan to provide increased benefits (determined on the basis of actuarial value); or Require the payment of benefits to the [Respondent], which are required to be paid to another alternate payee under another order previously determined to apply to the Plan.

The [Respondent] shall have the duty to notify the plan administrator(s) in writing of any change in his/her mailing address. It is the intention of the Court that the distribution by the Plan to the [Respondent] and the [Petitioner] shall be taxable on the income under the guidelines of IRS Rev. Rul. 2002–22.

Dated:_____
BY THE COURT:

DISCLAIMER

This document is for informational purposes only of the type of Domestic Relations Order used in connection with the division of martial property involving a nonqualified deferred compensation plan under Code Section 409A. It is provided as an aid to private legal counsel and should not be used except after proper consultation of legal counsel as to the party's particular circumstances.

(Specimen/Rev 1-1-2016/LRR) Copyright 2007–2021 Infosys McCamish Systems, LLC. All rights reserved. Used by permission. For more information or reprint/use permission, contact Richard_Magner@Infosys.com.

APPENDIX E
CHECKLIST FOR PERMISSIBLE DISTRIBUTIONS AND ACCELERATIONS
Under a Plan Designed to Comply with Section 409A

SECTION I. – USE FOR EMPLOYEES
1. Separation from service
2. Closely held, private, nonprofit company
3. Publicly traded company-note: six calendar month delay of distribution required for "specified employees" of such companies and most distributions other than death or disability
4. Fixed date/schedule
5. Death
6. Disability (disabled)
7. Change in effective ownership or control (change of control)
8. Unforeseeable emergency (financial hardship)
9. Plan termination/liquidation
10. Domestic relations order (DRO)
11. Payment to avoid federal, state and local "conflict of interest" laws
12. Payment of applicable employment (FICA) and withholding on distributions
13. Payment of amounts included because of failure to comply with Code Section 409A

14. Accelerated payment to lump sum for distributions of small amounts under Code Section 402(g)(1)(B) ($18,000 in 2017)
15. Payment of applicable state, local, and foreign taxes upon distribution
16. Payment to prevent a "nonallocation year" under Code Section 409A(p) with respect to ESOP sponsored by S corporation
17. Payment of applicable employment (FICA) and withholding because of benefit vesting under Code Section 457(f) plan

SECTION II. – USE FOR INDEPENDENT CONTRACTORS

1. Termination of the contract (separation from service) from publicly traded, closely held, private, nonprofit companies
2. Fixed date/schedule
3. Death
4. Disability (disabled)
5. Change in effective ownership or control (change of control)
6. Unforeseeable emergency
7. Plan termination/liquidation
8. Domestic relations order (DRO)
9. Payment to avoid federal, state, and local "conflict of interest" laws
10. Payment of applicable employment (FICA) and withholding on distributions
11. Payment of amounts included because of failure to comply with Code Section 409A
12. Accelerated payment of lump sum for distributions of small amounts under Code Section 402(g)(1)(B) ($18,000 in 2017)
13. Payment of applicable state, local, and foreign taxes upon distribution
14. Payment to prevent a "nonallocation year" under Code Section 409A(p) with respect to ESOP sponsored by S corporation
15. Payment of applicable employment (FICA) & withholding because of benefit vesting under Code Section 457(f) plan

Note: Most of the definitions for permissible distributions under Section 409A are unique and specific (e.g., "separation from service," which is even different between employees and independent contractors where separation from employment is described as "termination of the contract"), and a practitioner must refer to the specific definition involved to see if the event qualifies as a Section 409A permissible distribution. The definitions tend to be narrower than formerly used in such plans (e.g., "disabled").

Copyright 2007–2021 Infosys McCamish Systems, LLC. Used by permission. All rights reserved. For more Information or reprint/use permission, contact Richard_Magner@Infosys.com.

APPENDIX F
SAMPLE STATEMENTS FOR ATTACHMENT TO FEDERAL INCOME TAX RETURNS IN CONNECTION WITH CORRECTION OF DOCUMENTARY FAILURES PURSUANT TO NOTICE 2010-6

Sample Attachment for Service Recipient's Federal Income Tax Return Correction of Documentary Failure to Comply with Section 409A Pursuant to Notice 2010–6

Notice 2010–6 provision relied upon (choose one):
(they are briefly described in the Table of Contents of Notice 2010–6)
V.A   V.B   V.C   V.D   VI.A   VI.B   VII.A   VII.B
VII.C   VII.D   VII.E   VII.F   VIII   IX

Name(s) and taxpayer identification number(s) of individual(s) affected by the failure:
1.
2.
3.

Name of affected nonqualified deferred compensation plan:

Brief description of failure:

Correction by plan amendment (describe corrective amendment, include date of adoption):

Sample Attachment for Service Provider's Federal Income Tax Return Correction of Documentary Failure to Comply with Section 409A Pursuant to Notice 2010–6

Notice 2010–6 provision relied upon (choose one):
(they are briefly described in the Table of Contents of Notice 2010–6)
V.A   V.B   V.C   V.D   VI.A   VI.B   VII.A   VII.B
VII.C   VII.D   VII.E   VII.F   VIII   IX

Name of affected nonqualified deferred compensation plan:

Brief description of failure:

Correction by plan amendment (describe corrective amendment, include date of adoption).

APPENDIX G
SAMPLE STATEMENTS FOR ATTACHMENT TO FEDERAL INCOME TAX RETURNS IN CONNECTION WITH CORRECTION OF OPERATIONAL FAILURES

Sample Attachment to Service Recipient's Federal Income Tax Return
Correction of Operational Failure to Comply with Section 409A Pursuant to Notice 2008–113

Notice 2008–113 provision relied upon (choose one):

IV.A   IV.B   IV.C   V.B   V.C   V.D   VI.C   VI.D
VII.B   VII.C   VII.D

Name(s) and taxpayer identification number(s) of individual(s) affected by the failure:
1.
2.
3.

Name of affected nonqualified deferred compensation plan:
Brief description of failure (include date of failure and amount involved):
Correction (describe correction method, including date on which correction was completed and steps taken to avoid a recurrence and the date such steps were taken):
Statement of compliance:

The operational failure(s) described above is (are) eligible for correction under Notice 2008–113, and the service recipient and service provider(s) have taken all actions required and otherwise met all requirements for such correction.

Sample Attachment to Service Provider's Federal Income Tax Return Correction of Operational Failure to Comply with Section 409A Pursuant to Notice 2008–113

Notice 2008–113 provision relied upon (choose one):

IV.A   IV.B   IV.C   V.B   V.C   V.D   VI.C   VI.D
VII.B   VII.C   VII.D

Name of affected nonqualified deferred compensation plan:

Brief description of failure (include date of failure and amount involved):

Correction (describe correction method, including date on which correction was completed and steps taken to avoid a recurrence and the date such steps were taken):

Statement of compliance:

The operational failure(s) described above is (are) eligible for correction under Notice 2008–113, and the service recipient and service provider(s) have taken all actions required and otherwise met all requirements for such correction.

APPENDIX H
SUPER SUMMARY FOR CORRECTION OF OPERATIONAL VIOLATION OF SECTION 409A

Notice 2008–113 OPERATIONAL ERROR SUPER SUMMARY FOR CORRECTION OF NONQUALIFED RETIREMENT INCOME PLANS (Excludes Correction for Stock Right Failure)

NOTICE 2008–113 Correction Process Summary. *Do not use this summary as a substitute for the Notice or for a stock error.*	Error Corrected in Same Tax Year	Error Corrected in the Following Tax Year <u>*Noninsiders Only*</u>	Error Corrected Before End of Second Tax Year (aggregate amounts less than 402(g)(1)(B) limit)	Error Corrected Before End of Second Tax Year (aggregate amounts more than 402(g)(1)(B) limit)
UNDER-DEFERRALS OR EARLY PAYMENT WRONG YEAR	* EE must repay amounts *Noninsiders:* No interest *Insiders:* AFR interest if amount exceeds 402(g)(1)(B) limit * No 20 percent; no penalty interest tax. * Account may be adjusted for earnings & losses. <u>*Citation:*</u> IV.A.	* EE must repay amounts with interest. * Original payment included in income in year paid: repayment is deductible in year paid (excluding interest); future payment included in income when paid. * Account may be adjusted retroactively for earnings & losses. <u>*Citation:*</u> V.B.	* EE does *not* repay. * Error amount only included in income; 20 percent but no penalty interest tax. * EE's W-2 / 1040 amended as to erroneous payment in year of error <u>*Citation:*</u> VI.B.	* EE must repay. *Noninsiders:* No interest. *Insiders:* Interest. * Error amount only included in income; 20 percent but no penalty interest tax. * EE's W-2 / 1040 amended as to erroneous payment in error year; no deduction for repayment; future payment then not included in income. Account may be retroactively adjusted for earnings & losses. <u>*Citation:*</u> VII.B.

NOTICE 2008–113 Correction Process Summary. *Do not use this summary as a substitute for the Notice or for a stock error.*	Error Corrected in Same Tax Year	Error Corrected in the Following Tax Year *Noninsiders Only*	Error Corrected Before End of Second Tax Year (aggregate amounts less than 402(g)(1)(B) limit)	Error Corrected Before End of Second Tax Year (aggregate amounts more than 402(g)(1)(B) limit)
EARLY PAYMENT CORRECT YEAR (30 DAYS PRIOR OR 6-MONTH DELAY RULE VIOLATIONS)	* EE must repay amounts. Subsequent payment to EE must be delayed by same number of days paid early. * No 20 percent; no penalty interest tax. * Account must *not* be adjusted for earnings but *may* be for losses. *Citation:* IV.B.	* EE must repay amounts. Subsequent payment to EE must be delayed by same number of days paid early. * Early payment included in income in year paid; future payment not included in income unless distributed in a subsequent year to repayment, in which event repayment is deductible. * No 20 percent; no penalty interest tax. * Account must *not* be adjusted for earnings but *may* be for losses. *Citation:* V.C.	* EE does not repay. * Error amount only included in income; 20 percent but no penalty interest tax. * EE's W-2 / 1040 amended as to erroneous payment in error year. *Citation:* VI.B.	* EE must repay. Subsequent payment to EE must be delayed by days paid early. * Error amount only included in income; 20 percent but no penalty interest tax. * EE's W-2 / 1040 amended as to erroneous payment in error year; no deduction for repayment; future payment then not included in income. Account may be retroactively adjusted for earnings & losses. *Citation:* VII.C.

NOTICE 2008–113 Correction Process Summary. *Do not use this summary as a substitute for the Notice or for a stock error.*	Error Corrected in Same Tax Year	Error Corrected in the Following Tax Year *Noninsiders Only*	Error Corrected Before End of Second Tax Year (aggregate amounts less than 402(g)(1)(B) limit)	Error Corrected Before End of Second Tax Year (aggregate amounts more than 402(g)(1)(B) limit)
EXCESS DEFERRAL OR UNDER PAYMENT (LATE PAYMENTS)	* ER must pay amounts ER may pay reasonable TVM interest. * Excess deferral/under payment * Under payment corrected in same tax year *not* 409A violation so no tax is not 409A error and no relief. * No 20 percent; no penalty interest tax. * Account: Noninsiders: May be adjusted for earnings & losses. Insiders: Must be adjusted for earnings. *Citation:* IV.C.	* ER must pay excess amounts ER may *not* pay TVM interest. * ER corrective amounts included in income in year paid. * No 20 percent; no penalty interest tax. * Account must be adjusted retroactively for earnings & may adjust for losses back to error date. *Citation:* V.D. *Note: V.D. does not clearly address under payment. IRS has indicated this is an oversight and correction under V.D. is available.*	* ER must pay excess or under payment amounts. ER may not pay TVM interest. * Amount in error only included in income; 20 percent but no penalty interest tax. * EE's W-2 & 1040 amended to include payment. * Account: ER must distribute or forfeit earnings, but not retain; ER may reduce payment or ignore as to losses. *Citation:* VI.C.	* ER must pay excess or under payment amounts. ER may *not* pay TVM interest. * Error amount only included; 20 percent but no penalty interest tax. * EE's W-2 / 1040 amended for error year; no deduction for EE repayment; future payment then not included in income. * Account: ER must adjust for earnings & may adjust for losses. *Citation:* VII.D.

Copyright 2009–2021 Infosys McCamish Systems, LLC. Used by permission. All rights reserved. For more information or reprint/use permission, contact Richard_Magner@Infosys.com.

TABLE OF AUTHORITIES

AMERICAN BAR ASSOCIATION JOINT COMMITTEE ON EMPLOYEE BENEFITS ANNUAL MEETING REPORTS

2007 ABA JCEB Questions, Q&A 1, 153
2008 ABA JCEB Questions, Q&A 25, 65, 75
2008 ABA JCEB Questions, Q&A 27, 132
2008 ABA JCEB Questions, Q&A 35, 148
2008 ABA JCEB Questions, Q&A 40, 53
2008 ABA JCEB Questions, Q&A 41, 61
2009 ABA JCEB Questions, Q&A 18, 60
2009 ABA JCEB Questions, Q&A 19, 63
2009 ABA JCEB Questions, Q&A 20, 9
2009 ABA JCEB Questions, Q&A 21, 111
2009 ABA JCEB Questions, Q&A 22, 65
2009 ABA JCEB Questions, Q&A 25, 122
2009 ABA JCEB Questions, Q&A 29, 179
2009 ABA JCEB Questions, Q&A 32, 31, 132
2010 ABA JECB Questions, Q&A 25, 82
2010 ABA JECB Questions, Q&A 26, 81
2010 ABA JECB Questions, Q&A 27, 71
2010 ABA JECB Questions, Q&A 32 and 33, 74
2012 ABA JCEB Questions, Q&A 20, 49

AUTHORS AND COMMENTATORS

Baier, Richard C., 78, 176
Barker, Rosina B., 214
Belinkie, Sasha, 47

Berglund, Brian W., 214
Boekeloo, David, 10, 33
Collins, Michael J., 33
Fogelman, William P., 266
Hayday, Caroline, 47
Hogans, Daniel L., 5, 17, 21, 28, 33, 61, 97, 141, 164, 173
Hopkins, Robert, 10, 33
Kroh, Jeffrey W., 266
Morrison, Helen, 61, 62
O'Brien, Kevin P., 214
Oringer, Andrew L., 58
Phelan, John, 78, 176
Ranta, Keith, 260
Richards, John, 262
Richey, Louis R., 10, 33, 78, 176
Schmidt, William, 21, 31, 42, 173
Tackney, Stephen, 21, 42, 60, 211, 260, 261, 264
Van Fleet, Lisa A., 214
Wolff, Carolyn G., 214

ARTICLES

409A Failures: Correcting With and Without Notice 2008–113 (Barker and O'Brien), 214

Advisor's Guide to Nonqualified Deferred Compensation, The (Richey, Baier & Phelan), 78, 176

California Franchise Tax Board Statement, 100

Internal Revenue Code Section 409A: Ten Traps for the Unwary (Hogans and Collins), 33

Multiple Definitions of Substantial Risk of Forfeiture Create Confusion after Section 409A, but Notice 2007–62 Is Not the Answer (Boekeloo, Hopkins and Richey), 10, 33

Release Us from Confusion Over Nonqualified Deferred Compensation (Oringer), 58–59

Section 409A in Action (Berglund, Van Fleet, and Wolff), 214

Section 409A & Six Month Delay: Don't Forget Your Directors (Hayday and Belinkie), 47

TABLE OF AUTHORITIES **325**

View from Groom: An Open (or Closed) Section 409A Case (Kroh and Fogelman), 266

COURT CASES
Bond v. Marriott International, Inc., No. 15-1160 (4th Cir. 2016), 90
Davidson v. Henkel, 12-CV-14103, 2015 WL 74257 (E.D. Mich. Jan. 5, 2015), 95
Graphic Packaging Holding Co., Inc. v. Humphrey, 2010 U.S. App, LEXIS 23718, 50 E.B.C. 1289 (11th Cir. 2010), 147
Moran v. Davita, Inc., 441 F. App'x. 942 (3rd Cir. 2011), 52
Mozingo v. Trend Personnel, No. 15-11263 (5th Cir. App. Ct. Aug. 31, 2016), 161
Wilson v. Safelite Group, Inc., 930 F. 3rd 429 (6th Cir. 2019), 94–95

FEDERAL SECURITIES REGULATIONS
17 C.F.R. §§ 240.13d-3 and 16a-1(f) (2012), 255
17 C.F.R. § 240.16a-1(f), 256

FEDERAL STATUTES OTHER THAN INTERNAL REVENUE CODE
American Jobs Creation Act of 2004, 16, 271
Emergency Economic Stabilization Act of 2008, 76
Employee Retirement Income Security Act of 1974 (ERISA), 7, 89, 95, 161, 175, 187, 272, 307, 309
Fair Labor Standards Act, 154
Gulf Opportunity Zone Act of 2005 (GOZA), 177
Securities Exchange Act of 1934, 43, 178–179, 255, 256
Tax Reform Act of 2014, 276

INTERNAL REVENUE CODE
I.R.C. §§ 101(j), 161
I.R.C. § 104(a)(3), 153
I.R.C. §§ 162(m)(3), 409A(b)(3), 179
I.R.C. §§ 401(c)(4), 47
I.R.C. §§ 402(g)(1)(B), (4), 255
I.R.C. § 409A, 16

I.R.C. § 409A(a), 101, 102
I.R.C. § 409A(a)(1), 93
I.R.C. § 409A(a)(1)(A), 91
I.R.C. § 409A(a)(1)(a)(i), 133
I.R.C. § 409A(a)(1)(A)(ii), 94, 97, 98
I.R.C. § 409A(a)(1)(A)(i)(I), 13
I.R.C. §§ 409A(a)(1)(A)(i)(II) and (B), 93
I.R.C. §§ 409A(a)(1)(B)(i)(II), (b)(4)(A)(ii), 194
I.R.C. § 409A(a)(2), 16, 36
I.R.C. § 409A(a)(2)(A)(i), 38
I.R.C. § 409A(a)(2)(A)(i)-(vi), 70
I.R.C. § 409A(a)(2)(A)(v), 75, 76
I.R.C. § 409A(a)(2)(B)(ii), 71, 183
I.R.C. § 409A(a)(2)(C), 52, 183
I.R.C. § 409A(a)(3), 66, 85
I.R.C. § 409A(a)(4)(B)(iii), 120
I.R.C. § 409A(b), 179, 191
I.R.C. § 409A(b)(1), 177
I.R.C. § 409A(b)(2), 176, 177
I.R.C. § 409A(c), 100, 275
I.R.C. § 409A(d), 2, 4, 10, 33, 161
I.R.C. § 409A(d)(1), 5
I.R.C. §§ 416(i), 47
I.R.C. § 457A, 168
I.R.C. §§ 457(e)(11), 280
I.R.C. §§ 457(e)(12), 280
I.R.C. §457(f), 276
I.R.C. § 457(f), 278
I.R.C. §§ 3401(a), 195
I.R.C. §§ 3403, 196
I.R.C. §§ 6041(g)(1), 195
I.R.C. §§ 6051(a)(13), 195
I.R.C. §§ 6501(a), 264
I.R.C. §§ 6501(c)(2), 264
I.R.C. §§ 6501(e), 264
I.R.C. §§ 6601, 196

I.R.C. §§ 6651, 196
I.R.C. §§ 6662, 196
I.R.C. §§ 6672, 196
I.R.C. §§ 6721, 196
I.R.C. §§ 6722, 196

INTERNAL REVENUE SERVICE NOTICES

Notice 2002–8, 162
Notice 2005–1, 10
Notice 2005–1, Q&A 7, 11
Notice 2005–1, Q&A 15, 83
Notice 2005–1, Q&A 19, 275
Notice 2006–33, 179
Notice 2007–34, 158, 161–162
Notice 2007–62, 10, 33
Notice 2007–86, 275
Notice 2008–13, § III.G, 255
Notice 2008–62, 114, 277
Notice 2008–113, 91, 98, 100, 199, 200, 204, 206, 213–215, 229, 231–232, 234–236, 238–239, 241, 243–244, 246, 248, 250–251, 253–257, 262–263, 317–318
Notice 2008–113, § III.B, 263
Notice 2008–113, § III(H), 196
Notice 2008–113, § III.I, 257
Notice 2008–113, § IV.A, modified by Notice 2010–6, § XIII.A, 219, 241
Notice 2008–113, § IV.B, modified by Notice 2010–6, § XIII.A, 229, 248
Notice 2008–113, § IV.C, 224, 235
Notice 2008–113, §§ IV.D, IX.A, 254
Notice 2008–113, § IX, modified by Notice 2010–80, § III.H, 257
Notice 2008–113, § IX.B, 262
Notice 2008–113, modified by Notice 2010–6 and Notice 2010–80, 213
Notice 2008–113, § V.B, 221, 243
Notice 2008–113, § V.C, 231
Notice 2008–113, § V.C, modified by Notice 2010–6, § XIII.A, 250

Notice 2008–113, § V.D, 236
Notice 2008–113, § V.D, modified by Notice 2010–6, § XIII.B, 225
Notice 2008–113, §§ V.D and E, 206
Notice 2008–113, §§ V.E, IX.A, 254
Notice 2008–113, § VI.B, 232, 244, 251
Notice 2008–113, § VI.C, 226, 238
Notice 2008–113, § VII.B, 223
Notice 2008–113, § VII.C, 234, 246
Notice 2008–113, § VII.C, modified by Notice 2010–6, § XIII.A, 253
Notice 2008–113, § VII.D, 227, 239
Notice 2008–115, § III.A, 195
Notice 2009–8, 168
Notice 2010–6, 21, 58, 91, 100, 197, 210–211, 213–215, 219, 225, 229, 241, 248, 250, 253, 260–262, 264, 275, 315–316
Notice 2010–6, §§ III.C, V.A-C, VI.B, modified by Notice 2010–80, § III.B, 201
Notice 2010–6, §§ III.C, VI.A, VII.C, VII.F, VIII, IX, 205
Notice 2010–6, §§ III.C, VII.B, 205
Notice 2010–6, §§ III.C, XI.B, 207
Notice 2010–6, §§ III.E, F, 208
Notice 2010–6, § III.F, 196, 207
Notice 2010–6, § III.G, 206
Notice 2010–6, §§ III.G, XI.B-C, modified by Notice 2010–80, § III.A, 198
Notice 2010–6, § IV, 200
Notice 2010–6, modified by Notice 2010–80, 197–198, 201, 209
Notice 2010–6, § X, 210
Notice 2010–6, § XII, modified by Notice 2010–80, § III.E, 209
Notice 2010–80, 21, 54, 58, 85, 91, 197–198, 201, 206, 209, 213–214, 257
Notice 2010–80, § III.A, 206
Notice 2020–50, § 6, 182

PREAMBLES TO FINAL AND PROPOSED TREASURY REGULATIONS
Preamble, Part III.E.2, I.R.B. 2008–51 (Dec. 22, 2008), 264
Preamble to 2008 Proposed 409A Regulations § II, 99, 265, 266, 267

TABLE OF AUTHORITIES 329

Preamble to 2016 Proposed 409A Regulations, Section entitled "Proposed Effective Dates," 65, 66
Preamble to 2016 Proposed 409A Regulations § II.A, 169
Preamble to 2016 Proposed 409A Regulations § II.B, 28
Preamble to 2016 Proposed 409A Regulations § II.C.1, 139
Preamble to 2016 Proposed 409A Regulations § II.C.2, 138
Preamble to 2016 Proposed 409A Regulations § II.D, 128
Preamble to 2016 Proposed 409A Regulations § II.E, 155
Preamble to 2016 Proposed 409A Regulations § II.F, 114
Preamble to 2016 Proposed 409A Regulations § III.A, 40
Preamble to 2016 Proposed 409A Regulations § III.B, 42
Preamble to 2016 Proposed 409A Regulations § IV, 56
Preamble to 2016 Proposed 409A Regulations § IV, footnote 2, 292
Preamble to 2016 Proposed 409A Regulations §§ IV.C.2 and E, 286
Preamble to 2016 Proposed 409A Regulations § V.A, 56, 57, 58
Preamble to 2016 Proposed 409A regulations § V.B, 149
Preamble to 2016 Proposed 409A Regulations § V.B, 148
Preamble to 2016 Proposed 409A Regulations § VI, 73
Preamble to 2016 Proposed 409A Regulations § VI.A, 72
Preamble to 2016 Proposed 409A Regulations § VI.C, 82
Preamble to 2016 Proposed 409A Regulations § VI.D, 86
Preamble to 2016 Proposed 409A Regulations § VII, 94
Preamble to 2016 Proposed 409A Regulations § VIII, 2, 8
Preamble to 2016 Proposed 457 Regulations § III.B.1, 281
Preamble to 2016 Proposed 457 Regulations § III.C, 282
Preamble to 2016 Proposed 457 Regulations § III.D, 283
Preamble to 2016 Proposed 457 Regulations § III.E, 283
Preamble to 2016 Proposed 457 Regulations § IV.B.2, 290, 291
Preamble to 2016 Proposed 457 Regulations § IV.B.3, 291
Preamble to 2016 Proposed 457 Regulations § IV.C.2, 284
Preamble to 2016 Proposed 457 Regulations § IV.C.3, 287
Preamble to 2016 Proposed 457 Regulations § IV.E, 126, 288, 289
Preamble to 2016 Proposed 457 Regulations § V, 277
Preamble to Final 409A Regulations § VI.D (2007), 120
Preamble to Final 409A Regulations § II.B (2007), 27, 33, 56, 286
Preamble to Final 409A Regulations § III.G (2007), 11

Preamble to Final 409A Regulations § V.B (2007), 124
Preamble to Final 409A Regulations § VII.C.2.f (2007), 39
Preamble to Final 409A Regulations § VII.C.3.f (2007), 38
Preamble to Final 409A Regulations § VIII.H (2007), 74
Preamble to Final Section 409A Regulations § VIII(F) (2007), 90
Preamble to Treas. Reg. 1.409A-1 *et seq.*, I.R.B. 2007–19 (May 7, 2007), § II.B, 10

PRIVATE LETTER RULINGS
I.R.S. CCA Memo 20158013, 211
I.R.S. CCA Memo 200935029 (Aug. 28, 2009), 16, 85
PLR 9030028, 10, 33
PLR 9041026, 10, 33
PLR 201147038, 67
PLR 201221033, 67

REPORTS
H.R. Conf. Rep. No. 108–755, 737 (Oct. 22, 2004), 271
H.R. Conf. Rep. No. 108–755, 70777 (Oct. 22, 2004), 177
H.R. Conf. Rep. No. 108–775 (Oct. 22, 2004) pp. 514–15, 524 (§ 409A "funding" rules), 176

REVENUE PROCEDURES
Rev. Proc. 2008–50, §§ 6.02(5)(b), (c), 214
Rev. Proc. 2008–61, § 2.08, 194
Rev. Proc. 2013–3, § 3.01(46), 194

REVENUE RULINGS
Rev. Rul. 2002–22, 310
Rev. Rul. 2004–56, 71
Rev. Rul. 2010–27, 71

STATE STATUTE AND STATEMENT
California Franchise Tax Board Statement, Tax News (May, 2008), 100
Cal. Rev. Tax Code § 17501 as amended by AB 1173, 100

TREASURY REGULATIONS, FINAL

Treas. Reg. §§ 1.61-22, 158, 162
Treas. Reg. §§ 1.83-3(e), 147
Treas. Reg. §§ 1.83-3(e) and 1.409A-1(b)(4) and (l), 147
Treas. Reg. § 1.104-1(d), 153
Treas. Reg. §§ 1.401A-1(h)(1)(i), 1.409A-2(b), 1.409A-3(a), (i)(2)(i), (j)(1), (j)(4), 67
Treas. Reg. §§ 1.401(k)-1(d)(3)(iv)(E) and (F), 120
Treas. Reg. §§ 1.401(k)-1(d)(4), 81
Treas. Reg. § 1.409-2(b)(9) Examples 5 and 19, 196
Treas. Reg. § 1.409-1(c)(1)-(3), 133
Treas. Reg. §§ 1.409A-1, 1.409A-3, 16
Treas. Reg. §§ 1.409A-1–3, 101, 102
Treas. Reg. § 1.409A-1(a)(1), 5
Treas. Reg. §§ 1.409A-1(a)(1), (b), (c), 161
Treas. Reg. §§ 1.409A-1(a)(1), (b) and (c), 161
Treas. Reg. §§ 1.409A-1(a)(1) and (b)(1), 5
Treas. Reg. § 1.409A-1(a)(3), 164, 167
Treas. Reg. §§ 1.409A-1(a)(3), 164
Treas. Reg. §§ 1.409A-1(a)(3)(i) and (b)(8)(i), 165
Treas. Reg. § 1.409A-1(a)(3)(iv), 166
Treas. Reg. § 1.409A-1(a)(3)(v), 166
Treas. Reg. § 1.409A-1(a)(4), 27, 56, 279, 286
Treas. Reg. § 1.409A-1(a)(5), 12
Treas. Reg. §§ 1.409A-1(a) and (b), 161
Treas. Reg. § 1.409A-1(a)(b), 33
Treas. Reg. §§ 1.409A-1(a)-(b), 2, 4, 10
Treas. Reg. § 1.409A-1(b)(1), 7
Treas. Reg. § 1.409A-1(b)(3) and (4), 23
Treas. Reg. § 1.409A-1(b)(4), 26
Treas. Reg. §§ 1.409A-1(b)(4), 127, 281
Treas. Reg. §§ 1.409A-1(b)(4) and (9), 151
Treas. Reg. §§ 1.409A-1(b)(4) and (l), 147
Treas. Reg. §§ 1.409A-1(b)(4)(i)(F) and (9)(v)(D), 129
Treas. Reg. § 1.409A-1(b)(4)(ii), 17, 28

Treas. Reg. § 1.409A-1(b)(5), 136
Treas. Reg. § 1.409A-1(b)(5)(i), 144, 146
Treas. Reg. § 1.409A-1(b)(5)(i)(D), 137
Treas. Reg. § 1.409A-1(b)(5)(i)(E), 144, 145
Treas. Reg. § 1.409A-1(b)(5)(ii), 135
Treas. Reg. § 1.409A-1(b)(5)(iii), 138
Treas. Reg. § 1.409A-1(b)(5)(iv), 141, 142
Treas. Reg. §§ 1.409A-1(b)(5)(iv)(B)(2), 141
Treas. Reg. §§ 1.409A-1(b)(5)(iv)(B)(2)(iii), 141
Treas. Reg. § 1.409A-1(b)(5)(v), 143
Treas. Reg. § 1.409A-1(b)(5)(v)(H), 145
Treas. Reg. § 1.409A-1(b)(5)(v)(I), 206
Treas. Reg. § 1.409A-1(b)(6)(i), 147
Treas. Reg. § 1.409A-1(b)(8)(iii), 166
Treas. Reg. §§ 1.409A-1(b)(9), 127, 281
Treas. Reg. § 1.409A-1(b)(9)(i), 133
Treas. Reg. §§ 1.409A-1(b)(9)(iii) and (n), 130
Treas. Reg. §§ 1.409A-1(b)(9)(ii)-(iv), (h)(6), (m), (n), 134
Treas. Reg. §§ 1.409A-1(b)(9)(v), 153
Treas. Reg. § 1.409A-1(b)(9)(vi), 134
Treas. Reg. § 1.409A-1(b)(10)-(11), 155
Treas. Reg. §§ 1.409A-1(c), 108
Treas. Reg. § 1.409A-1(c)(1)-(3), 21
Treas. Reg. § 1.409A-1(c)(2), 98
Treas. Reg. §§ 1.409A-1(c)(2), 97
Treas. Reg. § 1.409A-1(c)(2)(i)(C)(2), 97, 173
Treas. Reg. § 1.409A-1(c)(3), 6, 15, 17, 97, 108
Treas. Reg. § 1.409A-1(c)(3)(i), 15, 21
Treas. Reg. §§ 1.409A-1(c)(3)(i) and (iii), 117
Treas. Reg. § 1.409A-1(c)(3)(iii), 21
Treas. Reg. § 1.409A-1(c)(3)(viii), 97
Treas. Reg. §§ 1.409A-1(c)(3)(viii), 97
Treas. Reg. § 1.409A-1(d), 31
Treas. Reg. § 1.409A-1(d)(1), 31, 124
Treas. Reg. § 1.409A-1(f), 8
Treas. Reg. § 1.409A-1(g), 8

Treas. Reg. § 1.409A-1(h)(1)(i), 39, 192
Treas. Reg. § 1.409A-1(h)(1)(ii), 42, 192
Treas. Reg. §§ 1.409A-1(h)(1)(i)-(ii), (h)(4), (h)(5), 38
Treas. Reg. § 1.409A-1(h)(2), 41
Treas. Reg. § 1.409A-1(h)(4), 39
Treas. Reg. § 1.409A-1(h)(5), 42
Treas. Reg. § 1.409A-1(i), 44
Treas. Reg. § 1.409A-1(i)(5), 51
Treas. Reg. §§ 1.409A-1(i)(5), 51
Treas. Reg. § 1.409A-1(i)(6)(i), 49
Treas. Reg. § 1.409A-1(i)(6)(ii), 49
Treas. Reg. § 1.409A-1(i)(6)(iii), 50
Treas. Reg. § 1.409A-1(i)(6)(iv), 50
Treas. Reg. §§ 1.409A-1(i)(6)(v), 51
Treas. Reg. §§ 1.409A-1(i) and (j), 46
Treas. Reg. § 1.409A-1(n)(2), 131
Treas. Reg. §§ 1.409A-2, 78
Treas. Reg. § 1.409A-2(a), 103
Treas. Reg. §§ 1.409A-2(a), 108
Treas. Reg. §§ 1.409A-2(a)(1), 88
Treas. Reg. § 1.409A-2(a)(3), 188
Treas. Reg. § 1.409A-2(a)(8), 110, 189, 190
Treas. Reg. § 1.409A-2(a)(13), 109
Treas. Reg. § 1.409A-2(a)(14), 114
Treas. Reg. §§ 1.409A-2(a) and (b), 187
Treas. Reg. § 1.409A-2(b), 111, 116
Treas. Reg. § 1.409A-2(b)(1), 116, 122
Treas. Reg. §§ 1.409A-2(b)(1), 124
Treas. Reg. § 1.409A-2(b)(2)(i), 108, 118, 121
Treas. Reg. §§ 1.409A-2(b)(2)(i), 59, 60, 124
Treas. Reg. § 1.409A-2(b)(2)(ii), 116, 117
Treas. Reg. § 1.409A-2(b)(2)(ii)(A), 172
Treas. Reg. §§ 1.409A-2(b)(2)(ii) and (iii), 75
Treas. Reg. § 1.409A-2(b)(2)(ii)(D), 118
Treas. Reg. § 1.409A-2(b)(2)(iii), 119
Treas. Reg. § 1.409A-2(b)(2)(iii) and (5), 119

Treas. Reg. § 1.409A-2(b)(7)(i), 64
Treas. Reg. § 1.409A-2(b)(7)(ii), 64
Treas. Reg. § 1.409A-3(a), 36, 62, 83
Treas. Reg. §§ 1.409A-3(a), 59
Treas. Reg. § 1.409A-3(a)(i)(3), 184
Treas. Reg. § 1.409A-3(c), 60
Treas. Reg. §§ 1.409A-3(c), 58, 60
Treas. Reg. §§ 1.409A-3(c), (d), (g) and (j)(4)(v), 217
Treas. Reg. § 1.409A-3(d), 54, 58, 62, 63, 246
Treas. Reg. § 1.409A-3(e), 148
Treas. Reg. § 1.409A-3(f), 66, 83, 84, 85, 190
Treas. Reg. §§ 1.409A-3(f), 85
Treas. Reg. § 1.409A-3(g), 67
Treas. Reg. §§ 1.409A-3(i)(1)(iv), 153
Treas. Reg. § 1.409A-3(i)(1)(v), 95, 154
Treas. Reg. §§ 1.409A-3(i)(3)(i)-(iii), 71, 183
Treas. Reg. § 1.409A-3(i)(4), 184
Treas. Reg. §§ 1.409A-3(i)(4), 52
Treas. Reg. §§ 1.409A-3(i)(4) (ii)-(vii) and (ix)-(xi), 70
Treas. Reg. §§ 1.409A-3(i)(4)(i)-(iii), 183
Treas. Reg. § 1.409A-3(i)(5), 75, 76
Treas. Reg. § 1.409A-3(i)(5)(iv)(A), 148
Treas. Reg. § 1.409A-3(j)(2), 71, 183
Treas. Reg. § 1.409A-3(j)(3), 73
Treas. Reg. §§ 1.409A-3(j)(4)(i), 74
Treas. Reg. §§ 1.409A-3(j)(4)(i) and (ix), 81, 183
Treas. Reg. §§ 1.409A-3(j)(4)(i) and (v), 74
Treas. Reg. §§ 1.409A-3(j)(4)(ii), 78, 79
Treas. Reg. §§ 1.409A-3(j)(4)(iv), 292
Treas. Reg. § 1.409A-3(j)(4)(ix), 82, 83
Treas. Reg. §§ 1.409A-3(j)(4)(ix), 162
Treas. Reg. §§ 1.409A-3(j)(4)(ix)(A), 81
Treas. Reg. § 1.409A-3(j)(4)(ix)(B), 81
Treas. Reg. § 1.409A-3(j)(4)(ix)(C), 81, 185
Treas. Reg. §§ 1.409A-3(j)(4)(vi), 86
Treas. Reg. § 1.409A-3(j)(4)(vii), 86

Treas. Reg. § 1.409A-3(j)(4)(viii), 186
Treas. Reg. §§ 1.409A-3(j)(4)(viii) & (xii), 186
Treas. Reg. § 1.409A-3(j)(4)(x), 87
Treas. Reg. §§ 1.409A-3(j)(4)(xi), 86
Treas. Reg. §§ 1.409A-3(j)(4)(xii), 52
Treas. Reg. §§ 1.409A-3(j)(4)(xiii), 85
Treas. Reg. § 1.409A-3(j)(4)(xiv), 88
Treas. Reg. §§ 1.409A-3(j)(6), 88
Treas. Reg. § 1.409A-6(a), 215
Treas. Reg. § 1.409A-6(a)(1)-(4), 271
Treas. Reg. § 1.409A-6(a)(1)(i), 269
Treas. Reg. § 1.409A-6(a)(1)(i), second sentence, 273
Treas. Reg. § 1.409A-6(a)(3), 274
Treas. Reg. §§ 1.409A-6(a)(4)(i)(C), 79
Treas. Reg. § 1.409A-6(a)(4)(iv), 272
Treas. Reg. § 1.409A-6(b), 275
Treas. Reg. § 1.409A-(b)(4)(ii), 28
Treas. Reg. §§ 1.7872-15, 158
Treas. Reg. § 31.3121(v)(2)-1(b)(4)(iv)(C), 12
Treas. Reg. § 1.409A-3(i)(3), 307

TREASURY REGULATIONS, PROPOSED

Prop. Treas. Reg. § 1.409A-1(a)(4) (2016), 169
Prop. Treas. Reg. § 1.409A-1(a)(5) (2016), 12, 13
Prop. Treas. Reg. § 1.409A-1(b)(4)(ii) (2016), 28
Prop. Treas. Reg. § 1.409A-1(b)(5)(iii)(A) (2016), 139
Prop. Treas. Reg. § 1.409A-1(b)(5)(iii)(E)(1) (2016), 138
Prop. Treas. Reg. § 1.409A-1(b)(9)(iii)(A)(1) (2016), 128
Prop. Treas. Reg. § 1.409A-1(b)(11) (2016), 155
Prop. Treas. Reg. § 1.409A-1(b)(13) (2016), 114
Prop. Treas. Reg. § 1.409A-1(h)(4) (2016), 40
Prop. Treas. Reg. § 1.409A-1(j)(13)(B) (2016), 86
Prop. Treas. Reg. § 1.409A-1(q) (2016), 56, 66
Prop. Treas. Reg. § 1.409A-1(q)(1)(2016), 65
Prop. Treas. Reg. § 1.409A-1(q)(2) (2016), 66
Prop. Treas. Reg. § 1.409A-1(q)(2016), 286

Prop. Treas. Reg. § 1.409A-3(b) (2016), 56
Prop. Treas. Reg. § 1.409A-3(d)(2) (2016), 57
Prop. Treas. Reg. § 1.409A-3(i)(5)(i)(A) (2016), 149
Prop. Treas. Reg. § 1.409A-3(j) (2016), 72
Prop. Treas. Reg. § 1.409A-3(j)(4)(iii)(B) (2016), 73
Prop. Treas. Reg. § 1.409A-3(j)(4)(ix)(C)(2) (2016), 82
Prop. Treas. Reg. § 1.409A-4, I.R.B. 2008-51 (Dec. 22, 2008), 91, 93, 94, 195, 211
Prop. Treas. Reg. § 1.409A-4(a)(1)(ii)(A), 99, 265, 266
Prop. Treas. Reg. §§ 1.409A-4(a)(1)(ii) and (a)(3), 264
Prop. Treas. Reg. § 1.409A-4(a)(1)(ii)(B) (2016), 94
Prop. Treas. Reg. § 1.457-11 (2016), 280
Prop. Treas. Reg. § 1.457-11(b) (2016), 281
Prop. Treas. Reg. § 1.457-11(d) (2016), 281
Prop. Treas. Reg. § 1.457-11(e)(1) (2016), 282
Prop. Treas. Reg. § 1.457-11(e)(2) (2016), 283
Prop. Treas. Reg. § 1.457-11(f) (2016), 283
Prop. Treas. Reg. § 1.457-12(a)(2) (2016), 278
Prop. Treas. Reg. § 1.457-12(c)(1) (2016), 291
Prop. Treas. Reg. § 1.457-12(c)(1)(i) (2016), 290
Prop. Treas. Reg. § 1.457-12(c)(1)(iv) (2016), 291
Prop. Treas. Reg. § 1.457-12(d)(1)(i) (2016), 280
Prop. Treas. Reg. § 1.457-12(d)(2) (2016), 284
Prop. Treas. Reg. § 1.457-12(d)(3) (2016), 287
Prop. Treas. Reg. § 1.457-12(e) (2016), 10, 33
Prop. Treas. Reg. § 1.457-12(e)(2) (2016), 288, 289
Prop. Treas. Reg. § 457-12(d) (2016), 279

INDEX

A

Acceleration of benefits
  beneficiary change and, 72–73
  cafeteria plan, 88
  cash-out distribution, 69
  cash-out of small benefits, 74
  change of control and, 75
  conflict of interest or foreign ethics laws and, 69, 73
  deferred compensation distributions, 69–70
  disability or death, 71–72
  dispute settlement and, 87–88
  domestic relations order, 69, 76–78
  election by service provider, 72–73, 74, 81
  employer termination/liquidation of plan, 79–81
  federal debt collection laws and, 86
  forfeiture or voluntary relinquishment of deferred compensation, 84–85
  impermissible service recipient discretion, 201
  installment or annuity payment cash-outs, 74–75
  loans prohibited, 83–84
  lump sum cash-out, 73–74
  nonallocation year and, 87
  offset provisions, 85–86
  pandemic emergency, 70–71, 181–192
  provision for plan termination, 81
  as security for loan or other amount due creditors, 84
  service recipient plan termination, 81–82
  substitute plans or benefits prohibited, 83
  substitution rule, 83
  tax-exempt entities and, 292
  tax withholding and, 86
  top hat plans, 89–90
  unforeseeable emergency, 70–71
  vesting, unforeseeable acceleration of, 69, 82–83
  violation of Section 409A and, 86
Account balance plan
  documentation requirements, 20
  grandfathering and, 274
  types of subject to Section 409A, 1–2
Aggregation rule
  deferrals and, 96
  federal income tax liability, 96
  other Section 409A applications, 97
  plan types for, 95–96
  service provider deferral elections, 108
Ambiguous terms, use of to define payment event, 198–200

Annualized recurring part-year compensation, 105
Anti-toggling rule, 59–61
  impermissible additional payment schedules, 202–203
Applicable covered employee, 177–179
Asset sales and separation from service, 39, 40

B

Beneficiary change, 72–73
Benefits
  acceleration of (*see* Acceleration of benefits)
  death (*see* Death benefits)
Board of directors, early distribution with consent of, 16
Bona fide death benefit plan, 3, 12, 157, 282
Bonus
  deferral and cancellation, 110–111
  discretionary, 181, 190
Bonus life insurance or annuity plan
  advantages of, 159
  defined, 158–159
  disadvantages of, 159–160
Breach of Section 409A
  aggregation rule, 95–97
  documentary violation, 97
  employer disclaimer of responsibility, 95
  enforcement of penalties, 196
  federal income tax consequences of, 93
  federal income tax structure, 91–93
  income tax due on, 92–93
  mediation of negative tax consequences, 100
  negative tax consequences, 92
  operational violation, 98–99
  prior federal income tax law and, 99–100
  service provider violation, 91
  service recipient responsible for payment of taxes due to, 94–95
  state personal income tax, 100
  statute of limitations, 264–265
  subsequent deferrals after, 99
  substantial risk of forfeiture, 94
Broad-based foreign retirement plan, 166

C

Cafeteria plan, 88
Cash basis rule for subsequent year, 109
Cash-out distribution
  acceleration of benefits, 69
  installment or annuity, 74–75
  lump sum, 73–74
  small benefits, 74
Change in ownership or effective control (CIC, COC)
  accelerated benefits, 69, 75
  defined for Section 409A, 75–76
  election to distribute by service provider, 75
  impermissible definition of, 202
  plan continuation following, 75, 79–80, 82
  as primary permissible distribution event, 35
Child college admission as impermissible distribution event, 16
CIC or COC (*see* Change in ownership or effective control)
Commissions, 1, 101, 103–104, 105, 198

Compensation
  covered, 1, 171–172, 215
  educational partial-year
    (*see* Recurring part-year
    compensation)
  subject to forfeiture, 107
  substantial risk of forfeiture and,
    28–31
Conflict of interest laws,
  acceleration of benefits to
  comply with, 69, 73
Correction, super summary for,
  319–322
Correction of Documentary
  Failures sample statements,
  315–316
Correction of operational errors,
  214. *See also* Di minimus error
  correction
Correction of Operational Failures
  sample statements, 317–318
Covenant not to compete,
  substantial risk of forfeiture
  and, 30
Covid-19 pandemic. *See* Pandemic
  emergency distributions

D

Death
  accelerated benefits, 69, 71–72
  beneficiary, 58
  payments made upon, 56
  as primary permissible
    distribution event, 35
Death benefit only (DBO) life
  insurance plans, 1, 12, 161, 162
Death benefits
  bona fide plans, 12, 282
  and death of beneficiary, 58
  specification of period of
    payment of, 57

Debt collection laws, offsets of
  deferred compensation to
  comply with, 86
Deferral elections. *See* Service
  provider deferral elections
Deferred amounts, tax
  consequences due to breach of
  Section 409A on, 93
Deferred compensation
  acceleration of benefits, 69–70,
    86–90
  amounts paid shortly after
    earned as not, 23
  checklist for structuring
    nonqualified, 293–294
  definition of, 4–6
  dispute settlement and,
    87–88
  employer account balance plans,
    101–102
  employer non-account balance
    plans, 102
  federal debt collection laws and,
    86
  foreign plans, 163–165
  forfeiture or voluntary
    relinquishment of, 84–85
  income amounts includable
    under Section 457, 290,
    291–292
  made in form of stock option,
    66
  nonallocation year and, 87
  participant account balance
    plans, 101
  present value of, 291
  replaced with split-dollar
    arrangement, 66
  tax withholding and, 86
Delayed payments, 63–64
De Minimis error correction, 214

Disability
  accelerated benefits, 69, 71–72
  definition of, 52
  impermissible definition of, 200
  leave of absence, 18, 38–39
  letter rulings, 193–194
  loans, 84
  plan access during pandemic, 184
  as primary permissible
    distribution event, 35
  stoppage of deferral
    contributions only-different
    definition, 52
Disability pay, 11–12
  bona fide disability pay plans,
    282–283
  separation from service and, 53
Discretionary bonus, 5, 109, 181,
  190
Dispute settlement, 87–88
Distribution events
  anti-toggling rule, 59–61
  asset sale, 39, 40
  benefit value as a basis for form
    of distribution, 64–65
  death of beneficiary and, 58
  delayed payments, 63–64
  disability, 52
  downturn in financial health, 63
  earliest of two or more
    permissible events, 59
  employee to independent
    contractor status change,
    41–42
  impermissible, 16
  independent contractors and
    separation from service, 40–41
  involuntary separation from
    service, 62
  late payments, 62–63
  leave of absence, 38–39
  marriage and, 61
  pandemic emergency, 70–71,
    181–191
  plan terminations, 35–36, 79–82
  primary permissible, 35–36
  publicly traded companies,
    43–44
  refusal or failure to make
    payment, 67
  rehire impact, 66–67, 118
  separation from service
    qualifications, 36–38
  service provider claim release
    and, 58–59
  six-month delay rule, 44–46
  small amounts, 64, 73–74, 215,
    312
  specified employees, identifying,
    44–51
  split-dollar arrangement, 66
  stock option, 66
  stock *vs.* cash payment, 65
  suspension of due to employee
    rehire, 66–67
  time and payment type, plan
    dictated, 53–54
Distribution restrictions,
  grandfathered amounts and,
  274–275
Dividend-equivalent distributions,
  147–148
Divorce, 19, 76, 77–78, 296, 303,
  307
Documentary errors
  ambiguous provisions and
    terms, 198–200
  amendment correction with
    limited recognition, 201–205
  amendment correction without
    income recognition, 200–201
  corrections requiring plan
    amendment, 205, 209–210
  limiting tax consequences, 197

linked plans, 207
new plan treatment, 208–209
Notice 2010-6, correcting without complying with, 210–211
Notice 2010-6 corrections, 207–208
plan amendment, correction by, 200–205
plan types not eligible for correction, 198
scriveners' error, 210
service provider income, 208–209
stock plans, 206
stock rights, 206
types of errors subject to correction, 197–198
Documentary violation, 97, 210–211
Documentation requirements, Section 409A
  account balance plan, 20
  all plans, 18–19
  elective deferral plan, 20
  employer non-account balance plan, 21
  error corrections, 315–316
  minimum requirements for, 18–21
  part-year compensation deferral elections, 113
  plans outside scope of, 17
  prohibited distribution events, 16
  provisions not permitted or advisable, 21
  publicly held employer plan, 19–20
  right to select time/ form of payment plan, 20
  tax consequences of violation of, 97
  timetable, 15
  written plans, 15
Domestic relations order (QDRO), 307–310
  acceleration of benefits, 69, 76–78
Downturn in financial health, 63

E

Early distribution with board of directors consent, 16
Educator recurring part-year compensation, 105
Effective dates
  compliance standards from 2005 through 2008, 275
  efforts to repeal Section 409A and, 276
  grandfathering, 269–275
  Section 409A, 269, 275
Election cancellation, 52, 110–111, 120, 182, 185–186
Election to defer. *See* Service provider deferral elections
Elective deferral plan
  documentation requirements, 20
E-mails, Section 409A documentation and, 18
Employee definition. *See* Service recipient
Employee stock purchase plan options, 135
Employer account balance plans, 101–102
Employer non-account balance plans
  documentation requirements, 21
  elections of time and form of payment, 107
  treatment under Section 409A, 102

Employer-owned life insurance policy, 161
Employment agreements
  fringe benefit arrangements, 151–153
  indemnification payments, 155
  legal fees, employment-related, 155
  legal settlements, 154
  Section 409A issues, 151
  self-insured medical coverage, 153
  tax gross-up payment, 153–154
Enforcement
  409A issues ruled on by IRS, 194
  auditing and enforcing, IRS current, 194
  IRS no-ruling position, 193–194
  penalties for Section 409A violation, 196
  reporting obligations of service recipient, 195
  timing requirements, 196
Evergreen elections, 106
Exceptions
  deferred compensation, 163–165
  to part-year compensation deferral elections, 111–112
  to plans subject to Section 409A, 3–4
  regulatory, 3–4
  severance plans, 127, 129
  statutory, 3
Excess benefit plans, 106
Excise taxes and acceleration of benefits, 69–70

F

Fair market value of stock, 139–141
Federal debt collection laws, 86
Federal Insurance Contributions Act (FICA), 86
Financial hardship. *See* Unforeseeable emergency
Financial health of service recipient, downturn in, 63
Fiscal year compensation deferral. *See* Service provider deferral elections
Fiscal year plans, 105
Foreign earned income, 167
Foreign ethics laws, acceleration of benefits to comply with, 73
Foreign plans
  broad-based retirement plan, 166
  deferred compensation exceptions, 163–165
  foreign earned income, 167
  foreign social security system, 166
  Sections 457A/409A compared, 167–168
  subject to Section 457A and Section 409A, 169
  tax equalization agreement, 165–166
  treaty exemption, 165
Foreign social security system, 166
Forfeiture
  compensation subject to, 28–31, 107
  rolling risk of, 125–126, 289–290
  substantial risk of (*see* Substantial risk of forfeiture)
Freezing plans (frozen plans), 78, 172, 190–191, 271
Fringe benefit arrangements, 151–153

Funding
　grandfathered plans, 179
　offshore trusts, 177
　requirements for, 175–176
　restricted period, 177–179
　trust assets as, 176–177

G

Grandfathering
　acceleration of benefits and, 83
　account balance plan and, 273–274
　amounts eligible for, 274–275
　distribution restrictions, 274–275
　domestic relations order and, 78
　effective dates, 269–275
　funding and, 179
　life insurance contract and, 272
　material modification, 269–271, 272–273
　non-account balance plan and, 274
　operational errors and, 215
　split-dollar life insurance, 158, 274
　tax consequences, 100
Grantor trusts, 175–176, 177

H

Haircut provisions, 16
Health care reimbursements, 152
Hogans, Daniel L., 17, 28, 61, 173

I

Impermissible distribution events, 16
Impermissible reimbursements, 203
Incentive stock options, 135–136
Income taxation, deferral of, 290
Indemnification payments, 155
　termination of contract (employment), 40, 42
Independent contractors
　definition (*see* Service recipient)
　separation from service and, 40–41
　status change from employee to, 41–42
　termination of contract (employment), 40, 42
Initial public offering, 50
In-kind benefits, impermissible, 203
Insider, definition for operational error correction purposes, 255–256
Investment commissions, 105
IRS examination, disqualification by, 264
　assessment of tax liabilities time-barred, 265–266
　audit status, service recipient, 260–261
　correction considered complete, 261
　correction program and taxpayer audit risk, 262
　service provider, 260
　service recipient, 259–260
　statute of limitations, 264–265, 266–267
　subsequent operational failure, 263
　taxpayer duty, 262
　tax-qualified retirement plan, 263–264

J
Joint life expectancies, 72–73

K
Key employee, 47, *See also* Specified employees, identifying
Key person life insurance policy, 161

L
Late payments, 62–63
Leave of absence, 38
Leaves of absence, 18, 38–39
 during pandemic, 192
Legal fees, employment-related, 155
Legal settlements, 154
Letter rulings, 193–194
Letter rulings, private, 329–355
Life insurance arrangements
 bonus life insurance or annuity plan, 158–160
 death benefit only (DBO) plan, 12, 162
 employer-owned life insurance, 161
 grandfathering, 272
 key person policy, 161
 split-dollar, 157–158, 162
Limited payment rule, 129
Linked plans, 106–107, 207
Linking plans, limitations on
 offsetting benefits, 172–173
 participant elections, nonqualified to qualified, 171–172
Loans, 83–84, 162

M
Marriage and distribution events, 61
Materially greater amounts, defined, 125–126
Mediation of negative tax consequences, 100
Mid-year start (pro rata rule), 104

N
Non-account balance plan, grandfathering and, 274
Nonallocation year, 87
Non-qualified deferred compensation
 benefit access during pandemic, 182–184
 checklist, 319–322
 disability pay and, 11–12
 plan types subject to Section 409A, 2
Non-qualified stock options, 135–136
 dividend equivalent rights, 144–145
 Section 409A, becoming subject to, 143–144
 stock split or stock dividend, 145
Nontaxable fringe benefits, 151–152
Non-vested amounts, tax consequences due to breach of Section 409A on, 93
Nonvested stock, service providers rights, 137
Notice 2010-6
 date of correction for, 207–208
 documentary errors, correcting, 197–198, 210–211, 315–316
 operational errors, correcting, 213–214
 plans not eligible for correcting documentary errors, 198
 relief without plan amendment, 198–200
 scriveners' errors and, 210

service provider income recognition, 208–209
service provider tax liability under, 91
stock plans and, 206

O

Officer, definition of, 256
Offset provisions
  acceleration of benefits, 85–86
  linking plans, limitations on offsetting benefits, 172–173
  salary advance, against deferred compensation, 16
Offshore trusts, funding with, 177
Operational errors
  analysis to determine, 215–217
  correction for, 213–214
  correction of de minimis errors, 214
  deferred amount greater than deferral election, 234–239
  deferred payment made before scheduled time, 239–246
  distribution in correct year but earlier than scheduled date, 246–253
  documentation and reporting of, 214
  earnings or losses adjustments by applicable deadline, 256–257
  exercise price of stock below fair market value, 253–255
  grandfathered plans and, 215
  insider, definition of, 255
  late distribution of previously deferred compensation, 223–227
  Notice 2008-113 reporting/ disclosure requirements, 257
  officer, definition of, 256

Section 402(g)(1)(B) deferral amount, 255
Section 409A, 217–223
separation from service payments during first six months, 228–234
Operational violation of Section 409A, 98–99
  super summary for correction, 319–322
Ownership or effective control
  change in acceleration of benefits, 75
  definition of, 75–76
  as primary permissible distribution event, 35

P

Pandemic emergency distributions, 70–71
  challenges created by, 181–182
  compensation reduction and, 186
  deferral election cancellation and, 185–186
  disability and, 184
  funding of rabbi trust and, 191
  leave of absence and, 192
  legislative or regulatory relief, 182
  nonqualified benefit plan access, 182–184
  performance-based bonus during, 188–190
  promise to pay reduced compensation later, 187
  reduced or canceled credits, 190
  separation of service and, 191–192
  temporary shutdown of all business operations and, 190

Pandemic emergency distributions, *continued*
  as unforeseeable emergency, 183–184
  voluntary plan termination and, 184–185
Participant account balance plans, 101
Participant definition. *See* Service recipient
Partnership arrangements subject to Section 409A, 10–11
Part-year compensation deferral elections, 111–114
  deadline for submission, 112
  documentation required, 113
  exceptions to, 111–112
  failure to meet timing rule, additional taxes for, 113–114
  making changes to, 113
  recurring part-year compensation, 286–287
  Section 409A requirements, 112
Payments
  death benefits, death of beneficiary, 58
  death benefits, specification of period for payment of, 57
  delayed, 63–64
  elections of time and form of, with respect to employer plans, 107
  indemnification, 155
  late, 62–63
  refusal or failure to make, 67
  service provider claim release and timing of, 58–59
  short-term deferral rule and timing of, 27, 31
  substantial risk of forfeiture and, 56
  tax gross-up, 153–154
  timing of, 55–56
  transaction-based compensation, 148–149
  transfer of property at substantial risk of forfeiture, 56
  upon death, 56
Performance-based compensation, 105, 109–110
  during pandemic, 188–190
Permissible distributions and accelerations checklist, 311–313
Phantom stock units, 146–147
Plans not subject to Section 409A, 3–4
Plans subject to Section 409A
  death benefits and, 12
  deferral of compensation and, 4–6
  determination of, 6
  disability pay and, 11–12
  exceptions to, 3–4
  general requirements for, 13
  legally binding treatment of, 6–7
  partnerships and, 10–11
  property acquisition or interest and, 9
  service provider for, 8
  service recipient for, 7–8
  tax-exempt entities (*see* Tax-exempt entities, plans of)
  types of, 1–2
  vacation leave and, 13
Plan termination
  accelerated benefits, 69
  pandemic emergency, 184–185
  as primary permissible distribution event, 35–36
Present value of deferred compensation, 291
Previously eligible participants, 104–105
Property acquisition or interest, plans subject to Section 409A and, 9

Publicly held employer plan documentation requirements, 19–20
Publicly traded companies
 separation from service, 43–44
 specified employees, 45–46

Q
QDRO. *See* Domestic relations order

R
Rabbi trust funding, 19, 175–179, 182, 270, 296
 during pandemic, 191
Railroad Retirement Act (RRTA), 86
Recurring part-year compensation, 11, 105, 111–112, 114, 286–287
Reduced or canceled credits during pandemic, 190
Regulatory exceptions to Section 409A, 3–4
Rehire, impact on distributions, 66–67
Reimbursement provisions, 203
Release, non-compete agreement, 201
Reporting
 aggregate plan deferral amounts, 96, 195
 federal W-2 (*see* Tax reporting, W-2)
 state income taxation (*see* Tax reporting, state income taxation)
Restricted period, 177–179
Restricted stock, 146–147
Restricted stock units, 146–147
Right to select time/form of payment plan documentation requirements, 20

Risk of forfeiture, substantial. *See* Substantial risk of forfeiture
Rolling risk of forfeiture, 125–126, 289–290

S
Safe harbor requirements, 120, 130–131
Sales commissions, 105
SARs. *See* Stock appreciation rights
Schmidt, William, 30
Scriveners' error, 210
Section 338, deemed asset sale under, 40
Section 409A plan documentation checklist, 295–299
Securities market, established, 43
Self-insured medical coverage, 153
Separation from service
 asset sales and, 39, 40
 change in status from employee to independent contractor, 41–42
 different payment schedules for voluntary and involuntary, 202
 disability pay and, 53
 distribution qualifications, 36–38
 during pandemic, 191–192
 impermissible definition of, 202
 independent contractor, 40–41
 involuntary, 62
 leaves of absence, 38–39
 operational errors and, 228–234
 as primary permissible distribution event, 35
 publicly traded companies, 43–44
 spin-off and, 39
 stock sale and, 39
 termination of employment presumptions, 36–38
Service provider, definition, 8

Service provider deferral elections
- annualized recurring part-year compensation, 105
- annuity payment types, 117–118
- beneficiaries, 8, 56, 72–73
- bonus deferral and cancellation, 110–111
- cancellation, 120
- cash basis rule for subsequent year, 109
- compensation subject to forfeiture, 107
- deferral of short-term deferral awards prior to vesting, 107–108
- definition of, 103
- different deferral percentages for different types of compensation, 121–122
- educator compensation, 105
- elections of time and form of payment with respect to employer plans, 107
- employee missed or late submissions, 112
- evergreen elections, 106
- exceptions to, 111–112
- excess benefit plans, 106
- fiscal year plans, 105
- flexibility, 122–124
- investment commissions, 105
- linked plans, 106–107
- mid-year start (pro rata rule), 104
- multiple subaccounts, 121
- nondiscretionary formula calculation method, 108
- pandemic emergency cancellations, 185–186
- partial deferral, 118
- part-year compensation, 111–114
- performance-based compensation, 105, 109–110
- periodic installments deferral, 118–119
- plan aggregation, 108
- previously eligible participants, 104–105
- rolling risk of forfeiture, 125–126
- sales commissions, 105
- Section 409A requirements, 112, 113
- single sum payment, 119
- subsequent election requirements, 114–119, 122–124
- 30-day rule, 104
- time frame for, 104–108

Service recipient, definition, 1, 7

Service recipient stock
- fair market value of, 139–141
- granting of stock rights, 136
- mandatory repurchase obligations, 139
- stock-based compensation, 137–138

Severance payments
- bona fide severance pay plans for purposes of Section 457, 280–281
- breach of Section 409A, 132–133
- collectively bargained, 134
- exempt from Section 409A, 127, 129
- foreign, 134
- form and type modifications, 132
- mitigation provision, 132
- nonqualified deferred compensation payments, 133
- rules used for, 128–129

termination for good reason, 130–131
voluntary termination, 130
window program, 134
Shareholder service providers (sole & majority) treatment, 28, 110, 145, 148
Short-term deferrals
amounts paid shortly after earned, 23
delay in payment situations, 27–28, 31
documentation of, 16
examples of, 26
rule defined, 24–26
Section 457 and, 284
service provider deferral elections, 107–108
substantial risk of forfeiture and, 28–31, 32–33
timing of payment, 27
vest and pay lump sum, 33
Shutdown, pandemic, 190
Sick leave plan, bona fide, 283
Six month delay rule
documentary errors, 203
exceptions to, 43–44
publicly held employer plan, 19–20
rehired employee cases and, 67
specified employees and, 44–46, 51–52
Small benefits, cash-out distribution of, 74
Specified employees, identifying
alternative approaches for, 45–46
claim for post-employment discrimination or retaliation, 51–52
default rules for, 44–45
following corporate transaction, alternative rules, 50–51
following initial public offering, 50
following spin-off, 50
public/nonpublic company transaction, following, 49
six-month delay rule, 44–46, 51–52
two public companies corporate transaction, following, 47–49
Specified time/fixed schedule as primary permissible distribution event, 35
Spin-offs
identifying specified employees following, 50
and separation from service, 39
401k Spill-over (401k wrap-around) plans, 171
Split-dollar life insurance arrangements
defined, 157
grandfathering and, 158, 274
termination of, 162
types of, 157–158
State income taxation, 77, 100, 217
Statutory exceptions to Section 409A, 3
Stock appreciation rights (SARs)
modification in terms of stock right, 142–143
Section 409A, becoming subject to, 143–144
Section 409A, structure to comply with, 145–146
transaction-based compensation rules, 149
Stock-based compensation
change in terms of stock right, 142–143
dividend-equivalent distributions, 147–148

Stock-based compensation, *continued*
  employee stock purchase plan option, 135
  fair market value of, 139–141
  incentive stock options, 135–136
  nonqualified stock options, 135–136, 143–146
  nonvested stock, service provider rights, 137
  phantom stock, 146–147
  restricted stock and restricted stock units, 146–147
  Sections 409A and ASC 718 compared, 141–142
  service recipient stock, 138–139
  stock appreciation rights (SARs), 136, 143–144
  stock rights granted before becoming service provider, 138
  transaction-based compensation payments, 148–149
  valuation date for restricted stock units, 147
Stock options
  substantial risk of forfeiture and, 66
  transaction-based compensation rules, 148–149
Stock sale and separation from service, 39
Stoppage of plan contributions
  stoppage of deferral contributions only, different definition, 66–67, 120
  stoppage of employer contributions, 120, 190–191, 297–298
  stoppage of participant elections to defer (*see* Service provider deferral elections)

Subsequent deferred election requirements, 114–119, 122–124
  impermissible discretion, 203–204
Substantial risk of forfeiture, 28–31
  breach of Section 409A tax consequences, 94
  definitions of, under Sections 409A, 83, and 457(f), 9, 32–33, 284–286
  example of, 32–33
  payment, transfer of property considered, 56
  service provider deferral elections, 107, 125–126
  tax-exempt organizations, 284–286, 287–289
Substitution rule, acceleration of benefits, 83

T

Tax consequences. *See* Breach of Section 409A
Tax equalization agreement exemption, 165–166
Tax-exempt entities, plans of
  acceleration of benefits to pay taxes, 292
  death benefit plans, bona fide, 282
  deferral of income taxation, 290
  deferred compensation defined in context of, 279
  disability pay plans, bona fide, 282–283
  income amounts includable under Section 457, 290, 291–292
  income subject to substantial risk of forfeiture, 287–289
  legally binding plans, 280
  non-qualified deferred compensation, 277
  plans not subject to Section 457, 279–280

present value of deferred compensation, 291
recurring part-year compensation, 286–287
rolling risk of forfeiture, 289–290
rules for taxable employers *vs.*, 278
Section 409A and, 9–10, 279
Section 457 and, 279
severance pay plans, bona fide, 280–281
short-term deferral rule, 284
sick leave plan, bona fide, 283
substantial risk of forfeiture, definition of, 284–286
vacation leave plan, bona fide, 13, 283
Tax gross-up payment, 153–154
Tax reporting
state income taxation, 77, 100, 217
W-2, 91, 195, 209, 219–221, 223, 225–227, 229, 232–233, 236–237
Tax withholding, 86
Termination of employment
examples of, 37–38
generally, 36
presumptions, 36–38
Termination of plans. *See* Acceleration of benefits, service recipient plan termination
30-day rule, 104
Top hat plans, 89–90
Transaction-based compensation payments, 148–149
Treaty exemption, 165
Trust assets, funding with, 176–177

U

Unforeseeable emergency
acceleration of benefits, 69, 71
distribution request form, 301–305
plan access during pandemic, 183–184
as primary permissible distribution event, 35
Section 409A, 70–71

V

Vacation leave plan, bona fide, 13, 283
Valuation methods for stocks, 139–141
Valuation of Privately Held Company Equity Securities Issued as Compensation (AICPA), 142
Vest and pay lump sum SERP, 33
Vested amounts, tax consequences due to breach of Section 409A on, 93
Vesting
deferral of short-term deferral awards prior to, 107–108
unforeseeable acceleration of, 69, 82–83
Voluntary salary deferrals, substantial risk of forfeiture and, 30
Voluntary service recipient plan terminations, 81–82, 184, 296

W

W-2 reporting for federal income tax purposes. *See* Tax reporting, W-2
401k Wrap-around plans (spill-over plans), 171
Window program, 134
Written plans, documentation requirements, 15. *See also* Documentation requirements, Section 409A